essentials

PowerPoint 2000
Basic

Linda Bird
Software Solutions
University of Rio Grande

Prentice Hall

A division of Pearson Education
Upper Saddle River, NJ 07458

PowerPoint 2000 Essentials Basic

International Standard Book Number: 1-58076-095-3

Library of Congress Catalog Card Number: 98-88895

Printed in the United States of America

First Printing: June 1999

03 02   8 7 6 5

Interpretation of the printing code: the rightmost double-digit number is the year of the book's printing; the rightmost single-digit number, the number of the book's printing. For example, a printing code of 00-1 shows that the first printing of the book occurred in 2000.

Trademark Acknowledgments

All terms mentioned in this book that are known to be trademarks or service marks have been appropriately capitalized. Prentice Hall cannot attest to the accuracy of this information. Use of a term in this book should not be regarded as affecting the validity of any trademark or service mark.

Microsoft is a registered trademark of Microsoft Corporation in the United States and in other countries. Some of the product names and company names used in this book have been used for identification purposes only and may be trademarks or registered trademarks of their respective manufacturers and sellers.

Screens reproduced in the book were created using Collage Plus from Inner Media, Inc., Hollis, NH.

PowerPoint 2000 Essentials Basic is based on **Microsoft PowerPoint 2000**.

Publisher:
Robert Linsky

Executive Editor:
Sunthar Visuvalingam

Series Editors:
Marianne Fox and
Larry Metzelaar

Annotated Instructor's Manual (AIM) Series Editor:
Linda Bird

Operations Manager:
Christine Moos

Director of Product Marketing:
Susan Kindel

Acquisitions Editor:
Chuck Stewart

Development Editor:
Joyce J. Nielsen

Technical Editor:
Asit Patel

Software Coordinator:
Angela Denny

Senior Editor:
Karen A. Walsh

Book Designer:
Louisa Klucznik

Design Usability Consultant:
Elizabeth Keyes

Project Editor:
Tim Tate

Copy Editor:
Nancy Sixsmith

Proofreader:
John Etchison

Indexer:
Angie Bess

Layout Technician:
Liz Johnston

Team Coordinator:
Melody Layne

Usability Testers:
Heather Fekete College of Business Administration, Butler University

Monica Hanlin College of Pharmacy, Butler University

Cathy Gilmore Shell Chemical Company

About the Author

Linda Bird specializes in corporate training and support through Software Solutions, her own company. She has successfully trained users representing more than 75 businesses, including several Fortune 500 companies. Her clients include Appalachian Electric Power Co., Borg Warner Automotive, Goodyear, Pillsbury, Rockwell Automation, and Shell Chemical. Her background also includes teaching at Averett College and overseeing computer training for a business training organization. She is currently associated with the University of Rio Grande.

Linda has written numerous books on PowerPoint, Word, and Windows 95. In addition, she has written instructor's manuals and contributed to books on most major software programs. She also authors monthly how-to articles for *Smart Computing* magazine and develops customized training manuals for client businesses.

Linda, a graduate of the University of Wisconsin, lives in Gallipolis, Ohio with her husband, Lonnie, and daughters, Rebecca and Sarah.

Dedication

I would like to dedicate this book to my husband, Lonnie, who is always supportive, and to Rebecca and Sarah, my truly amazing daughters.

Acknowledgments

Although the author is solely responsible for its content, this book and the *Essentials* series as a whole have been shaped by the combined experience, perspectives, and input of the entire authoring, editorial, and design team. We are grateful to the Series Editors, **Larry Metzelaar** and **Marianne Fox**, and to the College of Business Administration at Butler University for hosting the listserv on which the implications and value of every series element was thoroughly discussed and finalized even as this book was being written. They also hosted a November '98 seminar for the AIM authors and coordinated much of the usability testing at the Butler campus. We acknowledge **Robb Linsky** (Publisher, Que Education and Training) for having provided the initial direction and for having allowed the Essentials 2000 team to shape this edition as we saw fit. You, the reader, are the greatest beneficiary of this ongoing online collaborative effort.

Chuck Stewart adapted the original Que E&T *Essentials* series for corporate training. In early 1998, however, he began revamping the *Office 2000 Essentials* pedagogy to better serve academic needs exclusively. He enlisted the services of Series Editors Metzelaar and Fox because of their extensive background in courseware development, many years of classroom teaching, and innovative pedagogy. Early discussion with the Series Editors revealed the need for the three new types of end-of-chapter exercises you find in the *Office 2000 Essentials*. Chuck continued to provide ideas and feedback on the listserv long after handing over the executive editorship to Sunthar. Together, they completely overhauled the Essentials series, paying particular attention to pedagogy, content, and design issues.

Sunthar Visuvalingam took over as Executive Editor for the *Essentials* series in October 1998. He stepped into a process already in full swing and moved quickly to ensure "a level of collaboration rarely seen in academic publishing." He performed admirably the daunting task of coordinating an army of widely dispersed authors, editors, designers, and usability testers. Among the keywords that characterize his crucial role in forging a well-knit "learning team" are decisive leadership, effective communication, shared vision, continuous pedagogical and procedural innovation, infectious enthusiasm, dogged project and quality management, active solicitation of feedback, collective problem solving, transparent decision making, developmental mentoring, reliability, flexibility, and dedication. Having made his indelible mark on the *Essentials* series, he stayed on to shepherd the transition of the series to Alex.

Linda Bird (AIM Series Editor and author of both *PowerPoint Essentials* books) and **Robert Ferrett** (co-author of *Office Essentials*, all three *Access Essentials* books, and of the related *Learn* series) made significant contributions to enhancing the concept and details of the new series. A newcomer to the series but not to educational publishing, **Keith Mulbery** seized increasing ownership of *Essentials* and undertook the initiative of presenting the series at the April '99 National Business Education Association Convention.

Alex von Rosenberg, Executive Editor, manages the Computer Applications publishing program at Prentice Hall (PH). The PH team has been instrumental in ensuring a smooth transition of the *Essentials* series. Alex has been ably assisted in this transition by **Susan Rifkin**, Managing Editor; **Leanne Nieglos**, Assistant Editor; **Jennifer Surich**, Editorial Assistant; **Nancy Evans**, Director of Strategic Marketing; **Kris King**, Senior Marketing Manager; and **Nancy Welcher**, Media Project Manager.

Christine Moos, Operations Manager, and **Karen Walsh**, Senior Editor, worked hard with Sunthar and Alex to allow authors maximum flexibility to produce a quality product, while trying to maintain a tight editorial and production schedule. They had the unenviable task of keeping the book processes rolling while managing the complex process of transitioning the series to Prentice Hall. Book Designer **Louisa Klucznik** and Consultant **Elizabeth Keyes** spared no efforts in making every detail of the new design attractive, usable, consistent, and appropriate to the *Essentials* pedagogy. **Joyce Nielsen**, **Jan Snyder**, **Asit Patel**, **Nancy Sixsmith**, and **Susan Hobbs**—freelancers who had worked on earlier editions of the *Essentials* and the related *Learn* series in various editorial capacities—helped ensure continuity in procedures and conventions. **Tim Tate**, **Sherri Fugit**, **Melody Layne**, and **Cindy Fields** also asked sharp questions along the way and thereby helped us refine and crystallize the editorial conventions for the *Essentials* series.

A special thanks to **Joyce Nielsen** and **Nancy Sixsmith** for ensuring the quality of the book, **Asit Patel** for providing timely and valuable technical support, **Tim Tate** for shepherding the book through production, and **Sunthar Visuvalingam** for keeping everything on track.

Contents at a Glance

Table of Contents

Introduction

Introduction

Essentials courseware from Prentice Hall is anchored in the practical and professional needs of all types of students. This edition of the *Office 2000 Essentials* has been completely revamped as the result of painstaking usability research by the publisher, authors, editors, and students. Practically every detail—by way of pedagogy, content, presentation, and design—was the object of continuous online (and offline) discussion among the entire team.

The *Essentials* series has been conceived around a "learning-by-doing" approach, which encourages you to grasp application-related concepts as you expand your skills through hands-on tutorials. As such, it consists of modular lessons that are built around a series of numbered step-by-step procedures that are clear, concise, and easy to review. Explicatory material is interwoven before each lesson and between the steps. Additional features, tips, pitfalls, and other related information are provided at exactly the right place where you most expect them. They are easily recognizable elements that stand out from the main flow of the tutorial. We even designed our icons to match the Microsoft Office theme. The end-of-chapter exercises have likewise been carefully graded from the routine Checking Concepts and Terms to tasks in the Discovery Zone that gently prod you into extending what you learned into areas beyond the explicit scope of the lessons proper. Following, you find out more about the rationale behind each book element and how to use each to your maximum benefit.

How to Use This Book

Typically, each *Essentials* book is divided into seven or eight projects, concerning topics such as creating presentations, modifying presentations, formatting text and bullets, working with charts, and automating electronic slide shows. A project covers one area (or a few closely related areas) of application functionality. Each project is then divided into seven to nine lessons related to that topic. For example, a project on working with charts is divided into lessons explaining how to select an appropriate chart type; create a data chart; edit chart data; resize, move, and change chart types; choose a chart sub-type and format a chart; create an organization chart; and modify an organization chart. Each lesson presents a specific task or closely related set of tasks in a manageable chunk that's easy to assimilate and retain.

Each element in *PowerPoint 2000 Essentials Basic* is designed to maximize your learning experience. Here's a list of the *Essentials* project elements and a description of how each element can help you:

- **Project Objectives.** Starting with an objective gives you short-term, attainable goals. Using project objectives that closely match the titles of the step-by-step tutorials breaks down the possibly overwhelming prospect of learning several new features of PowerPoint into small, attainable, bite-sized tasks. Look over the objectives on the opening page of the project before you begin, and review them after completing the project to identify the main goals for each project.

- **Key Terms.** This book includes a limited number of useful vocabulary words and definitions, such as ***AutoContent Wizard***, ***annotation pen***, and ***slide transitions***. Key terms introduced in each project are listed in alphabetical order immediately after the objectives on the opening page of the project. These key terms are shown in bold italic, and are defined during their first use within the text. Definitions of key terms are also included in the glossary.

- **Why Would I Do This?** You are studying PowerPoint so that you can accomplish useful tasks in the real world. This brief section tells you why these tasks or procedures are important. What can you do with the knowledge? How can these application features be applied to everyday tasks?

- **Visual Summary.** This opening section graphically illustrates the concepts and features that you will learn in the project. Several figures, with ample callouts, show the final result of completing the project. This road map to your destination keeps you motivated as you work through the individual steps of each task.

- **Lessons.** Each lesson contains one or more tasks that correspond to an objective on the opening page of the project. A lesson consists of step-by-step tutorials, their associated data files, screen shots, and the special notes described as follows. Although each lesson often builds on the previous one, the lessons (and the exercises) were made to be as modular as possible. For example, you can skip tasks that you've already mastered, and you can begin a later lesson by using a data file provided specifically for its task(s).

- **Step-by-Step Tutorial.** The lessons consist of numbered, bold, step-by-step instructions that show you how to perform the procedures in a clear, concise, and direct manner. These hands-on tutorials, which are the "essentials" of each project, let you "learn by doing." Regular paragraphs between the steps clarify the results of each step. Also, screen shots are introduced after key steps for you to check against the results on your monitor. To revise the lesson, you can easily scan the bold numbered steps. Quick (or impatient!) learners may likewise ignore the intervening paragraphs.

- **Need to Know.** These sidebars provide essential tips for performing the tasks and using the application more effectively. You can easily recognize them by their distinctive icon and bold headings. It's well worth the effort to review these crucial notes again after completing the project.

- **Nice to Know.** Nice to Know comments provide extra tips, shortcuts, alternative ways to complete a process, and special hints about using the software. You may safely ignore these for the moment to focus on the main task at hand, or you may pause to learn and appreciate these tidbits. Here you find neat tricks and special insights to impress your friends and coworkers with!

- **If You Have Problems...** These short troubleshooting notes help you anticipate or solve common problems quickly and effectively. Even if you don't encounter the problem at this time, do make a mental note of it so that you know where to look when you find yourself (or others) in difficulty.

- **Summary.** This section provides a brief recap of the tasks learned in the project. The summary guides you to places where you can expand your knowledge, which may include references to specific Help topics or the Prentice Hall *Essentials* Web site (http://www.prenhall.com/essentials).

- **Checking Concepts and Terms.** This section offers optional True/False, Multiple Choice, Screen ID, and Discussion Questions that are designed to check your comprehension and assess retention. If you need to refresh your memory, the relevant lesson number is provided after each True/False and Multiple Choice question. For example, [L5] directs you to review lesson five for the answer. Lesson numbers may be provided, but only where relevant for other types of exercises as well.

- **Skill Drill Exercises.** This section enables you to check your comprehension, evaluate your progress, and practice what you learned. The exercises in this section build on and reinforce what has been learned in each project. Generally, the Skill Drill exercises include step-by-step instructions. At least one of the Skill Drill exercises requires you to use Help to learn how to learn on your own.

- **Challenge Exercises.** This section provides exercises that expand on or relate to the skills practiced in the project. Each exercise provides a brief narrative introduction followed by instructions. Although the instructions are written in a step-by-step format, the steps are not as detailed as those in the Skill Drill section. Providing less-specific steps helps you learn to think on your own. These exercises foster the "near transfer" of learning.

- **Discovery Zone Exercises.** These exercises require advanced knowledge of project topics or the application of skills from multiple lessons. Additionally, these exercises may require you to research topics in Help or on the Web to complete them. This self-directed method of learning new skills emulates real-world experience. We provide the cues, and you do the exploring!

- **Learning to Learn.** Throughout this book, you'll find lessons, exercises, and other elements highlighted by this icon. For the most part, they involve using or exploring the built-in Help system or Web-based Help, which is also accessible from the application. However, their significance is much deeper. Microsoft Office is so rich in features that cater to so many diverse needs that it's no longer possible to anticipate and teach you everything you might need to know. It's becoming increasingly important that, as you learn from this book, you also "learn to learn" on your own. These elements help you identify related—and perhaps more specialized—tasks or questions, and show you how to discover the right procedures or answers by exploiting the many resources already within the application.

- **Task Guide.** The Task Guide that follows the last project lists all the procedures and shortcuts that you learned in this book. It can be used in two complementary ways to enhance your learning experience. You can refer to it while progressing through the book, in order to refresh your memory on procedures learned in a previous lesson. Or, you can keep it as a handy real-world reference while using the application for your daily work.

- **Glossary.** Here, you find the definitions—collected in one place—of all the key terms defined throughout the book and listed on the opening page of each project. Use it to refresh your memory.

Typeface Conventions Used in This Book

We have used the following conventions throughout this book to make it easier for you to understand the material:

- Key terms appear in ***italic and bold*** the first time they are defined in a project.

- Text that you type, as well as text that appears on your computer screen as a warning, confirmation, or general information, appears in a special `monospace` typeface.

- Hotkeys, the underlined keys onscreen that activate commands and options, are also underlined in this book. Hotkeys offer a quick way to bring up frequently used commands.

How to Use the CD-ROM

The CD-ROM that accompanies this book contains all the data files for you to use as you work through the step-by-step tutorials, Skill Drill, Challenge, and Discovery Zone exercises provided at the end of each project. The CD contains separate parallel folders for each project. The filenames correspond to the filenames called for in this book. Here's how the files are named: The first three characters represent the software and the book level (such as PP1 for the *PowerPoint 2000 Essentials Basic*). The last four digits indicate the project number and the file number within the project. For example, the first file used in Project 1 would be 0101. Therefore, the complete name for the first file in the *PowerPoint 2000 Essentials Basic* book is PP1-0101.

Files on a CD-ROM are read-only; they cannot be modified in any way. In order to use the provided data files while working through this book, they must first be transferred to a read-write medium, where you may modify them. Because classroom and lab rules that govern the use of storage media vary from school to school, this book assumes the standard procedure of working with the file(s) on a 3.5-inch floppy.

A word of caution about using floppy disks: As you use a data file, it increases in size or automatically generates temporary work files. Ensure that your disk remains at least one-third empty to provide the needed extra space. Moreover, using a floppy for your work disk is slower than working from a hard drive. You will also need several floppy disks to hold all the files on the CD.

- **Saving to a 3.5-inch floppy disk.** For security or space reasons, many labs do not allow you to save to the hard drive at all. In Project 3, Lesson 1, you learn how to open a file from the CD-ROM and save it with a different name to a 3.5-inch floppy disk. This is the most portable solution because you can take your files with you easily from the classroom to the lab and back home to complete your exercise.

- **Copying to a 3.5-inch floppy disk.** Instead of opening and saving each data file individually as you start to work on it, you can copy one or more files to the floppy disk. Because Access does not have a Save As command for databases, the following is the only way to transfer Microsoft Access databases to a floppy:

    First, select the files on the CD that you want to copy and ensure that their combined size (shown on the status bar of the Explorer window) will fit into a 1.44MB floppy. Right-click on the selection with your mouse; choose Send To on the context menu that appears, and then choose 3 1/2 Floppy on the submenu. After copying, select the copied files on the floppy and right-click the selection with the mouse again. This time, choose Properties, choose the General tab on the Properties dialog box that appears, and then uncheck the Read-Only attribute at the bottom of this page. Because the original files on the CD-ROM were read-only, the files were copied with this attribute turned on. You can rename files copied in this manner only after you turn off the read-only attribute.

    Although you can use the same method to copy the entire CD contents to a large-capacity drive, it is much simpler to use the installation routine in the CD-ROM for the purpose. This automatically removes the read-only attribute while transferring the files.

- **Installing to a hard drive or Zip drive.** The CD-ROM contains an installation routine that automatically copies all the contents to a local or networked hard drive, or to a removable large-capacity drive (for example, an Iomega Zip drive). If you are working in the classroom, your instructor has probably already installed the files to the hard drive and can tell you where the files are located. You'll be asked to save or copy the file(s) that you need to your personal work area on the hard drive or to a floppy work disk.

Otherwise, run the installation routine yourself to transfer all the files to the hard drive (for example, if you are working at home) or to your personal Zip drive. You may then work directly and more efficiently from these high-capacity drives.

CD-ROM Installation Routine

If you were instructed to install the files on a lab computer or if you are installing them on your home computer, simply insert the CD-ROM into the CD-ROM drive. When the installation screen appears, follow these steps:

1. From the installation screen, click the Install button.

2. The Welcome dialog box displays. Click the Next button.

3. The Readme.txt appears. The Readme.txt gives you important information regarding the installation. Make sure that you use the scrollbar to view the entire Readme.txt file. When you finish reading the Readme.txt, click the Next button.

4. The Select Destination Directory displays. Unless instructed otherwise by your instructor, the default location is recommended. Click Next.

5. The Ready to Install screen appears. Click Next to begin the installation.

   A directory is created on your hard drive where the student files will be installed.

6. A dialog box appears, confirming that the installation is complete.

The installation of the student data files allows you to access the data files from the Start menu programs. To access the student data files from the Start menu, click Start, click Programs, and then click the *Essentials* title you installed from the list of programs. The student data files are in subfolders, arranged by project.

Uninstalling the Student Data Files

After you complete the course, you may decide that you do not need the student data files any more. If that is the case, you have the capability to uninstall them. The following steps walk you through the process:

1. Click on the Start menu, and then click Programs.

2. Click the *Essentials* title that you installed.

3. Click Uninstall.

4. Click one of the Uninstall methods listed:

   - Automatic—This method deletes all files in the directory and all shortcuts created.

   - Custom—This method allows you to select the files that you want to delete.

5. Click Next.

6. The Perform Uninstall dialog box appears. Click Finish. The Student data files and their folders are deleted.

The *Annotated Instructor's Manual*

The *Annotated Instructor's Manual* (*AIM*) is a printed copy of the student book—complete with marginal annotations and detailed guidelines, including a curriculum guide—that helps the instructor use this book and teach the software more effectively. The *AIM* also includes a Resource CD-ROM with additional support files for the instructor; suggested solution files that show how the students' files should look at the end of a tutorial; answers to test questions; PowerPoint presentations to augment your instruction; additional test questions and answers; and additional Skill Drill, Challenge, and Discovery Zone exercises. Instructors should contact Prentice Hall for their complimentary *AIM*. Prentice Hall can be reached via phone at 1-800-333-7945, or via the Internet at http://www.prenhall.com.

Project 1

Getting Started with PowerPoint

Objectives

In this project, you learn how to

➤ **Start PowerPoint**

➤ **Create a New, Blank Presentation**

➤ **Explore the PowerPoint Window**

➤ **Work with Toolbars and Menus**

➤ **Get Help**

➤ **Customize the Office Assistant**

➤ **Close Your Presentation and Exit PowerPoint**

Key terms introduced in this project include

- AutoLayout
- editing mode
- electronic slide show
- full menu
- hyperlink
- keyword
- Navigation pane
- Normal view
- Notes pane
- Office Assistant
- Outline pane
- personalized menus and toolbars
- placeholder
- presentation
- presentation graphics program
- Random Access Memory (RAM)
- ScreenTip
- short menu
- shortcut menu
- Slide pane

Why Would I Do This?

Microsoft PowerPoint 2000 is a powerful **presentation graphics program**. Presentation graphics software such as PowerPoint helps you structure, design, and present information to an audience so that it is catchy and visually appealing.

A **presentation** is simply a series of slides that contain visual information you can use to persuade an audience. Using PowerPoint, you can effectively and efficiently create professional-looking handouts, overheads, charts, and so on. Whether you are developing a marketing plan, reporting progress on a project, or simply conducting a meeting, PowerPoint can help you create powerful presentations quickly. And after you initially develop a presentation, you can jazz it up by adding and modifying text, charts, clip art, and drawn objects.

You can deliver PowerPoint presentations in various ways—by using printed handouts, 35MM slides, or overhead transparencies. Probably the most popular way to show a presentation, however, is to display it as an **electronic slide show**. An electronic slide show is a predetermined list of slides that are displayed sequentially. You can show the list onscreen or by using a Liquid Crystal Display (LCD) panel and an overhead projector to cast the image from your computer onto a large screen. As you learn PowerPoint, you'll probably think of many ways you can use the program to communicate information to others effectively.

In this project, you get a jump-start on working with PowerPoint. You learn the basics of starting PowerPoint and of creating a new presentation. You also see how to find help by using the **Office Assistant**, PowerPoint's online Help system, so that you learn the program quickly and easily.

Visual Summary

To get you up and running with PowerPoint, you'll start the program and find your way around the PowerPoint window. You'll also create a new, blank presentation and use the Slide pane to enter text. To find out more about the program, you'll use the Office Assistant to tap into the Help system (see Figure 1.1).

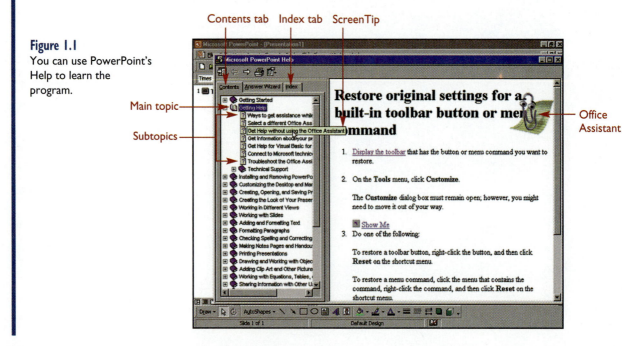

Figure 1.1
You can use PowerPoint's Help to learn the program.

When you finish developing the sample presentation, it will look similar to the one shown in Figure 1.2.

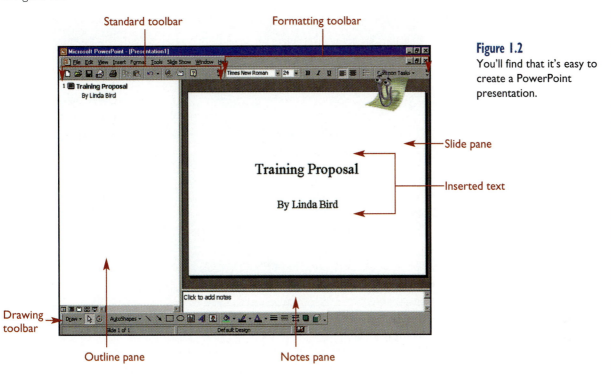

Standard toolbar   Formatting toolbar

Figure 1.2
You'll find that it's easy to create a PowerPoint presentation.

Slide pane

Inserted text

Drawing toolbar

Outline pane   Notes pane

It's easy to communicate effectively when you use PowerPoint presentations. So grab your mouse and let's get going!

Lesson 1: Starting PowerPoint

Most people like choices. Fortunately, Microsoft offers you a variety of methods you can use to start PowerPoint. One of the easiest methods to use is to click the Windows Start button and then choose Microsoft PowerPoint from the Programs menu. In this lesson, you start PowerPoint by using this method.

To Start PowerPoint

❶ Move the mouse pointer to the Start button at the left edge of the Windows taskbar, and then click the left mouse button.
The Start button's popup menu displays (see Figure 1.3).

continues ▶

To Start PowerPoint   (continued)

Figure 1.3
You can start PowerPoint by using the Windows Start button.

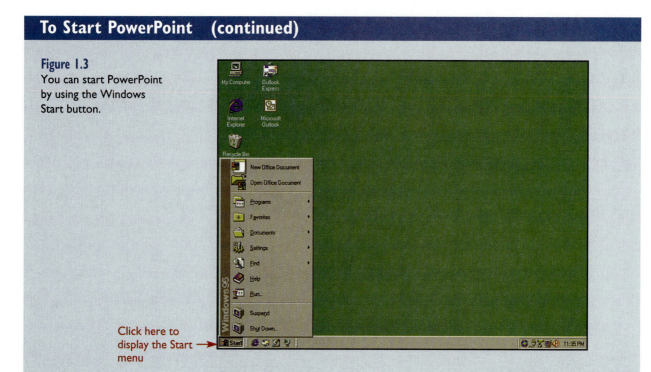

Click here to
display the Start
menu

2 Move the mouse pointer to the Programs menu item.

A listing of available programs displays. Don't panic if the ones on your system don't match those shown in this book, however. The programs listed just reflect the ones installed on your system.

> ❌ If you don't see Microsoft PowerPoint on the Programs submenu, move the mouse pointer over the Microsoft Office folder. Then click the PowerPoint icon from the Microsoft Office submenu.

3 Move the mouse pointer to Microsoft PowerPoint, and then click the left mouse button.

PowerPoint is loaded into the computer's working area—*Random Access Memory (RAM)*—and displays on your screen (see Figure 1.4). Random Access Memory is the temporary storage space that a computer uses for programs that it's currently working on.

As you scan the PowerPoint window, you probably notice that many screen components are similar to other Windows programs. For example, the menu bar, title bar, and toolbars look similar to other programs that you may have used. (If you're not sure where PowerPoint's commands and features are located, don't worry—you will take a tour of the PowerPoint application window shortly.)

Additionally, PowerPoint displays a startup dialog box designed to help you quickly create presentations. Unless the feature has been turned off, usually the Office Assistant appears on the screen as well.

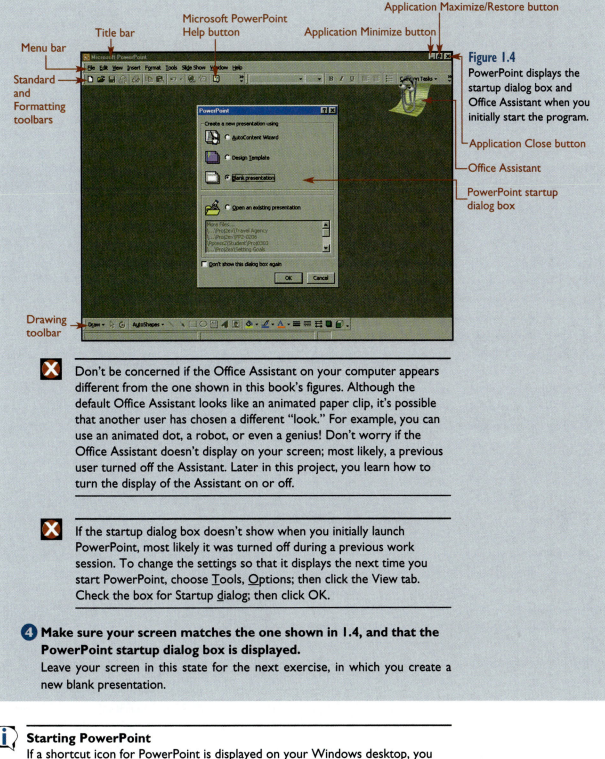

Menu bar

Title bar

Microsoft PowerPoint
Help button

Application Minimize button

Application Maximize/Restore button

Standard
and
Formatting
toolbars

Figure 1.4
PowerPoint displays the
startup dialog box and
Office Assistant when you
initially start the program.

Application Close button

Office Assistant

PowerPoint startup
dialog box

Drawing
toolbar

X Don't be concerned if the Office Assistant on your computer appears
different from the one shown in this book's figures. Although the
default Office Assistant looks like an animated paper clip, it's possible
that another user has chosen a different "look." For example, you can
use an animated dot, a robot, or even a genius! Don't worry if the
Office Assistant doesn't display on your screen; most likely, a previous
user turned off the Assistant. Later in this project, you learn how to
turn the display of the Assistant on or off.

X If the startup dialog box doesn't show when you initially launch
PowerPoint, most likely it was turned off during a previous work
session. To change the settings so that it displays the next time you
start PowerPoint, choose Tools, Options; then click the View tab.
Check the box for Startup dialog; then click OK.

---

4 **Make sure your screen matches the one shown in 1.4, and that the
PowerPoint startup dialog box is displayed.**
Leave your screen in this state for the next exercise, in which you create a
new blank presentation.

Starting PowerPoint
If a shortcut icon for PowerPoint is displayed on your Windows desktop, you
can start PowerPoint by double-clicking it. You can also right-click the icon to
display a *shortcut menu*, which is a list of context-sensitive commands that you
display by right-clicking an object. After the shortcut menu is displayed, choose
Open from the displayed menu to start PowerPoint.

Many systems are also set up to automatically display the Microsoft Office
Shortcut Bar on the Windows desktop. This bar contains buttons that you can
use to launch Microsoft Office programs, including PowerPoint.

Lesson 2: Creating a New Blank Presentation

Now that you've launched PowerPoint, the stage is set for creating your first presentation! The PowerPoint startup dialog box provides three options for quickly creating a new presentation: using the AutoContent Wizard, using a design template, or starting completely from scratch by using a blank presentation.

This lesson focuses on creating a new presentation from the ground up. (In Project 2, you learn how to use a template or the AutoContent Wizard to speed up the process.) Try creating a presentation from scratch now.

To Create a New Blank Presentation

1 **In the PowerPoint startup dialog box that is still open from Lesson 1, click the Blank presentation button; then choose OK.**

> ✕ Don't despair if you accidentally closed PowerPoint's startup dialog box or if it didn't display when you launched PowerPoint. Just choose File, New from the menu to display the New Presentation dialog box. On the General tab, click the Blank Presentation icon; then choose OK. Continue with Step 2 of this lesson.

The New Slide dialog box displays with 24 predefined layout options called *AutoLayouts* (see Figure 1.5). Each AutoLayout includes *placeholders*, which are areas on a slide that can accept different types of objects, such as graphics and text. For example, the Title Slide AutoLayout contains areas for the slide's title and subtitle. Using the AutoLayouts takes considerably less time than individually defining the format for each slide.

Figure 1.5
You can quickly create a slide for your presentation with preset formatting.

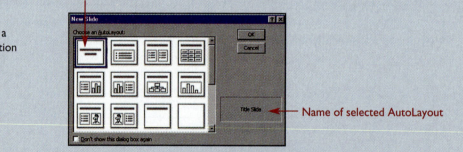

Selected AutoLayout

Name of selected AutoLayout

2 **Single-click several of the AutoLayouts.**
A darkened border appears around the border of an AutoLayout when you select it. Also notice that the name of each AutoLayout displays in the lower-right corner of the New Slide dialog box when you click the associated AutoLayout.

3 **When you finish experimenting, click on the Title Slide AutoLayout; then choose OK.**
Your first presentation slide displays on your desktop in *Normal view*. This tri-pane view includes a Slide pane, an Outline pane, and a Notes pane (see Figure 1.6). Each of the three panes represents a way to work with your pre-

sentation. You use the *Slide pane* to see how each slide appears and to add text, graphics, or other objects to the slide. In contrast, you use the *Outline pane* to organize the content of the entire presentation and to get a feel for the overall flow. Finally, you use the *Notes pane* to develop speaker notes. For now, you use only the Slide pane to enter your text.

As you develop your presentation, you will probably use the Normal view to enter text and graphics, as well as to quickly scan the presentation's entire flow and content. Because of this versatility, Normal view is a handy all-purpose view.

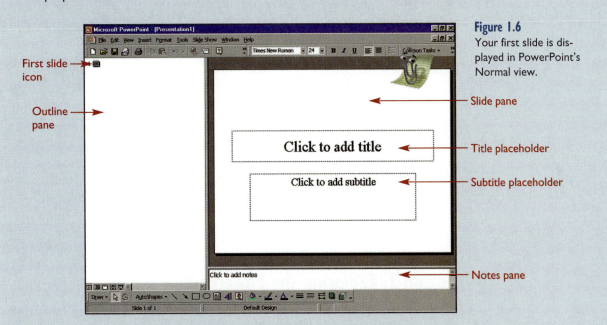

Figure 1.6
Your first slide is displayed in PowerPoint's Normal view.

❹ **In the Slide pane, click in the title placeholder (the upper place-holder). (If you're unsure where the title placeholder is located, refer to Figure 1.6.)**
The title placeholder is activated in *editing mode* and appears with a rope-like border. When a placeholder is in editing mode, it simply means that you can enter or edit text in the placeholder.

❺ **Type `Training Proposal`.**
Your text is entered in the title placeholder. It also appears next to the first slide icon in the Outline pane. Don't panic if you make a mistake as you enter the text. You can make corrections as you do in a word processing program—just press `Del` or `Backspace`.

❻ **Click in the subtitle placeholder (the lower placeholder); then type `By`, followed by *your name*.**
Notice that the text you enter on the slide is simultaneously displayed beside the first slide icon in the Outline pane. This helps you see how the text you enter relates to the rest of the presentation when you develop multiple-slide presentations.

continues ▶

To Create a New Blank Presentation   (continued)

X If a red squiggly line appears beneath a word (such as your name), don't worry. PowerPoint flags possible typos or misspellings with the red line so that you can correct them. In this case, PowerPoint just doesn't recognize your name—you can safely ignore the red line.

7 **Click in the Slide pane outside the subtitle placeholder.**
The placeholder is deselected and is no longer in editing mode.

Congratulations! You just developed your first presentation (refer to Figure 1.1, if necessary, to see how it should look). To build the presentation further, you could add more slides and text. For now, though, leave the presentation in its present state so that you can "take a tour" of PowerPoint's application window.

i **Entering Text**
When you initially display a Title (or Bulleted List) slide, you don't have to click in a placeholder in order to enter text. Instead, just start typing; the upper placeholder is automatically activated in editing mode. To move the insertion point to the next placeholder, press and hold down Ctrl, and then press ↵Enter. Release both keys.

Lesson 3: Exploring the PowerPoint Window

Now that you have started PowerPoint and created a simple presentation from scratch, it's time to become familiar with the PowerPoint application window, or screen. Even if you've worked with previous versions of PowerPoint or other Windows software, you will find some changes in PowerPoint 2000. Come along as we take you on a tour...

To Explore the PowerPoint Window

1 **Compare the location of the screen components listed in Figure 1.7 with those on your computer.**
The title bar, located at the very top of the window, includes the Application Minimize, Maximize/Restore, and Close buttons. The menu bar includes the main menu commands, as well as the current presentation's Minimize, Maximize/Restore, and Close buttons.

The Standard and Formatting toolbars are represented by the row of buttons beneath the menu bar. The Drawing toolbar is displayed at the bottom of the screen; it includes buttons for drawing objects on your slide. (You will see shortly how to use the toolbar buttons.)

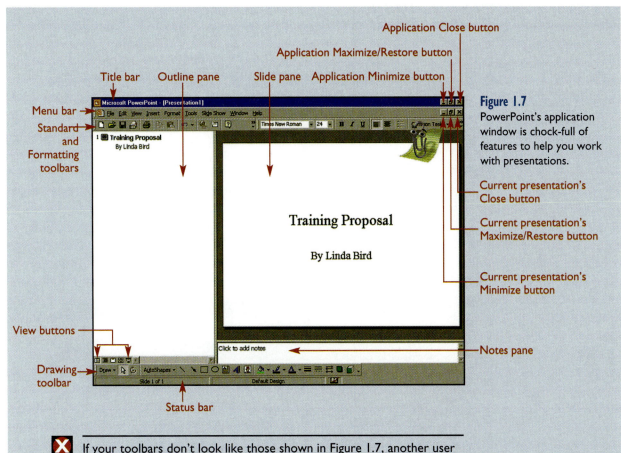

Figure 1.7
PowerPoint's application window is chock-full of features to help you work with presentations.

If your toolbars don't look like those shown in Figure 1.7, another user probably customized their appearance—perhaps without even realizing it! That's because PowerPoint adapts to the way you work by placing the most frequently-used commands on the toolbars and menus. Later in this project, you learn how to reset your toolbars and menu commands so that they match those shown in the book.

The main part of the application window is reserved for the presentation itself. Currently, the presentation is shown in Normal view, which was discussed in the previous lesson. (You see how to switch to other PowerPoint views in Project 2.)

Now try working with PowerPoint's toolbar buttons.

2 **Rest your mouse pointer over each of the toolbar buttons on the Standard, Formatting, and Drawing toolbars.**
As you rest your mouse pointer over each button, a *ScreenTip* displays the name of the button (see Figure 1.8). Thus, ScreenTips are a handy way to become familiar with the toolbar buttons.

continues ▶

To Explore the PowerPoint Window   (continued)

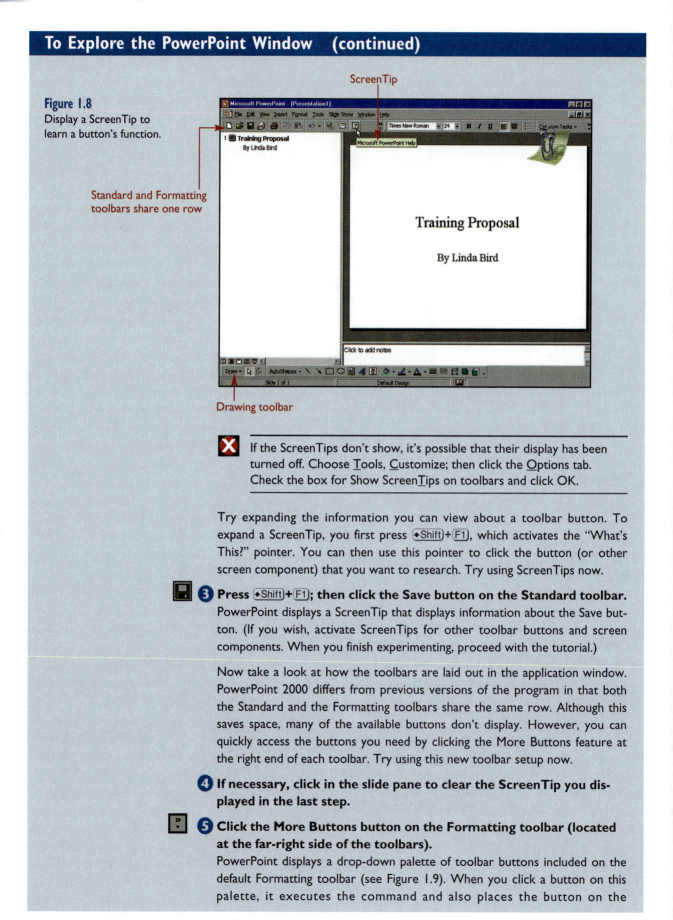

Figure 1.8
Display a ScreenTip to learn a button's function.

ScreenTip

Standard and Formatting toolbars share one row

Drawing toolbar

If the ScreenTips don't show, it's possible that their display has been turned off. Choose Tools, Customize; then click the Options tab. Check the box for Show ScreenTips on toolbars and click OK.

Try expanding the information you can view about a toolbar button. To expand a ScreenTip, you first press ⬆Shift+F1, which activates the "What's This?" pointer. You can then use this pointer to click the button (or other screen component) that you want to research. Try using ScreenTips now.

3 **Press ⬆Shift+F1; then click the Save button on the Standard toolbar.**
PowerPoint displays a ScreenTip that displays information about the Save button. (If you wish, activate ScreenTips for other toolbar buttons and screen components. When you finish experimenting, proceed with the tutorial.)

Now take a look at how the toolbars are laid out in the application window. PowerPoint 2000 differs from previous versions of the program in that both the Standard and the Formatting toolbars share the same row. Although this saves space, many of the available buttons don't display. However, you can quickly access the buttons you need by clicking the More Buttons feature at the right end of each toolbar. Try using this new toolbar setup now.

4 **If necessary, click in the slide pane to clear the ScreenTip you displayed in the last step.**

5 **Click the More Buttons button on the Formatting toolbar (located at the far-right side of the toolbars).**
PowerPoint displays a drop-down palette of toolbar buttons included on the default Formatting toolbar (see Figure 1.9). When you click a button on this palette, it executes the command and also places the button on the

Formatting toolbar for future use. For example, if you typically use the Text Shadow button (which isn't included on the default setup for the Formatting toolbar), you can choose it from the palette.

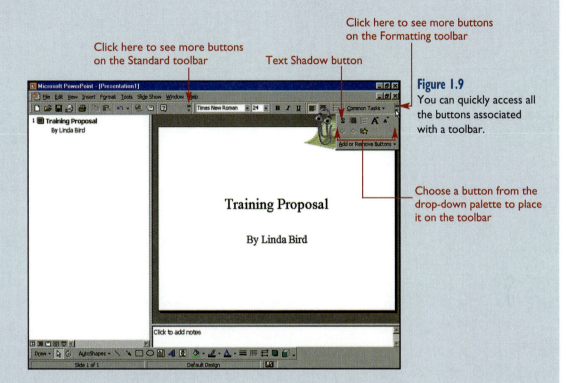

Click here to see more buttons on the Standard toolbar

Text Shadow button

Click here to see more buttons on the Formatting toolbar

Choose a button from the drop-down palette to place it on the toolbar

Figure 1.9
You can quickly access all the buttons associated with a toolbar.

6 Click the Text Shadow button on the Formatting toolbar's More Buttons palette.

The Text Shadow button is displayed on the Formatting toolbar. Additionally, if you had text selected, the Text Shadow effect would have been applied to it.

Now take a look at the menu commands in PowerPoint. As in other Windows programs, you execute a command by clicking a command on the menu bar and then clicking the command you want from the submenu. PowerPoint 2000, however, gives you the option of using either short or full menus. The *short menu*, true to its name, displays an abbreviated list of commonly used commands. The *full menu* includes all of PowerPoint's commands.

By default, the short menu displays first. After a momentary delay, the full menu displays, which keeps the most commonly used commands handy. Try using this new menu setup now.

7 Click the Insert menu on the menu bar; then rest the mouse pointer over the word Insert until a full menu of choices displays.

The short menu displays first, showing a list of the most commonly used commands (see Figure 1.10). When you rest the mouse pointer momentarily over the menu command, however, the full menu displays (see Figure 1.11).

continues ▶

To Explore the PowerPoint Window   (continued)

Figure 1.10
The short menu displays initially when you choose a command...

Figure 1.11
...but PowerPoint provides quick access to the full menu when you momentarily rest your pointer over the command.

❌ If the menus on your computer don't appear exactly like those shown in the book, don't worry. PowerPoint 2000 includes adaptable, or personalized, menus. This simply means that the program shows the commands at the top of each pull-down menu that you use the most frequently. Because the program automatically customizes the menus to the way you work, it's likely that your menus will display slightly different commands than those shown in the figures.

8 **Click outside the pull-down menu to close it without choosing any commands.**
Leave PowerPoint running for the next tutorial, in which you learn to work with toolbars.

ⓘ **Working with Menus**
There are a couple of alternative methods of displaying the full menus. First, you can rest your mouse pointer on the double down arrows at the bottom of the pull-down menu. Second, you can double-click a main menu command to quickly display the full menu that is associated with it.

Lesson 4: Working with Toolbars and Menus

By now, you should be feeling more comfortable with using ScreenTips to display information about toolbar buttons, and displaying short and full menus. In this lesson, you expand your knowledge as you work with PowerPoint's Common Tasks button and learn to customize toolbars.

To Work with Toolbars and Menus

1 **Make sure that PowerPoint is running and your new presentation is displayed in Normal view.**

Now you're ready to display the Common Tasks menu. True to its name, this menu includes frequently used commands, such as adding a new slide. Try displaying this menu now.

2 **Click the Common Tasks button on the far right side of the Formatting toolbar.**

The Common Tasks menu displays, showing a list of three frequently used tasks (see Figure 1.12).

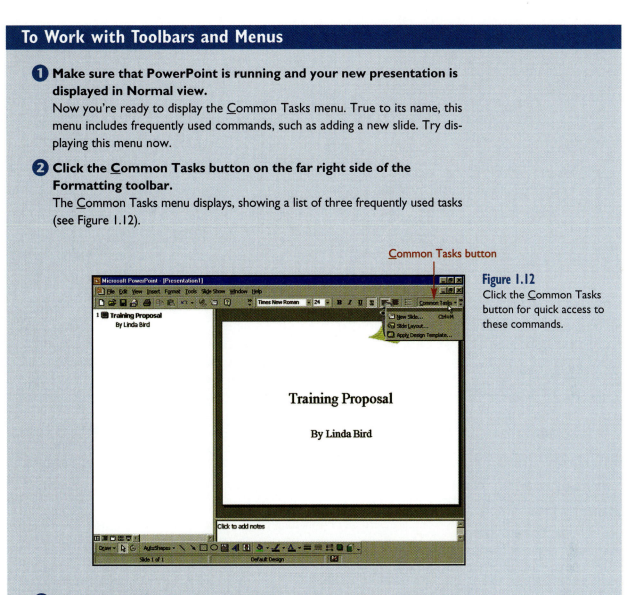

Common Tasks button

Figure 1.12
Click the Common Tasks button for quick access to these commands.

3 **Click outside the Common Tasks menu to close it without choosing any of the commands.**

Now turn your attention to the *personalized menus and toolbars* included in PowerPoint. PowerPoint's capability to adapt to an individual's work habits by automatically changing the display of menus and toolbar buttons is advantageous because the commands shown are those you use the most. To ensure that your screens display the same way as the figures shown in this book, the personalized menus are turned off, and the Standard and Formatting toolbars are separated to keep all the buttons handy.

4 **Choose Tools, Customize from the menu; then click the Options tab.**

The Options page of the Customize dialog box displays (see Figure 1.13). You use this dialog box to control how PowerPoint's adaptable menus and toolbars work. For example, you can change the settings so that only the full menus show or you can separate the Standard and Formatting toolbars.

continues ▶

To Work with Toolbars and Menus (continued)

Figure 1.13
You can control the way your toolbars and menus operate.

Uncheck this box to separate the toolbars

Uncheck this box to turn off personalized menus

Click here to reset your toolbars and menus

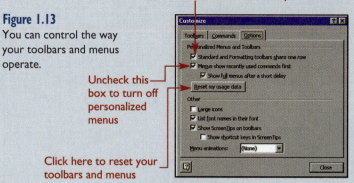

First, erase the record of which commands you (or another person) used in PowerPoint. When you do this, PowerPoint reverts back to the original toolbar and menu commands.

5 **Click the Reset my usage data button.**
The Office Assistant displays a message, warning you that resetting usage data will erase the record of commands you used.

6 **Click Yes to confirm your action.**

7 **Uncheck the following boxes: Standard and Formatting toolbars share one row and Menus show recently used commands first.**
Turning off these options separates your Standard and Formatting toolbars. It also ensures that PowerPoint's full menus display.

8 **In the Customize dialog box, click Close.**
The Standard and Formatting toolbars appear on separate rows (see Figure 1.14) and all the buttons associated with each toolbar display. Because all the figures in this book are shown using this toolbar layout, it's a good idea to leave your screen this way.

Figure 1.14
Separate the Standard and Formatting toolbars for quick access to all their buttons.

Standard toolbar

Formatting toolbar

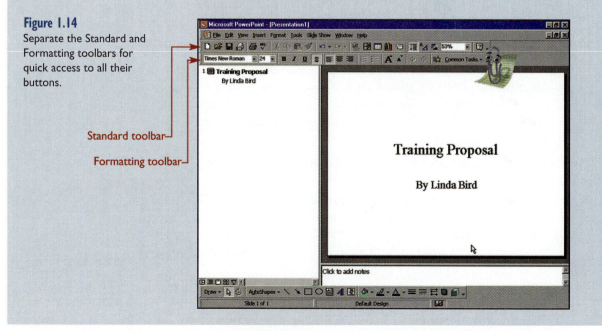

Leave your presentation open for the next lesson, in which you learn how to get help in PowerPoint.

ⓘ Using Keyboard Shortcuts to Open Menus

If you're a keyboard fan, you'll be glad to know that you don't have to use the mouse every time you want to access the menus. Instead, press Alt and the menu command's underlined letter to open the pull-down menu. To choose a command on the pull-down menu, just press the underlined letter associated with the command. For example, you can press Alt+I to open the Insert menu; then press H to choose the Chart command on the Insert menu.

⟨?⟩ Lesson 5: Getting Help

Have you ever wished for a personal computer trainer—someone to personally guide you through a new software program? Fortunately, PowerPoint 2000 includes an electronic version of such a person—the Office Assistant. Although not a full-blown substitute for a personal computer trainer, the Office Assistant can bring up a list of subjects related to a question you type.

You can choose Help, Microsoft PowerPoint Help to display the Office Assistant. Alternatively, you can click the Microsoft PowerPoint Help button on the Standard toolbar or simply press F1. Once the Office Assistant is displayed, you can easily bring up context-sensitive help. Try using this handy feature now.

To Get Help

❶ Choose Help, Microsoft PowerPoint Help.
Alternatively, click the Microsoft PowerPoint Help button. No matter which method you choose, though, the Office Assistant displays a message balloon. You can enter a question in the text box area of the balloon, and then have the Office Assistant find all the information related to your inquiry (see Figure 1.15). This balloon also sometimes includes a list of Help topics related to whatever features you used most recently. (If the Office Assistant is already displayed on your screen, just single-click it to display the balloon.)

continues ▶

To Get Help   (continued)

Type your question here   Message balloon

Figure 1.15
You can use the
Office Assistant to find
information.

Click here to see
options related to the
Office Assistant

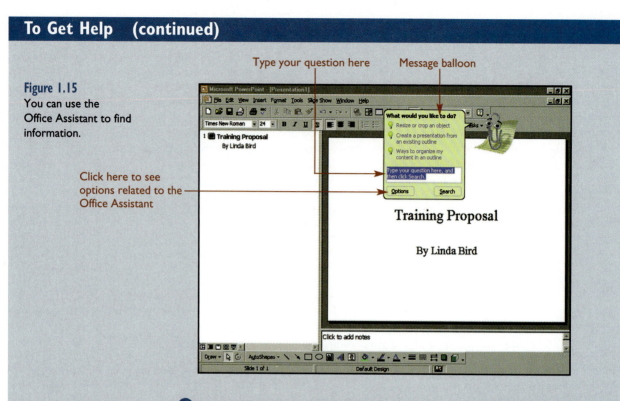

2 **In the text box area, type** How do I reset my toolbars? **and click**
Search.
A list of related topics displays (see Figure 1.16). You can click the topic you
want to display help about or you can click the See more... button to view
additional topics.

Figure 1.16
The Office Assistant
answers your question by
displaying related topics.

List of topics produced
by the search

Click here to see
additional topics

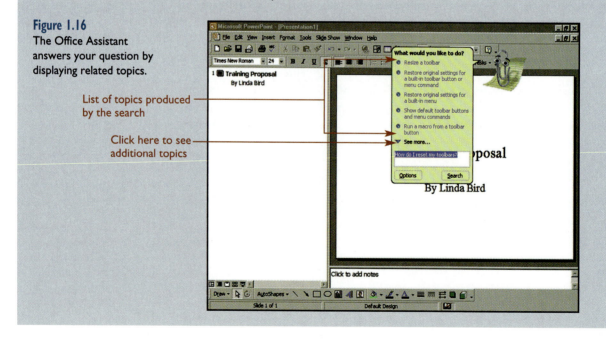

❸ From the list, click `Restore original settings for a built-in toolbar button or menu command.`

The Microsoft PowerPoint Help window for this topic displays (see Figure 1.17). Don't be concerned that the Help window displays on top of your PowerPoint application window and that the screen looks a bit cluttered. When you eventually close the Help window, PowerPoint will display your presentation in the Normal view again. If the Office Assistant displays on top of the Help window, just drag the Assistant to another location.

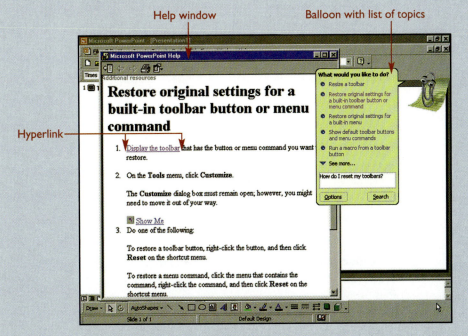

Figure 1.17
The PowerPoint Help window gives you step-by-step instructions.

You can read the information included in the topic or view related topics. You can also click a *hyperlink* in the dialog box. Hyperlink text is underlined and shown in a contrasting color, and a special "helping hand" pointer displays whenever you move the mouse pointer over the hyperlink text. You can click a hyperlink to display related information. Try using a hyperlink now.

❹ Move your mouse pointer over the `Display the toolbar` **hyperlink in the Help window until the hand pointer displays; then click.**

The PowerPoint Help window displays information related to the hyperlink—in this case, how to show or hide a toolbar (see Figure 1.18).

continues ▶

To Get Help   (continued)

Figure 1.18
Click a hyperlink to jump
to related information.

Show button   Back button

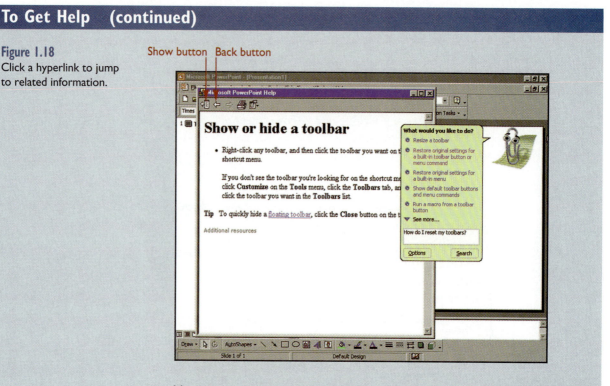

Now try returning to the previous screen by using the Back button that
displays in the PowerPoint Help window.

5 **Click the Back button in the PowerPoint Help window.**
The previous Help screen displays. Notice that the Forward button is now
activated. As you probably guessed, you can easily scroll between Help topics
by using the Forward and Back buttons.

Now see how to access PowerPoint's Help Contents and Index pages.

6 **Click the Show button in the PowerPoint Help window.**
PowerPoint splits the Help window into two panes, so that you can access Help
in alternative ways (see Figure 1.19). The left pane is called the *Navigation
pane* because it helps you navigate through various topics by topic or
keyword. For example, instead of asking questions of the Office Assistant, you
can find the information topically on the Contents page—much as you would
use a book's table of contents. You can also use PowerPoint's alphabetical
listing of topics found on the Index page. To display the Contents or Index
pages, just click the associated tab.

Now you're ready to use the Contents page to find information. A book icon
represents each topic; you can double-click the icon to display subtopics
related to the main topic. Try using the Contents page now.

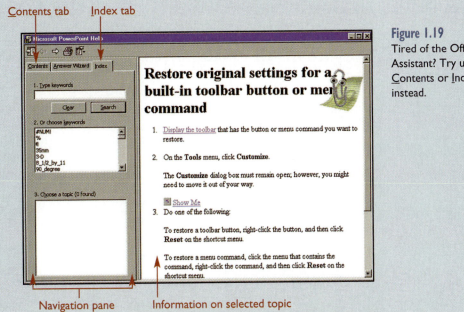

Figure 1.19
Tired of the Office Assistant? Try using the Contents or Index pages instead.

(7) **Click the Contents tab to display it; then double-click the Getting Help book icon.**

A list of subtopics appears, as shown in Figure 1.20. Don't worry if you can't view the entire name of a subtopic, because you can rest your mouse pointer over the topic until the full name displays. When you find the topic you want, click its icon to see information about the topic.

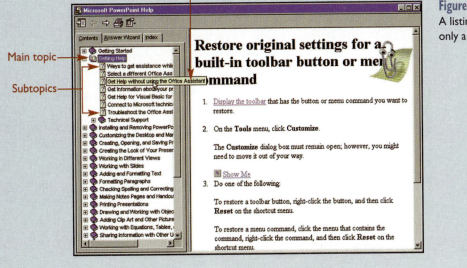

Figure 1.20
A listing of subtopics is only a double-click away.

continues ▶

To Get Help (continued)

8 **Rest your mouse pointer over the** `Get Help without using the` `Office Assistant` **subtopic until the full name of the topic appears, and then click.**

The information related to the topic displays in the right pane of the Help window (see Figure 1.21). If you want, spend a minute or two clicking on other topics on the <u>C</u>ontents page and reading the associated information. Practice closing an open book icon by double-clicking it.

Figure 1.21
Click a subtopic to see related information.

Information related to the chosen subtopic

Selected subtopic

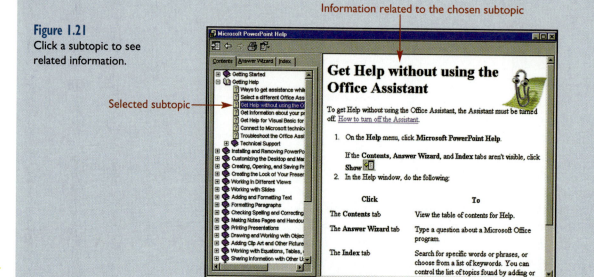

Now try using the <u>I</u>ndex, which includes an alphabetical list of topics (or *keywords*) that you can use to find all related topics. For example, if you enter the keyword `Print`, PowerPoint may find more than 40 topics related to the word, and then display them in the Help window. You can click a topic to select it and display its associated Help screen.

9 **Click the <u>I</u>ndex tab; then click in the <u>T</u>ype keywords text box and enter** `Save`. **Choose <u>S</u>earch.**

A list of topics related to the keyword displays in the C<u>h</u>oose a topic section of the dialog box, as shown in Figure 1.22.

You can click a topic on the C<u>h</u>oose a topic list to see related information in the right pane. Try using this feature now.

10 **In the C<u>h</u>oose a topic list, click** `Save a presentation`.

Information about the topic displays in the right pane of the Help window (see Figure 1.23).

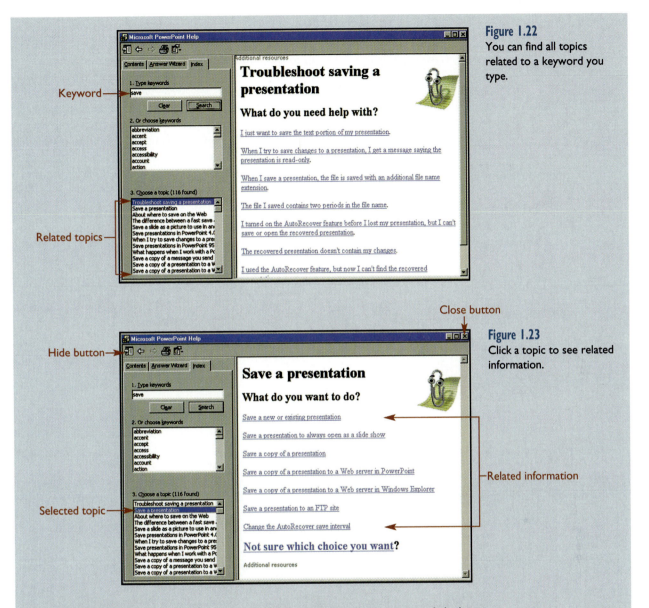

Figure 1.22
You can find all topics related to a keyword you type.

Keyword

Related topics

Close button

Figure 1.23
Click a topic to see related information.

Hide button

Selected topic

Related information

To redisplay a single pane in the PowerPoint Help window, you can click the Hide button. To completely close the PowerPoint Help window, click its Close button in the upper-right corner of the window.

11 **Click the Hide button to close the Navigation pane. (If you're unsure where the Hide button is located, refer to Figure 1.23.)**

12 **Close the PowerPoint Help window by clicking its Close button (refer to Figure 1.23).**
The PowerPoint Help window closes and your presentation redisplays in Normal view. Keep the presentation open for the next lesson, in which you explore options specifically related to using the Office Assistant.

Finding Help on the Web

If you're like most users, you'll probably rely heavily on PowerPoint's built-in Help system to find ways to work with the program more effectively. If you absolutely can't find the information you need within PowerPoint, however, you have another option: You can tap into the resources available on the World Wide Web. Assuming that you have Internet access, you can choose <u>H</u>elp, Office on the <u>W</u>eb. Perform whatever steps you usually do to connect to the Web (such as entering your password). PowerPoint automatically displays Microsoft's Web site for PowerPoint. After you're connected to the Web, you can use hyperlinks (and the Back and Forward buttons on the toolbar) to move between Web sites. When you finish cruising the Web, click the Close button to disconnect from the Web and redisplay PowerPoint.

Lesson 6: Customizing the Office Assistant

As with many PowerPoint 2000 features, you can customize the Office Assistant to match the way you work. In fact, you can choose an Assistant other than the default "Clippit"—perhaps one that better matches your personality (such as the "Genius"). Fortunately, Office 2000 includes a few Assistants that you can use instead of Clippit. In this lesson, you learn how to choose a different appearance for the Assistant.

As handy as the Office Assistant is, you may find that you prefer to use the PowerPoint Help window without the Assistant. To give you plenty of options, you can temporarily hide the Office Assistant and then redisplay it during a work session. But if this doesn't fit the bill, you can instead turn off the feature completely. Try exploring these options now.

To Customize the Office Assistant

1 Choose <u>H</u>elp, Microsoft PowerPoint <u>H</u>elp, and then click <u>O</u>ptions in the Office Assistant's balloon.

The Office Assistant dialog box displays. You use this dialog box to change the Assistant's settings, turn off the Assistant, or change the way the Assistant appears.

2 Click the <u>G</u>allery tab.

The <u>G</u>allery page of the Office Assistant dialog box displays, as shown in Figure 1.24. You can scroll through the available Assistants by clicking the <u>N</u>ext and <u>B</u>ack buttons.

Figure 1.24
You have a choice of several different Office Assistants.

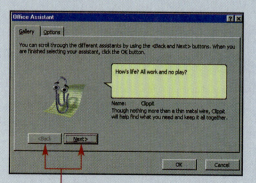

Click these buttons to scroll through the available Assistants

3 **Click the Next and Back buttons until you see the Assistant that you want to use; then click OK.**

The Assistant changes to the one you chose. Now try temporarily hiding (and then redisplaying) the Assistant.

4 **Choose Help, Hide the Office Assistant.**

The Assistant is no longer displayed, but it is only a mouse click away. You can quickly redisplay it by choosing Help, Show the Office Assistant or by clicking the Microsoft PowerPoint Help button. Try redisplaying the Assistant now.

5 **Choose Help, Show the Office Assistant.**

The Assistant displays in the PowerPoint application window. Now turn off the Assistant completely by changing settings in the Office Assistant dialog box.

6 **Click the Office Assistant to display its balloon (if necessary), and then click the Options button.**

The Office Assistant dialog box displays.

7 **Click the Options tab in the Office Assistant dialog box, if necessary; then uncheck the box for Use the Office Assistant. Click OK.**

The Office Assistant is no longer displayed onscreen. At first glance, this command appears to duplicate the command to temporarily hide the Assistant (as you did in Step 4). However, when the Office Assistant is completely turned off, pressing F1 (or choosing Help, Microsoft PowerPoint Help) displays only the Microsoft PowerPoint Help window—not the Office Assistant. Try using this command now to see the difference.

8 **Choose Help, Microsoft PowerPoint Help.**

The Microsoft PowerPoint Help window displays, complete with the Navigation pane. Notice that the Office Assistant is not displayed, however. In fact, the Office Assistant is turned off for the remainder of the book. (You're welcome to continue to use the Assistant if you've grown particularly fond of it. Just remember that your computer screen won't match some of the figures in the book.)

9 **Click the Close button in the Microsoft PowerPoint Help window to close it.**

The Help window is cleared. Leave PowerPoint open for the next lesson.

Getting Help

Even if you turned off the Office Assistant for the work session, you can easily turn it back on again—just choose Help, Show the Office Assistant.

Besides answering your questions, the Office Assistant can give you help in other ways. For example, the Assistant provides tips on how to use features more effectively in PowerPoint. You know when the Assistant has a tip for you because a yellow light bulb appears near the Assistant. Click the light bulb to see the tip. This is especially helpful when you develop new presentations because the Assistant gives you ideas on clip art or other items to include in your presentation.

If you want to know more about the Assistant, including ways to customize the feature for the way you work, explore the Getting Help list of subtopics on the Contents page.

Lesson 7: Closing Your Presentation and Exiting PowerPoint

Now you're ready to close your presentation and exit PowerPoint. Closing a presentation and clearing it from memory is similar to clearing your desk at school or work to make room for another project. And if closing a presentation is similar to clearing off your desk, exiting the entire program is like leaving your office.

Remember—any presentation exists only in RAM until you save it, and the presentation you created in this lesson is no exception. Unless you save the presentation to a permanent storage location, such as a disk or drive, closing it also permanently clears it from your computer. Because of this, you typically should save most presentations before closing them. Because you won't need the presentation you created in Lesson 2 anymore, however, you learn how to clear this presentation without saving it.

This lesson also covers how to properly exit the PowerPoint program. You can exit PowerPoint in a couple of ways: by clicking the Application Close button or choosing File, Exit from the menu. (If you plan to complete the Skill Drill, Challenge, and Discovery Zone exercises at the end of this project, simply start PowerPoint again. If you finish working, you should also shut down Windows and turn off the computer.) Try closing your presentation and exiting PowerPoint now.

To Close Your Presentation and Exit PowerPoint

1 **Choose File, Close.**
PowerPoint displays a message asking if you want to save the presentation (see Figure 1.25). Any time you make changes to a presentation and then attempt to close it without saving your revisions, PowerPoint displays this message.

X The exact appearance of the message that displays depends on whether or not the Office Assistant is shown. If you redisplay the Assistant, the message appears in the Assistant's balloon. If not, the message appears in the message box shown in Figure 1.25.

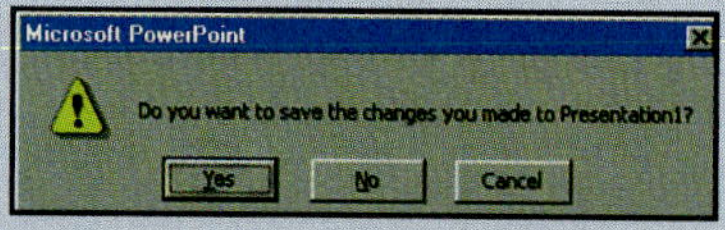

Figure 1.25
PowerPoint always asks if you want to keep unsaved changes.

Microsoft PowerPoint

Do you want to save the changes you made to Presentation1?

Yes   No   Cancel

2 **Choose No.**
PowerPoint clears the presentation from memory. Now you're ready to exit the program.

3 **Click the Application Close button.**
Alternatively, you can choose File, Exit from the menu. The PowerPoint program closes and the Windows desktop (or another open application) redisplays.

It's also important to properly exit Windows before turning off the computer. The best way to do this is to use (ironically enough) Windows' Start button.

(Be sure you close all other open applications before proceeding. If you don't know if another program is running or not, see your instructor for help.)

4 **Click the Start button, and then choose Sh<u>u</u>t Down from the menu.**
The Shut Down Windows dialog box displays. You use this dialog box to control how to shut down or restart Windows.

5 **Make sure that the <u>S</u>hut down option button is chosen, and then click OK.**
Windows closes temporary files and clears them from memory. This process generally takes a few seconds, so be patient during the process. It's important to wait until Windows indicates that you can turn off the computer.

6 **Wait until the `It's now safe to turn off your computer` message displays (or ask your instructor if Windows has cleared).**
After you receive confirmation, you can turn off your computer.

7 **Turn off your computer's main unit, monitor, and any other hardware (such as speakers or a printer).**

Summary

Congratulations! In this project, you learned the basics of starting PowerPoint and creating a new presentation. You also became familiar with the PowerPoint window and navigated the program's toolbars and menus. You acquired skills for researching Help topics and using the Office Assistant. Finally, you learned how to properly exit PowerPoint and shut down Windows.

To expand on your knowledge, spend a few minutes exploring Help on these topics. Additionally, complete some of the Skill Drill, Challenge, and Discovery Zone exercises.

Checking Concepts and Terms

True/False

For each of the following, check *T* or *F* to indicate whether the statement is true or false.

__T __F **1.** You can get help by using PowerPoint's Window Assistant. [L5]

__T __F **2.** Closing a presentation and exiting PowerPoint are the same. [L7]

__T __F **3.** If power to your computer is interrupted, you lose everything in Random Access Memory (RAM). [L1]

__T __F **4.** By default, PowerPoint includes both short and full menus for each menu command. [L4]

__T __F **5.** By default, PowerPoint menus and toolbars change which commands display automatically to reflect the ones you use the most frequently. [L4]

Multiple Choice

Circle the letter of the correct answer for each of the following.

1. PowerPoint's Normal view includes the
_____ component. [L2]

   a. Slide pane

   b. Outline pane

   c. Notes pane

   d. all of the above

2. You develop a presentation in PowerPoint by
_____. [L2]

   a. creating a new one completely from scratch

   b. using the AutoContent Wizard

   c. using a template

   d. any of the above

3. Which of the following is true regarding
PowerPoint's menus? [L3–4]

   a. They adapt to the user's work habits by displaying
the most commonly used commands near the top.

   b. You must use the mouse to access their commands.

   c. By default, the long, or full, menus display first.

   d. all of the above

4. Which of the following is true regarding
PowerPoint's toolbars? [L4]

   a. You cannot change which buttons display unless
you reinstall PowerPoint.

   b. By default, the Standard and Formatting toolbars
appear on the same row.

   c. You cannot display the toolbars and the Office
Assistant at the same time.

   d. All toolbars appear at the top of the PowerPoint
application window.

5. To exit PowerPoint, _____. [L7]

   a. simply turn off the computer

   b. choose File, Close

   c. click the Application Close button

   d. press Esc

Screen ID

Identify each of the items shown in Figures 1.26 and 1.27.

Figure 1.26

A. Application Maximize/
Restore button

B. Office Assistant

C. Menu bar

D. Formatting toolbar

E. Common Tasks button

F. Application Close
button

G. Title bar

H. Application Minimize
button

I. Standard toolbar

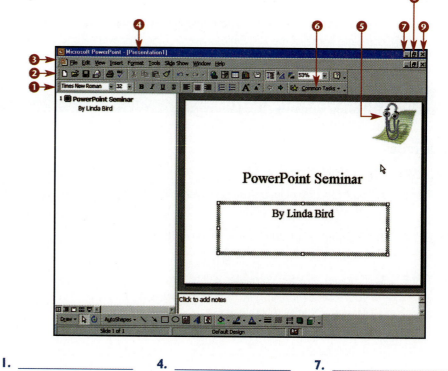

1. _____   4. _____   7. _____

2. _____   5. _____   8. _____

3. _____   6. _____   9. _____

Figure 1.27

J. Status bar

K. Drawing toolbar

L. Outline pane

M. Presentation Close
button

N. View buttons

O. Slide icon

P. Presentation Minimize
button

Q. Mouse pointer

R. Slide pane

S. Presentation Maximize/
Restore button

T. Subtitle placeholder

U. Notes pane

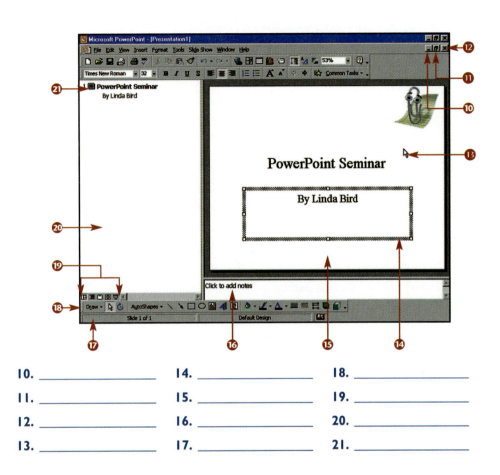

10. _____	14. _____	18. _____
11. _____	15. _____	19. _____
12. _____	16. _____	20. _____
13. _____	17. _____	21. _____

Discussion Questions

1. Why do you think Microsoft designed PowerPoint's toolbars and menus to adapt to users' work habits? What are the advantages of such a system? What are the disadvantages? [L4]

2. In what ways is the Office Assistant "user-friendly"? How does a feature such as the Office Assistant encourage people to use online Help? Why is a Help system that is easy to use also cost-effective for businesses? [L5–6]

3. List the three parts, or panes, used in Normal view. Discuss the advantages and disadvantages of this type of view. [L2–3]

Skill Drill

Skill Drill exercises reinforce project skills. Each skill that is reinforced is the same, or nearly the same, as a skill presented in the project. Detailed instructions are provided in a step-by-step format.

1. Starting and Exiting PowerPoint

As the first person in your office who has used PowerPoint 2000, you're determined to learn the ins and outs of the program. To do so, you decide to practice the different ways to start and exit PowerPoint. [L1, 7]

1. On the Windows desktop, click the Start button to display the menu. Choose Programs, and then click Microsoft PowerPoint from the submenu.

2. If the startup dialog box displays in PowerPoint, clear it by clicking its Cancel button.

3. Click PowerPoint's Application Close button (on the far right end of the title bar) to exit the program.

4. Now try starting the program by using a shortcut icon (if available on your system): Double-click the PowerPoint shortcut icon on the Windows desktop.

5. In the startup dialog box, choose Blank Presentation and click OK.

6. Close the blank presentation by choosing File, Close. (If you're prompted to save the presentation, choose No.)

7. Choose File, Exit to exit PowerPoint. Leave Windows open if you plan to complete the remaining Skill Drill exercises.

2. Creating a New Blank Presentation

You need to quickly produce a flyer for a company picnic. Because it's quick and easy to create a presentation in PowerPoint, you decide to use it to make the flyer. [L2]

1. Start PowerPoint. In the startup dialog box, choose Blank Presentation, and then choose OK.

2. Make sure the Title Slide AutoLayout is chosen in the New Slide dialog box (the first AutoLayout on the top row). Click OK to create a blank slide using this type of AutoLayout.

3. In the Slide pane, click in the title placeholder. Type Company Picnic!.

4. Click in the subtitle placeholder. Type Raccoon Creek Park. Press ↵Enter to move the insertion point to the next line. Type April 17 and press ↵Enter. Type 5:00 p.m.–9:00 p.m.

5. Click outside the placeholders. Keep the presentation open for the next exercise.

3. Exploring the PowerPoint Application Window

Your computer instructor has hired you part-time to assist other students during an open lab. You're new to PowerPoint, however, and are worried that you won't remember the toolbar buttons' functions. To brush up on the program's commands, you spend a few minutes using ScreenTips. [L3]

1. In the open PowerPoint window, rest your mouse pointer over each toolbar button on the Standard, Formatting, and Drawing toolbars until a ScreenTip displays. Note the name of each button.

2. Click the Common Tasks button on the Formatting toolbar. Write down the name of the three commands listed. Click in the Slide pane area to close the toolbar without activating any commands.

3. Locate the More Buttons button on the Standard and Formatting toolbars. Click the button to see

what buttons (or commands) are shown on the palette. Click in the Slide pane area to close the palette without activating any commands.

4. Press ⇧Shift+F1 to activate the What's This? pointer. Click the New button on the Standard toolbar. Read the ScreenTip associated with the button. Repeat the process for at least five other buttons.

5. Choose File, Close, and then click No to close the presentation without saving it.

4. Using the Office Assistant

You stay late one night at the office to learn a few new features in PowerPoint. To use your time efficiently, you decide to use PowerPoint's Office Assistant to find the information you need. [L5]

1. In the open PowerPoint screen, choose Help, Show the Office Assistant to display the Office Assistant (if necessary).

2. In the Assistant's balloon, type How do I create a presentation?. Click Search.

3. Click Create a new presentation on the list of topics displayed in the Assistant's balloon.

4. Read the information displayed in the Microsoft PowerPoint Help window. When you finish, close the Help window.

5. Display the Assistant, if necessary. Click the Assistant to display the balloon.

6. Type How can I get help? in the text box area, and then choose Search.

7. Click the `Ways to get assistance while you`
`work` option button. (If you wish, click the hyperlinks
listed in the Help window. Click Back to move to
the previous screen.)

8. When you finish reading the information, close the
Help window. Leave PowerPoint open for the next
exercise.

5. Changing the Office Assistant Options

Although you find that the Office Assistant is handy, you want to exert more control over
this feature. For example, sometimes you want to research information in the Help window without using the Assistant. To become more familiar with ways to work with the
Assistant, you practice hiding and redisplaying the Assistant. You also change the way the
Assistant appears onscreen. [L6]

1. In the open PowerPoint screen, choose Help, Hide
the Office Assistant.

2. Redisplay the Office Assistant by choosing Help,
Show the Office Assistant.

3. Hide the Assistant a second time. Try an alternative
method of redisplaying it: Click the Microsoft
PowerPoint Help button.

4. Hide the Assistant a third time. Press F1 to show
the Assistant again.

5. Click the Assistant to display the balloon, and then
click the Options button. In the Office Assistant dialog box, click the Gallery tab.

6. Click the Back button to scroll through the display of
the available Assistants. When you find one you like,
click OK.

7. Display the Office Assistant dialog box again; then
click the Options tab.

8. Turn off the display of the Assistant for the remainder of your work session by clearing the Use the
Office Assistant box. Click OK to accept your
choice. Keep PowerPoint open for the next exercise.

6. Using Help Without the Office Assistant

Your boss sent you off to a PowerPoint class so that you can become the "PowerPoint
guru" in your office. You learned a lot in the class, but you realize that there are many features in the program that the instructor didn't have time to cover. So that you don't disap-
point your boss (who now thinks that you know everything there is to know about
PowerPoint), you spend some time using the Help window to research PowerPoint
features. [L5-6]

1. Make sure that the Office Assistant is turned off. (If
you didn't complete the previous exercise in its
entirety, work through Steps 7–8 now to turn the
Assistant off.)

2. Press F1 to display the Microsoft PowerPoint Help
window. Click the Contents tab, if necessary, to display the Contents page.

3. Double-click the book icon for Clip Art to display
the list of subtopics associated with this topic. Click
the first subtopic listed; then read the displayed
information.

4. In the Navigation pane, click the second subtopic
listed. Read the associated information. Repeat this
process for each of the subtopics for Clip Art.

5. Double-click the Clip Art book icon to hide the list
of subtopics.

6. Click the Index tab to display the Index page. In the
Type keywords box, type `Print`. Click Search.

7. Click the first topic listed on the Choose a topic list.
Read the associated information.

8. Repeat Step 7 for at least four additional topics.
When you're finished, close the Microsoft
PowerPoint Help window.

7. Changing Toolbar Options

One of the great features of PowerPoint 2000 is its capability to create personalized
menus and toolbars that reflect the commands you use most frequently. However, a

friend of yours is upset because the constantly changing menus and toolbars confuse him. To help him out, you help him reset the toolbars and menus to the way they were originally when the program was first installed. [L4]

1. Choose Tools, Customize to display the Customize dialog box.

2. Click the Options tab to display the Options page.

3. Click the Reset my usage data button. Choose Yes to confirm your action, and then close the dialog box.

4. Use the ScreenTips to research the name and function of each toolbar button on the Standard and Formatting toolbars. Leave PowerPoint open if you plan to complete the Challenge or Discovery Zone exercises.

Challenge

Challenge exercises expand upon or are somewhat related to skills presented in the lessons. Each exercise provides a brief narrative introduction, followed by instructions in a numbered step format that are not as detailed as those in the Skill Drill section.

I. Researching Help Topics with the Office Assistant

One of the Help Desk employees for your company is on vacation, and you've been asked to cover for him. To answer questions that some of your co-workers ask about PowerPoint, you rely on the Office Assistant. [L5]

1. Choose Help, Show the Office Assistant to display the Office Assistant (if necessary). Then, use the Assistant to research the following topics:

   - How to create a new presentation
   - How to print a presentation
   - How to save a presentation
   - How to open an existing presentation
   - Which AutoLayouts are available in PowerPoint
   - How to format text with bold or italic
   - What views are available in PowerPoint
   - How to create speaker notes
   - How to insert Clip Art on a slide

2. Write down the steps to performing at least two of these actions, and then try out the steps in PowerPoint.

3. Explain verbally to another user the steps involved in performing two other actions you researched. If possible, have the user complete the steps on a computer as you "talk" him or her through the actions. Keep PowerPoint open for the next exercise.

2. Researching Help Topics Without the Office Assistant

The Help Desk employee decided to extend his vacation an additional week, so you're in charge of answering more questions about PowerPoint. To access Help more quickly, you decide to turn off the Office Assistant and use the PowerPoint Help window without the Assistant. [L5–6]

1. Turn off the Office Assistant (make sure that you don't simply hide the Assistant), and then display the Microsoft PowerPoint Help window.

2. Using the Contents page of the dialog box, research the following topics:
- How to add bullets or numbering to text
- How to remove or interrupt bullets and numbering
- How to print a slide
- How to print an outline
- How to print on a black-and-white printer
- How to find and use PowerPoint Introduction, the online tutorial

3. Using the Index page of the Help window, research the following topics:
- How to change the typeface or font
- How to draw on a slide
- How to add a video to your presentation
- How to add music to your presentation

4. Work another user step-by-step through the following topics, using information that you gleaned from the Help window:
- Creating a new blank presentation
- Saving the presentation
- Printing the presentation
- Closing the presentation
- Running PowerPoint Introduction, the online tutorial

Keep PowerPoint open if you plan to complete the remainder of the Challenge exercises.

3. Resetting the Office Assistant, Toolbars, and Usage Data

You're the Information Systems Manager for a small manufacturing plant. You support 50 end users and have recently upgraded the entire plant to Office 2000. To keep the computer systems uniform in their setup throughout your facility, you decide to have all the users reset their toolbars and usage data.   [L4]

1. Work through the steps necessary to reset your usage data on your own system. Write down the exact sequence that your end users must follow to reset the data on their systems.

2. Complete the steps necessary to separate the Standard and Formatting toolbars onto different rows. Write down the steps as you complete them.

3. Work through the steps on your system that are necessary to change the Office Assistant's appearance back to "Rocky." Then complete the steps necessary to turn off the Assistant (so that your users can have direct access to the Microsoft PowerPoint Help window). Write down the steps you followed.

4. Complete the steps necessary to display only long menus.

5. Create a written page that outlines the steps necessary to reset usage data, separate the Standard and Formatting toolbars, display only long menus, and turn off the Office Assistant. Give the page to another user and see if he or she can successfully complete the actions by following your written directions. Keep PowerPoint open if you plan to complete the remainder of the Challenge exercises.

[?] 4. Creating and Printing New Presentations

Your boss wants you to create some motivational and safety flyers to post around your building. To create the flyers quickly, you decide to develop a series of one-slide presentations in PowerPoint. [L2, 5]

1. If necessary, use PowerPoint's Help to brush up on creating a new blank presentation. Then use Help to find out how to print a presentation slide.

2. Create a new blank presentation. Choose the Title Slide AutoLayout for the first (and only) slide. Enter Don't Forget! in the slide's title placeholder. Then type Safety is our #1 priority! in the subtitle placeholder. Print the slide, and then close the presentation without saving it.

3. Using the previous step as a guide, create another flyer. Enter If You Don't Know… Ask! in the title placeholder. Print the slide, and then close the presentation without saving it.

4. Create a third flyer. In the title placeholder, enter We're part of the same team!. Print the slide, and then close the presentation without saving it. Keep PowerPoint open if you plan to complete the remainder of the Challenge exercises.

5. Creating and Printing a New Presentation

You work for the registrar's office at a local college. To get ready for fall registration, your boss wants you to develop signs to help direct students to the various college departments. [L2]

1. Create a new blank presentation. Choose the Title Slide AutoLayout for the first (and only) slide. Enter Accounting Department in the slide's title placeholder. Type Room 100 in the subtitle placeholder. Print the slide, and then close the presentation without saving it.

2. Using the preceding step as a guide, create a slide for each of the following departments. Print each slide, and then close the presentation without saving it.

Enter in title placeholder:	Enter in subtitle placeholder:
Business Department	Room 112
Computer Science Department	Room 120
Drafting Department	Room 125
Industrial Technology Department	Room 132
Nursing Department	Room 145
Production Control Department	Room 154

Keep PowerPoint open if you plan to complete the remainder of the Challenge exercises.

[?] 6. Researching Help on the World Wide Web

You're writing a paper on PowerPoint 2000 for your Computer Science class and you've exhausted the Help information included in the program. To obtain more data, you decide to get some help from Microsoft's Web sites. [L5]

1. Make sure that you have Web access and that your equipment is set up to connect to the Web. (If you have questions, see your instructor.)

2. Choose <u>H</u>elp, Office on the <u>W</u>eb. Complete whatever steps are necessary on your system to connect to the Web.

3. Explore Microsoft's Web sites for PowerPoint. If you're having trouble locating the correct site, try entering `www.microsoft.com` to access Microsoft's home page.

4. Research and write down at least five tips and tricks for working with PowerPoint that you didn't know.

5. Disconnect from the Web; then try out the new tips in PowerPoint 2000.

6. Share the information you learned with at least one other person in your class. If you wish, write a short paper on what you learned.

Discovery Zone

Discovery Zone exercises require advanced knowledge of topics presented in Essentials lessons, the application of skills from multiple lessons, or self-directed learning of new skills.

1. Working with Toolbars and Keyboard Shortcuts

You've been asked to do some assistant teaching for an upcoming PowerPoint class. However, the class is covering intermediate subjects, such as working with toolbars and keyboard shortcuts. So that you'll be ready for the class, you decide to research and practice working with toolbars.

Using PowerPoint's Help system, find out how to perform the following:

- Hide a toolbar's display
- Redisplay a toolbar
- Move a toolbar
- Change toolbar buttons
- Restore default toolbars

After you research the information, perform the actions listed previously. Then restore the toolbars to their original settings.

Next, find out which keyboard shortcuts are available by tapping into PowerPoint's Help system.

Using the Microsoft PowerPoint Help window or the Office Assistant, find out the following:

- How to show or hide shortcut keys in the ScreenTips
- Which shortcut keys you can use to move around in a presentation
- Which shortcut keys you can use to work with an outline
- Which shortcut keys you can use to work with menus
- Which shortcut keys you use to open, save, and print a presentation

(*Hint*: Type `Use Keyboard Shortcuts` in the Office Assistant balloon to quickly find a comprehensive list of shortcut keys.)

Try out the keyboard shortcuts listed in Help. Then develop a list of the shortcuts that you think you will use most often. Copy and share the list with others in your class. [L4–5]

[?] 2. Working with Shortcut Menus

You always look for more efficient methods of getting around software programs such as PowerPoint. Because PowerPoint 2000 works with Windows 95/98/NT, you strongly suspect that you can use shortcut menus to access commonly used commands.

Using the Office Assistant or the Microsoft PowerPoint Help window, find out how to use shortcut menus. Create a new blank presentation and display it in Normal view. Then, display the shortcut menu for the Slide pane. Write down the commands that appear on the shortcut menu. Click outside the menu to close it without executing any commands.

Next, display shortcut menus for the Outline pane, the Notes pane, and the Standard toolbar. Write down the commands included on each menu.

Finally, enter your name in the title placeholder of your slide. With the placeholder in edit mode, display the shortcut menu for the text.

Share your observations about shortcut menus with at least one other person in your class. If necessary, demonstrate how to use the shortcut menu. Close the presentation without saving it.   [L5]

3. Creating Presentations

As you worked with PowerPoint in this project, you probably thought of several presentations that you want to create using the program. Use the knowledge you gained to develop and print at least three single-slide presentations. Base each presentation on the Title Slide AutoLayout.

Create one of each of the following types of presentations:

- A presentation to use in a business setting
- A presentation to promote an upcoming event
- A sign to direct people to a certain location in your business

If you forget how to perform a particular action in PowerPoint, use Help to brush up on the concepts. Print each presentation, and then close it.   [L2]

[?] 4. Working in Help and on the Web

The World Wide Web includes tremendous resources and information related to working with PowerPoint. Think of three topics in PowerPoint you want to know more about. Research all the information about the topics that you can by using PowerPoint's built-in Help system. Write down what you learn. Next, connect to the World Wide Web to find supporting data for your topics. If necessary, go to Microsoft's home page to find hyperlinks to PowerPoint. If you are familiar with performing a search on the Web, you can also search for other PowerPoint Web sites.

Organize in outline form the information you find, and share the information with at least one other person. If you are particularly ambitious, create a presentation that includes the information you found. (*Hint*: You add new slides to a presentation by choosing New Slide from the Common Tasks palette. You'll probably want to add slides based on the Bulleted List AutoLayout.) Print the presentation, and then close it.   [L5]

Creating Presentations

Objectives

In this project, you learn how to

➤ **Use a Template to Create a Presentation**

➤ **Use the AutoContent Wizard to Create a Presentation**

➤ **Explore PowerPoint's Views**

➤ **Move Among Slides in Normal View**

➤ **Run an Electronic Slide Show**

➤ **Use the Slide Show Shortcut Keys**

➤ **Save Your Presentation**

➤ **Print a Presentation**

Key terms introduced in this project include

- AutoContent Wizard
- clip art
- context sensitive
- footer area
- grayscale
- keyboard shortcuts
- output
- pure black and white
- templates
- thumbnail
- views
- wizards

Why Would I Do This?

The more tools you have in your PowerPoint toobox, the better equipped you are to use the program effectively. In Project 1, you learned one tool, or method, for creating a new presentation: developing it totally from scratch. PowerPoint also includes two other ways for easily creating a new presentation: using a template and relying on the AutoContent Wizard. In this project, you learn how to use these two alternative methods.

No matter how you initially create a presentation, you'll work with it by using the various perspectives, or **views**, which PowerPoint provides. You learn how to switch between these views and choose the most appropriate one as you modify your presentation. You also see how to move among slides in both Normal and Slide Show views. Finally, you learn how to save and print your presentation.

Visual Summary

In this project, you learn easy-to-use methods to create a presentation. For example, you use the New Presentation dialog box to select a design template on which to base your presentation, as shown in Figure 2.1.

Figure 2.1
You can use the New Presentation dialog box to create a presentation based on a template.

Click this tab to find the AutoContent Wizard

Select a template from this list

View a template's design here

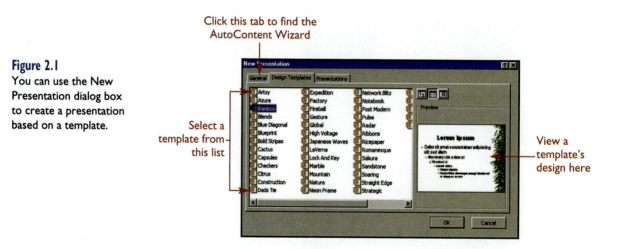

You also learn how to use the **AutoContent Wizard** to create a presentation that includes a preset design and sample content (see Figure 2.2).

After you develop your presentation, you learn how to display it in each of PowerPoint's views. When you finish, you'll have created, saved, and printed a presentation similar to the one in Figure 2.3. Try working with these features now.

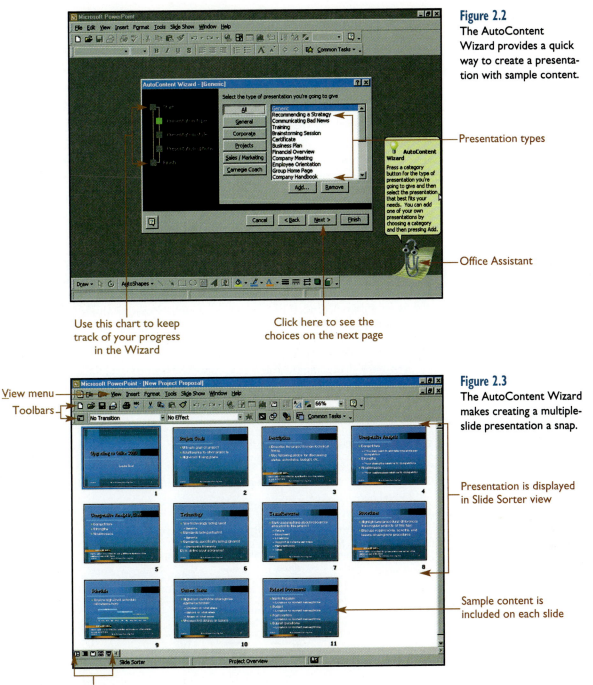

Figure 2.2
The AutoContent Wizard provides a quick way to create a presentation with sample content.

Presentation types

Office Assistant

Use this chart to keep track of your progress in the Wizard

Click here to see the choices on the next page

Figure 2.3
The AutoContent Wizard makes creating a multiple-slide presentation a snap.

View menu

Toolbars

Presentation is displayed in Slide Sorter view

Sample content is included on each slide

View buttons

Lesson 1: Using a Template to Create a Presentation

PowerPoint includes a number of predesigned **templates** (sometimes called design templates), upon which you can base your presentation. You can think of a template as a blueprint that PowerPoint uses to create slides. The template includes the formatting, color, and graphics necessary to create a particular "look."

Because these templates were created by professional graphic artists, you can use a template to create a presentation with a consistent, well-designed look. Using a template is helpful because you can concentrate on content rather than spending your time and effort on layout and design. You can choose a template when you initially create a presentation or apply one to an existing presentation. In Project 6, you'll learn to apply different templates to an existing presentation. For now, concentrate on developing a new presentation based on a template. Try working with templates now.

To Use a Template to Create a Presentation

❶ Start PowerPoint, if necessary, and clear PowerPoint's Startup dialog box.

❷ Choose <u>F</u>ile, <u>N</u>ew from the menu bar.
The New Presentation dialog box displays. This dialog box, like many others in PowerPoint, includes multiple tabs. In fact, the layout of this dialog box is reminiscent of tabbed file folders in a file cabinet. To bring a dialog box page to the front, just click the associated tab.

❸ Click the Design Templates tab.
The Design Templates page of the dialog box displays (Figure 2.4). You can single-click to select a template and preview it—right within the New Presentation dialog box.

Figure 2.4
The New Presentation dialog box gives you access to many templates.

Click this tab to access PowerPoint's templates

Large icons button
Details button
List button

❹ Single-click the High Voltage template.
PowerPoint displays a *thumbnail*—a miniature slide that represents the selected template in the Preview area, as shown in Figure 2.5.

❺ Single-click several other templates to preview them. When you're finished experimenting, choose Azure, and then click OK.
PowerPoint displays the New Slide dialog box, so that you can choose the AutoLayout for your opening slide. By default, PowerPoint selects the Title Slide AutoLayout for your initial slide. (If you need a refresher course on AutoLayouts and placeholders, refer to Project 1, Lesson 2.)

Figure 2.5
PowerPoint helps you choose the right template by letting you see a preview.

Selected template

Thumbnail

> ❌ Don't worry if the templates listed on your system look different from the listing shown in this book. Most likely, PowerPoint is displaying the templates in either Large Icon or Details view. To make your screen resemble that shown in Figure 2.5, click the List button in the New Presentation dialog box.
>
> Most of PowerPoint's templates are installed the first time you use them, so they're probably already installed on your system. (If not, see your instructor for help.)
>
> If you have more templates than those shown in this book, you probably have "leftover" templates from previous versions of PowerPoint, or ones that were customized and saved by another user on your system. Consider yourself lucky—this just means that you have more templates from which to choose!

> ❌ If the Azure template isn't available on your system, choose another one.

6 **Click OK to create a new slide based on the Title Slide AutoLayout.**
PowerPoint creates a new presentation based on your selected template and displays it in Normal view (see Figure 2.6). Note that the slide includes placeholders—just as it did when you created a new blank presentation in Project 1. This presentation differs, however, because the slide background, colors, formatting, and graphics are already in place. All you have to add is the content.

7 **Click in the title placeholder, and then type New Products.**
The text is entered in the placeholder—just as when you worked with a new blank presentation. In Project 3, you learn how to add additional slides to presentations that you create. For now, close this presentation without saving it so that you can learn how to use PowerPoint's AutoContent Wizard.

8 **Choose File, Close; then choose No in the message box.**
The presentation closes without being saved. Keep PowerPoint open for the next lesson.

continues ▶

To Use a Template to Create a Presentation   (continued)

Figure 2.6
PowerPoint's templates help you quickly create a presentation with a certain "look and feel."

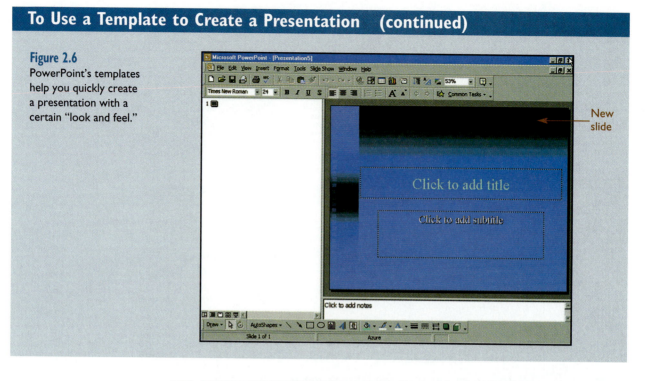

New slide

Although it's most common to choose a template or launch the AutoContent Wizard from the New Presentation dialog box, there's another choice. You can choose AutoContent Wizard or Design Template from PowerPoint's Startup dialog box when you initially launch the program.

Lesson 2: Using the AutoContent Wizard to Create a Presentation

Another way to create a presentation is to use the AutoContent Wizard. The AutoContent Wizard is a tool that helps you create presentations that include sample content as well as an underlying template. Microsoft's **wizards** are interactive tools that guide you step-by-step through a process that might otherwise be complicated or awkward—and the AutoContent Wizard is no exception. Just as with other Microsoft wizards, you make choices on each page. You then click Next to advance to the subsequent page, Back to display the previous page, or Finish to quickly complete the presentation. (You can also click Cancel at any time to quit the entire process.)

You can use the AutoContent Wizard to quickly create presentations on recommending a strategy, conducting training, reporting progress, and so on. In the following tutorial, you use the AutoContent Wizard to create a presentation to recommend that your organization upgrade to Office 2000. Try using this handy tool now.

To Use the AutoContent Wizard to Create a Presentation

1 Choose File, New, and then click the General tab of the New Presentation dialog box.

PowerPoint includes an icon for the AutoContent Wizard on this page. You can quickly launch the wizard by double-clicking this icon.

2 Double-click the AutoContent Wizard icon.

The first of five AutoContent Wizard dialog boxes displays, as shown in Figure 2.7. Notice that the chart on the left side of the dialog box helps track your progress as you create a presentation. The buttons at the bottom of the dialog box help you move between AutoContent dialog boxes (or even cancel the wizard).

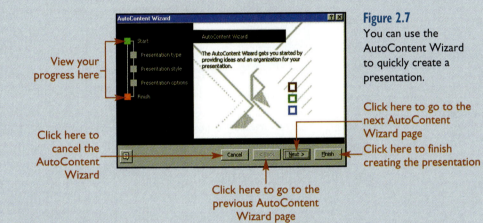

View your progress here

Click here to cancel the AutoContent Wizard

Click here to go to the previous AutoContent Wizard page

Figure 2.7
You can use the AutoContent Wizard to quickly create a presentation.

Click here to go to the next AutoContent Wizard page

Click here to finish creating the presentation

3 Click the Next button.

The Presentation type page of the AutoContent Wizard displays. You can use this page to determine the type of presentation that best fits your needs.

4 Click the All button to display the entire list of predesigned presentations.

All presentation types are shown in the list box on the right side of the dialog box (see Figure 2.8). You can limit the type of presentation listed by clicking one of the category buttons.

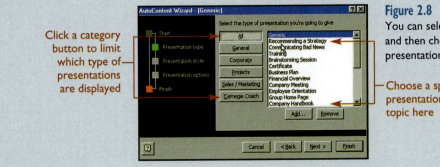

Click a category button to limit which type of presentations are displayed

Figure 2.8
You can select a category, and then choose a specific presentation.

Choose a specific presentation topic here

continues ▶

To Use the AutoContent Wizard to Create a Presentation (continued)

5 **Click several of the category buttons to see what sample presentations they include. When you finish experimenting, choose the Projects button.**

The presentations associated with this category display.

6 **Click Project Overview, and then choose Next.**

The third AutoContent dialog box displays (see Figure 2.9).

Figure 2.9
On this page, choose the type of output you plan to use.

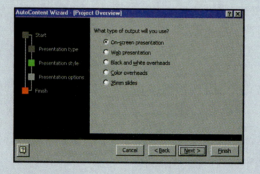

You can use this dialog box to choose the general type of **output** you want. For example, if you're running a brainstorming session or meeting, you can choose the On-screen presentation option. In contrast, if you want to publish the presentation to the World Wide Web, choose Web presentation. Because the most common use for PowerPoint is to develop onscreen presentations, this option is preselected.

7 **Make sure the On-screen presentation option button is selected, and then choose Next.**

The Presentation options page of the AutoContent Wizard dialog box displays, as seen in Figure 2.10. You use this page to add a title to your presentation. You can also add items to the **footer area** of each slide—the place at the bottom of the slide. For example, you can add your company name or a slide number to each slide.

Figure 2.10
You can include footer information on your slides.

Check this box to include the current date

Check this box to include the slide number

Add your title here

Add footer text here

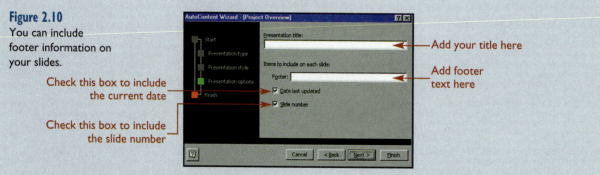

8 **Click in the Presentation title text box, and then type** Upgrading to Office 2000.

9 **Click in the Footer text box, type** By the Information Technology Team, **and then click Next.**

The final page of the AutoContent Wizard displays.

10 **Read the displayed information, and then choose Finish to view your presentation.**

The AutoContent Wizard creates the presentation and displays it in Normal view, as shown in Figure 2.11. As you recall from Project 1, this view includes an Outline pane, a Slide pane, and a Notes pane. Additionally, the information you entered in the wizard is automatically included in the title slide. The remainder of the presentation is created as a series of slides with major topics and subtopics. These suggested topics serve as a blueprint for your presentation.

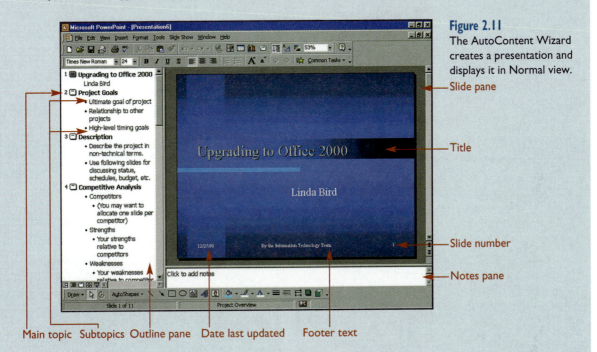

Figure 2.11
The AutoContent Wizard creates a presentation and displays it in Normal view.

Main topic   Subtopics   Outline pane   Date last updated   Footer text

Keep this presentation open for the next lesson, in which you learn how to use PowerPoint's different views.

ⓘ **Creating Presentations**

If you want to quickly create a presentation with the sample content in place, but you don't want to work through the page-by-page choices in the AutoContent Wizard, you're in luck. Just choose File, New, and then click the Presentations tab. Double-click an icon to create a new presentation with the sample content included.

Lesson 3: Exploring PowerPoint's Views

After you create a presentation, you can view it in a number of different ways: Normal view, Slide view, Outline view, Slide Sorter view, Notes Page view, or as a Slide Show. So that you can quickly learn the purpose of each view, the following table describes the best uses for each view.

Use	To
Normal view	Get an overview of your entire presentation, work with the outline, notes, or individual slide elements.
Slide view	Work with one slide at a time on the entire screen, add or change text or graphics, or draw shapes.
Outline view	Work with the text in traditional outline form.
Slide Sorter view	Display miniatures (thumbnails) of all slides, including text and graphics. Use this view to change the slide order, add transitions, and set timings for electronic slide shows.
Notes Page view	Display a page in which you can create speaker notes for each slide.
Slide Show	Display your presentation as an onscreen electronic slide show.

Your presentation should currently be displayed in Normal view. You can change to a different PowerPoint view by using the <u>V</u>iew menu or clicking a view button. In this exercise, you practice by using both methods. Now, try changing the view of the presentation.

To Explore PowerPoint's Views

❶ In the open presentation, rest the mouse pointer on any of the view buttons (see Figure 2.12).

In a second or two, a ScreenTip displays, indicating the view button's name.

Figure 2.12
You can use the view buttons to get a different perspective on your presentation.

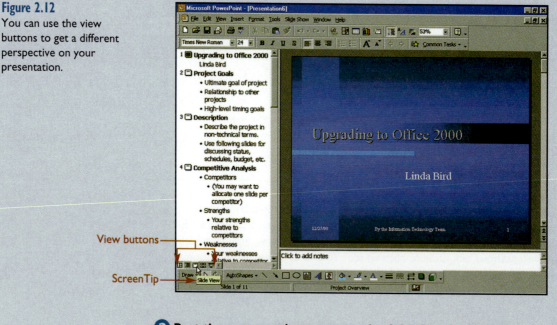

View buttons

ScreenTip

❷ Rest the mouse pointer over each of the five view buttons.
A ScreenTip identifies each button.

❸ Click the Outline View button.
The presentation displays as a traditional outline, with main topics and subtopics listed for each slide. The Slide and Notes panes still display, but they change size and location (see Figure 2.13).

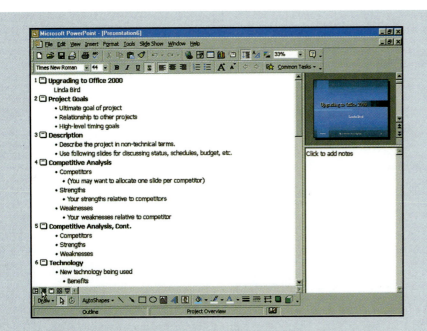

Figure 2.13
Outline view gives you an overview of your presentation's text.

4 Click the Slide View button.

The selected slide displays full-screen (see Figure 2.14). Slide view is best to use when you want to work with slide elements that might otherwise be hard to see or modify. For example, this is a good view to use to insert electronic pictures (commonly called *clip art*) or to draw pictures on the slide.

Selected slide

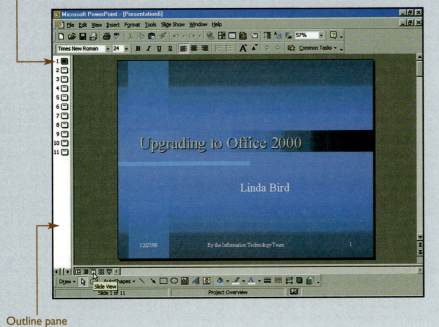

Figure 2.14
Use Slide view to work more efficiently with individual slide elements.

Outline pane

continues ▶

To Explore PowerPoint's Views (continued)

5 **Click the Slide Sorter View button, or choose View, Slide Sorter from the menu.**

Your presentation displays as a series of miniature slides (see Figure 2.15). The Slide Sorter view is an excellent view to use to add, delete, or rearrange slides. You can also add slide transitions and animation effects in this view by using the Slide Sorter toolbar. (You learn more about working with slide transitions and animation effects in Project 7.)

Figure 2.15
You can use Slide Sorter view to display your presentation as miniature slides.

Slide Sorter toolbar

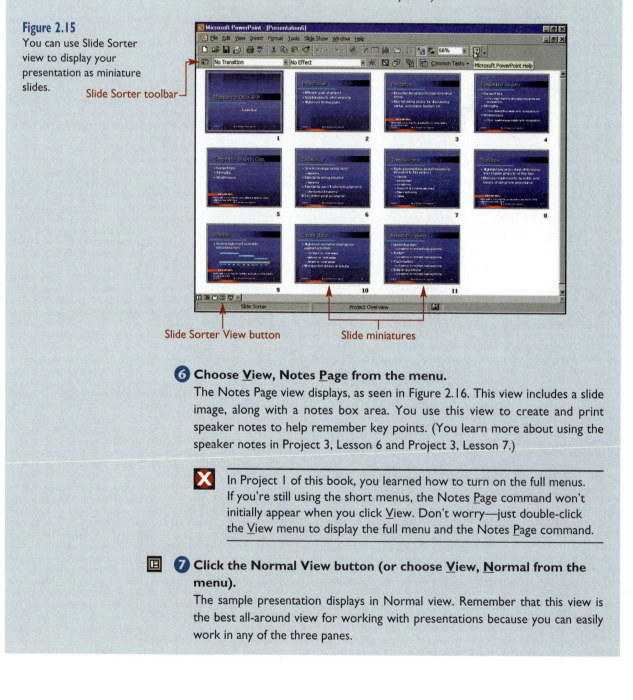

Slide Sorter View button   Slide miniatures

6 **Choose View, Notes Page from the menu.**

The Notes Page view displays, as seen in Figure 2.16. This view includes a slide image, along with a notes box area. You use this view to create and print speaker notes to help remember key points. (You learn more about using the speaker notes in Project 3, Lesson 6 and Project 3, Lesson 7.)

> **X** In Project 1 of this book, you learned how to turn on the full menus. If you're still using the short menus, the Notes Page command won't initially appear when you click View. Don't worry—just double-click the View menu to display the full menu and the Notes Page command.

7 **Click the Normal View button (or choose View, Normal from the menu).**

The sample presentation displays in Normal view. Remember that this view is the best all-around view for working with presentations because you can easily work in any of the three panes.

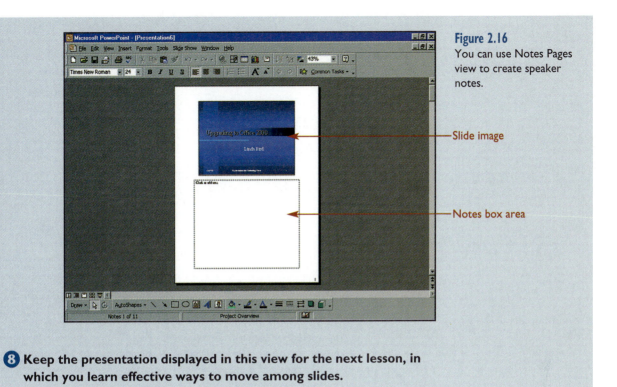

Figure 2.16
You can use Notes Pages view to create speaker notes.

Slide image

Notes box area

8 **Keep the presentation displayed in this view for the next lesson, in which you learn effective ways to move among slides.**

Working with Views

Some of PowerPoint's views can be accessed only via the view buttons; others are listed on the Yiew menu (but don't have a corresponding view button). For example, you can display Outline view by clicking a view button, but PowerPoint doesn't list Outline view as a menu item. In contrast, you can display your presentation in Notes Page view only by using the Yiew, Notes Page command. Luckily, the most popular views (such as Normal and Slide Sorter views) are accessible either way.

Lesson 4: Moving Among Slides in Normal View

After you create a presentation, you need to know how to move around it efficiently. For example, you may need to move quickly to the first or last presentation slide, or "page through" the presentation slide by slide. To get you up to speed on how to move around within a presentation, we show you some efficient methods. First, you'll be guided through using **keyboard shortcuts**, which are simply the keys you can press on the keyboard to perform actions. Then, you'll see how to perform the same actions with the mouse. As you work more and more with PowerPoint, you'll probably find which method best complements your work habits. Try experimenting with these methods now.

To Move Among Slides in Normal View

1 **Make sure your presentation displays in Normal view, and then press** `PgDn`.

The second presentation slide displays. You can press `PgDn` to move quickly through a presentation slide by slide; you can press `PgUp` to display the previous slide.

2 **Press** `PgUp`.

The first presentation slide displays. Try moving quickly to the end of the presentation by using a keyboard shortcut that (almost) universally displays the end of a worksheet, document, or presentation: `Ctrl`+`End`.

3 **Press** `Ctrl`+`End`.

The last presentation slide displays in the Slide pane. Notice that the last slide is selected simultaneously in the Outline pane. Now try displaying the first presentation slide.

4 **Press** `Ctrl`+`Home`.

The first presentation slide displays. Now that you are familiar with some common keyboard shortcuts, try your hand at performing the same actions with the mouse.

To move among slides using the mouse, you can use buttons on the vertical scrollbar in the Slide pane. For example, you can click the Next Slide or Previous Slide button. Alternatively, you can drag the scroll box on the vertical scrollbar to move to the relative location within your presentation (Figure 2.17).

Figure 2.17
You can use the Next Slide and Previous Slide buttons to quickly move among slides.

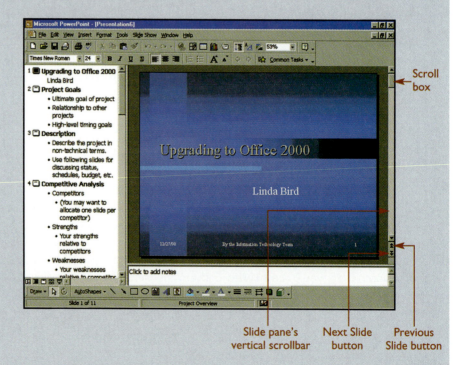

Scroll box

Slide pane's vertical scrollbar   Next Slide button   Previous Slide button

5 **Click the Next Slide button at the bottom of the Slide pane's vertical scrollbar (refer to Figure 2.17).**

The second slide in your presentation displays.

6 **Click the Previous Slide button at the bottom of the Slide pane's vertical scrollbar.**

The first presentation slide redisplays. Now try using the scroll box to move to a relative location in your presentation. For example, if you want to display the fifth slide in a ten-slide presentation, drag the scroll box approximately halfway down the vertical scrollbar.

7 **Click the Slide pane's vertical scroll box, and then drag it up and down slowly.**

A ScreenTip displays to the left of the scrollbar. This is a handy feature because the ScreenTip shows the slide number, total number of slides, and current slide title (see Figure 2.18). Furthermore, when you release the mouse button, the slide indicated by the ScreenTip displays.

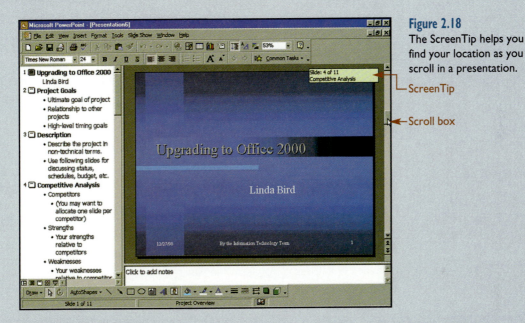

Figure 2.18
The ScreenTip helps you find your location as you scroll in a presentation.

ScreenTip

Scroll box

8 **Stop at Slide 4, Competitive Analysis, and then release the mouse button.**

The slide shown in the ScreenTip becomes the active slide and is shown in Normal view. Now try moving to a different slide by selecting a slide icon in the Outline pane.

9 **Move your mouse pointer over the icon for Slide 3 in the Outline pane until a four-headed arrow displays (see Figure 2.19).**

10 **Click the icon for Slide 3 in the Outline pane.**

The third slide is selected in the Outline pane and it displays concurrently in the Slide pane.

11 **Press Ctrl+Home to display the first presentation slide. Keep your presentation open for the next exercise.**

continues ▶

To Move Among Slides in Normal View (continued)

Figure 2.19
You can select a slide icon in the Outline pane to move quickly to the corresponding slide.

Slide icons

Four-headed arrow

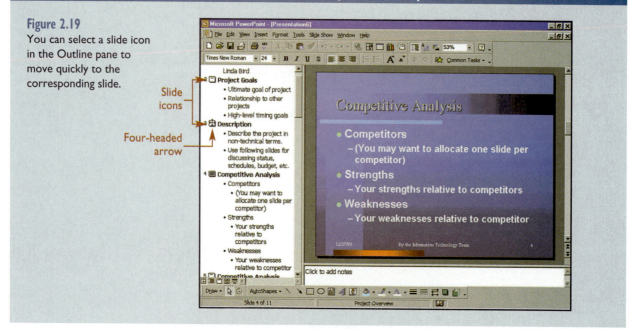

Lesson 5: Running an Electronic Slide Show

As you work with PowerPoint, you soon discover that one of the most popular and effective means of displaying a presentation is an electronic slide show. You can run a slide show as a handy method of checking the presentation's content and flow, or to actually show the presentation to an audience by using an LCD panel and overhead projector. You can also create an onscreen, self-running presentation for use at trade shows or on your company's intranet. In this lesson, you learn the basics of running a slide show. In the next tutorial, you find out how to use shortcut keys to navigate more efficiently within the slide show.

To Run an Electronic Slide Show

1. **Make sure that Slide 1 in the open presentation is displayed in Normal view.**

2. **Click the Slide Show button (or choose View, Slide Show).**
   The electronic slide show begins. Notice that the first slide displayed is the one that was active when you began the show—Slide 1.

3. **Click the left mouse button.**
   The next slide in the presentation displays. (If you prefer to use the keyboard, you can press ↵Enter or PgDn to advance to the next slide. Similarly, you can press ←Backspace or PgUp to move back one slide.)

   Advancing through the entire slide show is easy—just keep clicking the left mouse button until the presentation again displays in the last view you used (such as Normal view). For now, however, practice some ways to jump between slides in a slide show.

Here's how to do this: You can use the shortcut menu (sometimes called a pop-up menu) to move effectively in a slide show. Shortcut menus are displayed by right-clicking the mouse, and are **context sensitive**. Context sensitive means that the menu displays the commands that are related to the area of the screen that you click.

4 **Click the right mouse button.**
The slide show shortcut menu displays (see Figure 2.20). This menu includes commonly used commands that help you control a running slide show. Although you activate the shortcut menu by pressing the right mouse button, you choose commands with the left mouse button.

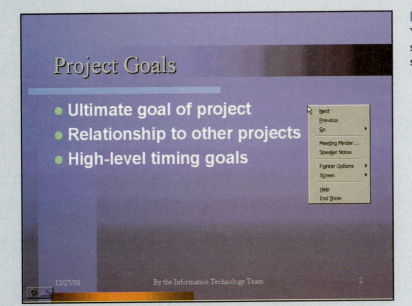

Figure 2.20
You can control a running slide show by using the shortcut menu.

5 **Choose Previous from the shortcut menu.**
Slide I displays. Notice that you can also move forward in a presentation by choosing Next from the shortcut menu.

6 **Right-click the mouse to display the shortcut menu; then choose Go, Slide Navigator.**
The Slide Navigator dialog box displays. Because this dialog box shows all the slide titles, you can use it to move quickly to any slide in your presentation.

7 **Double-click Slide 7, Team/Resources.**
The presentation displays Slide 7.

8 **Right-click the mouse, and then choose End Show from the shortcut menu. (You can also end a slide show by pressing ⏎Enter.)**
PowerPoint displays the presentation in Normal view—the view you used most recently before you started the electronic slide show. Keep this presentation open for the next lesson, in which you learn slide show shortcut keys.

If the shortcut menu doesn't display when you right-click the mouse, choose Tools, Options, and then click the View tab in the Options dialog box. In the Slide show section, check the box for Popup menu on right mouse click, and then choose OK.

Lesson 6: Using the Slide Show Shortcut Keys

When you present your slide show to a live audience, it's useful to know as many ways as possible to move among your slides. For example, you want to quickly display a slide that includes production or sales figures—even if it's not the next slide in the sequence.

In Lesson 5, you learned how to launch an electronic slide show and some basic ways to move among the slides. In this lesson, you build on that knowledge by learning keyboard shortcuts. You can use keyboard shortcuts to move between slides in a presentation or to blank out a current slide so that the audience's attention is redirected to you. Try using some of these keyboard shortcuts now.

To Use the Slide Show Shortcut Keys

1 **Display the first presentation slide in Normal view, and then press** F5.

F5 is the keyboard shortcut you can use to launch a slide show. Now try viewing the keyboard shortcuts that are available when you run a slide show.

2 **Press** F1.

The Slide Show Help dialog box displays, showing a list of available shortcut keys to help you get around the slide show (see Figure 2.21).

Figure 2.21
Press F1 while running a slide show to display a list of keyboard shortcuts for your slide show.

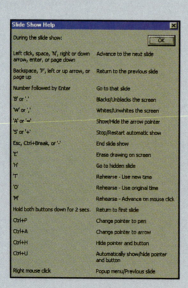

3 **Click OK to close the Slide Show Help dialog box, and then press** N.

The next slide displays. In a similar fashion, pressing P displays the previous slide.

4 Press P.
PowerPoint displays the previous slide in your electronic slide show.

You can also display a certain slide seamlessly by pressing the slide's number, followed by ↵Enter. This method is quicker than using the Slide Navigator, and your audience doesn't see the command onscreen. Try using this method to move to another slide now.

5 Press 4, and then press ↵Enter.
The presentation displays Slide 4, Competitive Analysis.

Now try using some of the other functions associated with keyboard shortcuts. For example, you can use keyboard shortcuts to clear the screen so that it doesn't distract the audience during your presentation. To do this, you can press B to blacken the screen or W to white it out. The screen remains blank until you press B or W a second time to redisplay the screen. Try using this helpful feature now.

6 Press B to blacken the screen, and then press B again.
The display toggles between the screen and blackened views. (If you want to, try pressing W to white out the screen before continuing with the tutorial.)

Now try a quick and easy way to end your slide show.

7 Press ↵Enter.
The slide show ends and the presentation again displays in Normal view. Keep the presentation open for the next lesson, in which you learn to save it.

Lesson 7: Saving Your Presentation

So far, the presentation you developed exists only in Random Access Memory (RAM)—the working area of the computer. RAM only retains its contents as long as power is supplied to your computer. Therefore, if power is interrupted to your computer, you'll lose everything.

When you save the presentation from RAM to one of the computer's permanent storage areas (a floppy disk, the hard drive, or a network drive), however, you have a stored copy. This saved file can be opened, used, and revised at a later time.

When you initially save a file, you must tell PowerPoint the name and storage location for the presentation—just as you label a file before placing it in a filing cabinet. PowerPoint 2000 allows you to use long filenames so that you can accurately describe a file's contents. You can use up to 255 characters, including spaces, so you can give a presentation descriptive names such as `Annual Meeting, 2000` or `Presentation to Stockholders`. However, you cannot use certain characters such as / \ > < * ? " | : and ;.

You use the File, Save or File, Save As commands to save a presentation. Use File, Save As when you first save a presentation, or when you change the name, drive, or folder of a saved presentation. Use File, Save to quickly update a file that was previously saved. You can also click the Save button on the Standard toolbar.

In this lesson, you save the sample presentation to your floppy disk—drive A—so make sure that you have a disk in this drive before starting the tutorial.

To Save Your Presentation

1 **In the open presentation, choose File, Save As from the menu bar.**
The Save As dialog box displays (see Figure 2.22). You use this handy dialog box to indicate the name and location for your file.

Figure 2.22
You use the Save As dialog box when you first save a file.

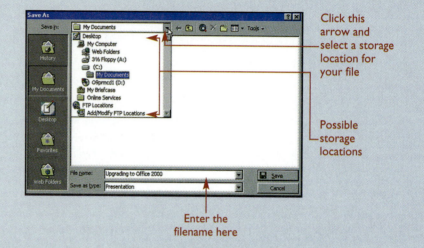

Click this arrow and select a storage location for your file

Possible storage locations

Enter the filename here

2 **Click the Save in drop-down list arrow (refer to Figure 2.22).**
PowerPoint displays a list of available storage locations for your computer. This list may vary from computer to computer, depending on which drives are installed (and whether or not your computer is on a network).

> **✕** It's possible that your instructor has another file location in mind for you to save your presentation—such as a subfolder in the My Documents folder on your hard drive. If you don't know where to save the presentation, ask your instructor.

3 **Click 3 1/2 Floppy (A:).**
Drive A is selected as the storage location for your presentation.

4 **Move the mouse pointer to the File name text box area.**
The pointer changes to an I-beam, indicating that this is an area that can accept text. However, before you can enter text, you must "set" the I-beam.

5 **Click in the text box area, and then drag over the default filename (`Upgrading to Office 2000`).**
The default filename is selected. When text is selected, you can quickly replace it by simply typing in new text. As you enter the new text, the original text is replaced.

6 **Type `New Project Proposal`, and then click the Save button.**
That's all there is to it! Your presentation is saved as `New Project Proposal` on the floppy disk. Notice that the name also appears in the Title bar. You now have a permanent copy of your presentation stored for later use (and you're safe from losing data due to power outages, surges, and so on).

However, if you make changes to the presentation (either now or later), you should choose File, Save or click the Save button to update the stored file. When you do, the presentation is automatically updated, using the same file-name and location. In other words, the existing file is replaced rather than creating a second copy of it.

Keep your saved presentation open for the next tutorial, in which you learn how to print it.

Lesson 8: Printing a Presentation

One common way to output, or produce, a presentation is to print it. You can print your entire presentation, including the slides and outline, in color, **grayscale**, or **pure black and white**. Grayscale includes shades of white, gray, and black. In contrast, when you choose the pure black and white option, PowerPoint converts all gray areas to black or white.

Printing an outline is particularly useful because it helps you see the overall flow and sequence of the presentation. Because the main purpose of the outline is to view the content, the printout shows only the text you entered—no graphics are shown.

You can print the presentation as a series of slides. Of course, your slides show graphics and backgrounds as well as text. In this lesson, you learn how to preview your presentation in grayscale, and how to print outlines and slides. Try your hand at printing now.

Checking the Printer Selection

Before you print a presentation, it's a good idea to make sure that the correct printer is selected. The Name text box in the Printer section of the Print dialog box shows the current printer. If the printer listed is not the one you want, click the drop-down arrow to the right of the Name box, and then select a different one. This feature makes it easy to change printers, especially if you work on a network and have a variety of printers available.

To Print a Presentation

❶ In the New Project Proposal presentation, choose File, Print.
The Print dialog box displays (see Figure 2.23).

> **X** You cannot display the Print dialog box by clicking the Print button on the Standard toolbar. Clicking the Print button automatically sends the current presentation to the printer with no further confirmation from you! Instead, be sure to choose File, Print from the menu so that you can access the Print dialog box.

You can use this dialog box to make choices about the type of output (slides versus outline, for example), the number of copies, and the print range.

continues ▶

To Print a Presentation   (continued)

Figure 2.23
You make choices about
output in the Print dialog
box.

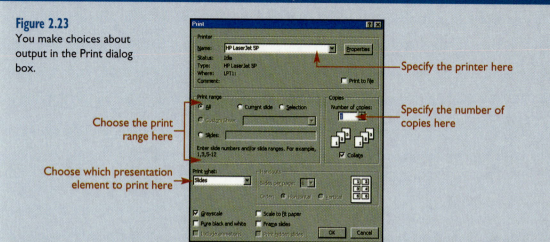

Specify the printer here

Specify the number of
copies here

Choose the print
range here

Choose which presentation
element to print here

2 **Click the drop-down arrow to the right of the Print what text box.**
A drop-down list displays the various ways that you can print your presentation.

3 **Select Outline View.**
Outline View is shown as the current selection in the Print what text
box. Make sure that the correct settings are selected so that the entire
presentation will print as an outline.

4 **In the Number of copies text box, make sure that the number of
copies is set to 1.**

5 **In the Print range area, make sure that the All option button is
selected.**

6 **Choose OK.**
This choice accepts the print settings and prints the outline.

You can also print your presentation as slides. However, unless you have
access to a color printer, it's a good idea to see how your presentation will
look in grayscale (shades of black, gray, and white) before printing it.

If you want to print only one slide (rather than the entire presentation), it's
easiest to move the insertion point to the slide you want so that PowerPoint
can identify it as the current slide.

With those concepts in mind, try printing a slide now.

7 **In the open presentation, press Ctrl+Home to move the insertion
point to the first slide—the Title slide.**
Moving the insertion point to this slide makes it the current slide. Try displaying
this slide in grayscale so that you can see how it will print.

8 **Click the Grayscale Preview button on the Standard toolbar.**
The slide displays in grayscale so that you can get an idea of how it will look
when printed. A Slide Miniature displays in color, as shown in Figure 2.24.

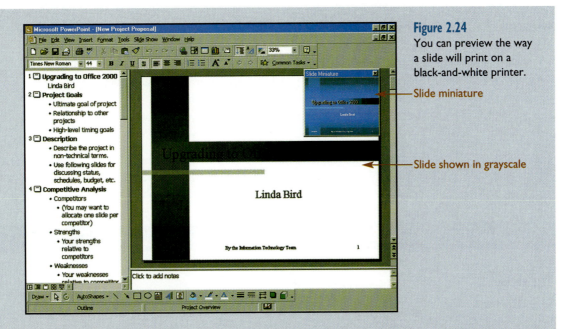

Figure 2.24
You can preview the way
a slide will print on a
black-and-white printer.

— Slide miniature

— Slide shown in grayscale

Now, change options in the Print dialog box so that the slide prints properly.

9 **Choose File, Print.**
The Print dialog box displays.

10 **In the Print range section, click the Current slide option button so that only one slide will print.**
Next, you need to confirm that you are printing slides and that they will print in grayscale—not color.

11 **Make sure that Slides displays in the Print what text box area and that the Grayscale check box is selected.**
Printing in grayscale optimizes the look of color slides for printing on black-and-white printers. (Don't make the mistake of choosing Pure black and white. This option makes your printer change all gray tones to black or white!)

12 **Click OK to print the current slide.**
This choice accepts the print settings and prints the slide.

13 **Choose File, Save, and then close the presentation.**
The changes you made to the presentation (such as modifying the print settings) are saved, and the presentation is cleared from memory.

Keep PowerPoint open if you plan to complete the Skill Drill, Challenge, and Discovery Zone exercises at the end of this project. Otherwise, make sure to exit PowerPoint and shut down Windows properly before turning off your computer.

Printing Specific Slides
You can also select a specific slide to print by typing the slide number in the Slides text box of the Print range area. This text box also enables you to "pick and choose" slides by entering the slide numbers separated by commas. For example, entering 1-3,5,8 in the Slides text box prints only those slides.

Summary

You covered quite a bit of ground in this lesson. First, you learned two methods of creating a new presentation: using a design template and using the AutoContent Wizard. You explored PowerPoint's views and learned how to switch between them. You learned how to navigate among slides in Normal view. You also launched a slide show and used keyboard shortcuts to move around in the show. Finally, you learned how to save and print a presentation.

To expand on your knowledge, spend a few minutes exploring Help on these topics. Additionally, complete some of the Skill Drill, Challenge, and Discovery Zone exercises.

Checking Concepts and Terms ✓

True/False

For each of the following, check *T* or *F* to indicate whether the statement is true or false.

__T __F **1.** PowerPoint includes 15 different views that you can use to work with your presentation. [L3]

__T __F **2.** You can click the Print button on the Standard toolbar to quickly display the Print dialog box. [L8]

__T __F **3.** You can create a new presentation based on a template. [L1]

__T __F **4.** The Slide Sorter View button automatically sorts your slides alphabetically. [L3]

__T __F **5.** Outline view, Normal view, and Slide Show are just different ways of viewing the same set of slides. [L3]

__T __F **6.** The Office Assistant Wizard creates the structure and suggested content of a presentation based on the choices you make. [L2]

__T __F **7.** The first time you save a presentation, you must name it and indicate a file location. [L7]

__T __F **8.** To move among PowerPoint slides in Normal view, you must use the mouse. [L4]

__T __F **9.** The Normal view includes only two panes: the Outline pane and the Normal pane. [L3–4]

__T __F **10.** You can print a presentation only in grayscale. [L8]

Multiple Choice

Circle the letter of the correct answer for each of the following.

1. The best reason for printing a presentation as an outline is _____. [L8]

a. to check logical flow and content

b. to view graphics

c. to view the colors and background used on a slide

d. none of the above

2. To save an existing file with a new name or location, _____. [L7]

a. click the Save button on the toolbar

b. choose File, Save

c. choose File, Save As

d. choose Tools, Save As

3. _____ is a PowerPoint view. [L3]

a. Normal

b. Slide Sorter

c. Notes Page

d. all of the above

4. The most commonly used view in PowerPoint 2000 is _____.[L3–4]

a. Preview

b. Normal

c. Grayscale

d. Miniature

5. To create a new presentation with sample content already in place, use the _____. [L1–2]

a. SampleContent Wizard

b. QuickFormat Wizard

c. AutoContent Wizard

d. PowerPoint Wizard

6. Which of the following statements is true? [L8]

a. You can't print your presentation as slides—only as an outline.

b. You must display the presentation in Slide Sorter view before opening the Print dialog box.

c. You can print a presentation from a running slide show.

d. You can print your presentation as slides, an outline, or notes pages.

7. Which of the following statements is true? [L1]

a. Templates include formatting, colors, and graphics.

b. You can base a new presentation on a template by clicking the Template button.

c. You use the Template Wizard to create a new presentation based on a template.

d. none of the above

8. You should _____ before you print to a black-and-white printer. [L8]

a. make sure that the correct printer is selected in the Print dialog box

b. preview the presentation in grayscale

c. check the Grayscale box in the Print dialog box

d. all of the above

9. When printing, you can set _____. [L8]

a. the number of copies

b. which presentation item you want to print (such as slides or outline)

c. which slides to print

d. all of the above

10. To output your presentation, you can _____. [L8]

a. print it as an outline

b. print it as slides

c. use it as an onscreen slide show

d. all of the above

Screen ID

Identify each of the items shown in Figure 2.25.

Figure 2.25

A. Notes pane

B. Normal View button

C. Slide Show button

D. Grayscale Preview button

E. Slide View button

F. Slide pane

G. Outline View button

H. Outline pane

I. Slide Sorter View button

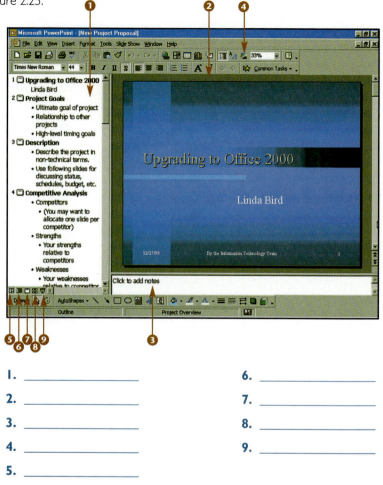

1. _____   6. _____

2. _____   7. _____

3. _____   8. _____

4. _____   9. _____

5. _____

Discussion Questions

1. Compare and contrast the three main methods of developing a presentation: creating one from scratch, using a template, and using the AutoContent Wizard. [L1–2]

2. Give several examples of presentations that you might need to develop at school or work. Find out which AutoContent Wizard presentation works best for each. [L2]

Skill Drill

Skill Drill exercises reinforce project skills. Each skill reinforced is the same, or nearly the same, as a skill presented in the project. Detailed instructions are provided in a step-by-step format.

1. Using Help

One of your friends wants you to come over and help him learn PowerPoint. In preparation for the session, you decide to use Help to find out more about creating presentations. Specifically, you research how to create presentations by using a template or using the AutoContent Wizard. [L1–2]

1. Start PowerPoint, and then choose Help, Microsoft PowerPoint Help. If necessary, click the Show button to split the Help window into two panes.

2. Click the Contents tab in the Microsoft PowerPoint Help window. Double-click the Creating Presentations icon.

3. Click the `Create a new presentation` subtopic. Read the information associated with the subtopic.

4. In the right pane, click the `Create a presentation based on a design template` subtopic. Read the information associated with the subtopic.

5. Click the Back button, and then click the `Create a presentation based on suggested content and design` subtopic in the right pane. Read the information associated with the subtopic.

6. On a piece of paper, write down the pros and cons for using a template and for using the AutoContent Wizard.

7. Close the Microsoft PowerPoint Help window. Leave PowerPoint open if you plan to complete additional exercises.

2. Using a Template to Create a Presentation

You work for a sports equipment company. Your boss wants to call a meeting to brainstorm ideas for a new product line. To remind everyone about the meeting, your boss asks you to develop a catchy flyer. You decide to create a one-slide presentation in PowerPoint, showing the appropriate information. [L1]

1. Start PowerPoint, if necessary, and then choose File, New. Click the Design Templates tab.

2. Single-click each of the templates available to preview them. Write down the names of the three templates you like the best.

3. Click the Notebook template, and then click OK.

4. In the New Slide dialog box, make sure that the Title Slide AutoLayout is selected, and then click OK.

5. Click in the title placeholder. Enter `Brainstorming Meeting!`

6. Click in the subtitle placeholder. Enter `Conference Room A`. Press `⏎Enter`. On the second line, enter `Tuesday, 8:00 a.m.`

7. Choose View, Black and White to display your slide in grayscale.

8. Choose File, Print to display the Print dialog box.

9. Make sure that the Print range is set to All. Confirm that the Number of copies is set to 1. Check that the Print what text box is set to `Slides`. Finally, check the Grayscale box.

10. Click OK to print a copy of your slide. Close the presentation without saving it. If you plan to complete additional exercises, leave PowerPoint open.

3. Using the AutoContent Wizard to Create a Presentation

Because you attended a PowerPoint class, everyone in your department now considers you a PowerPoint expert. For this reason, your co-workers want you to convince management to buy the "latest and greatest" computers for them. You decide to use PowerPoint to present your ideas at a staff meeting to show that purchasing new computers would be cost-effective. Because you need to prepare the presentation by tomorrow, you decide to use the AutoContent Wizard. [L2]

1. In PowerPoint, choose File, New. Click the General tab, and then double-click the AutoContent Wizard icon. Click Next to advance past the opening page of the wizard.

2. On the second page of the wizard, click All to display the entire list of presentations. Scroll down the list and choose `Selling Your Ideas`. Click Next.

3. On the third page, make sure that the On-screen presentation option is selected, and then click Next.

4. On the fourth page, enter `Improving Productivity` as the presentation title. Enter `By`, and then type your name in the Footer text box.

5. On the same page, make sure that the Date last updated and Slide number boxes are checked. Click Next.

6. Click Finish to create the presentation and display it in Normal view. Leave your presentation open for the next Skill Drill exercise, in which you use PowerPoint's views.

4. Exploring PowerPoint's Views

To get a better idea of what sample content the AutoContent inserted in the presentation you created in the previous exercise, you decide to switch between views and move between slides. [L3]

1. Make sure that the presentation you created in the previous Skill Drill exercise is open in Normal view. Review the purpose for each of the views.

2. Display a ScreenTip for each of the view buttons.

3. Click each of these view buttons: Outline View, Slide View, and Slide Sorter View.

4. From the menu, choose View, Normal.

5. Choose View, Slide Sorter.

6. Choose View, Notes Page.

7. Click the Normal View button. Leave the presentation displayed in this view for the next exercise, in which you move among slides.

5. Moving Among Slides in Normal View

To move effectively between presentation slides in Normal view, you practice using both keyboard shortcuts and mouse commands. [L4]

1. Make sure that your presentation is open in Normal view, and that the first presentation slide displays.

2. Press PgDn as many times as necessary to completely advance through your presentation. Press PgUp three times to move backward in your presentation by three slides.

3. Click one of the slide icons in the Outline pane. Notice that the corresponding slide displays simultaneously in the Slide pane. Repeat the process with other slide icons.

4. Press Ctrl + Home to display the first presentation slide. Press Ctrl + End to show the last presentation slide.

5. Drag the scroll box in the Slide pane's vertical scrollbar upward until **Slide: 4 of 5, Benefits** displays in the ScreenTip. Release the mouse button to display Slide 4.

6. Click the Next Slide button to advance to the next presentation slide. Click the Previous Slide button to show the previous slide.

7. Press Ctrl + Home to show the first presentation slide. Leave the presentation open for the next exercise, in which you run an electronic slide show.

6. Running an Electronic Slide Show

To preview the way your presentation will look when you present it at the meeting, you decide to display it in Slide Show view. You also review the Slide Show shortcut keys and practice using them so that you're prepared for your talk. [L5–6]

1. Make sure that the first presentation slide is displayed in Normal view, and then click the Slide Show button.

2. Press F1 to display the Slide Show Help dialog box. Look over the list of keyboard shortcuts you can use to move between slides in a slide show. Write down the ones you think that you will use the most and click OK to clear the dialog box.

3. Advance completely through the slide show by left-clicking the mouse six times. (The presentation should again display in Normal view.)

4. Press F5 to start the slide show a second time. Practice using the following keyboard shortcuts:

   - Press ↵Enter and N to advance to subsequent slides.

   - Press ←Backspace and P to move to the previous slide.

   - Press 4 and ↵Enter to display Slide 4.

   - Press B to blacken the screen, and then press B a second time to display the slide show again.

   - Press ↵Enter to end the slide show.

   Keep your presentation open for the next exercise, in which you save and print it.

7. Saving and Printing Your Presentation

You're giving your presentation using a computer other than the one you developed it on. Because of this (and to have a permanent copy), you save the presentation to a disk. You also print the presentation as an outline so that you can check the flow and content. [L7–8]

1. Make sure that you have a disk in the floppy disk drive. With the presentation you developed in the previous exercises open, choose File, Save As.

2. Click the Save in drop-down list arrow, and then choose 3 1/2 Floppy (A:) from the list.

3. Select the name in the File name text box, and then type Our Plan for Getting New Computers as the file's name. Click Save.

4. Print the presentation as an outline. Choose File, Print. In the Print dialog box, click the Print what drop-down list arrow and choose Outline View.

5. Make sure that the Number of copies is set to 1. Click OK to print the presentation.

6. Click the Save button on the Standard toolbar to update the changes you made to the presentation.

7. Choose File, Close to close the presentation. Keep PowerPoint open if you plan to complete the Challenge or Discovery Zone exercises. If not, exit PowerPoint and shut down Windows properly before turning off your computer.

Challenge

Challenge exercises expand on or are somewhat related to skills presented in the lessons. Each exercise provides a brief narrative introduction, followed by instructions in a numbered-step format that are not as detailed as those in the Skill Drill section.

1. Researching Help Topics

You were asked to give a short training session for other employees on how to get up and running with PowerPoint. To help develop your training manual, you use Help to find out more about using the AutoContent Wizard and design templates. [L1–2]

1. In PowerPoint, choose Help, Microsoft PowerPoint Help. Click the Show button, if necessary, to split the dialog box into two panes.

2. Click the Index tab. Type AutoContent in the Type keywords text box, and then click Search. Research the following topics related to the AutoContent Wizard. Make notes of what you learn and try out the techniques in PowerPoint.

   - Add a template to the AutoContent Wizard
   - Create your own template
   - Apply a design template to an existing presentation

3. Use PowerPoint's Help window to research the following topics related to printing a presentation. Make complete notes of what you learn and try out the techniques in PowerPoint.

   - Printing an outline with and without formatting
   - Setting up the slide size and orientation for printing
   - Preview and change what the slides will look like when printed in black and white.

4. To practice presenting the information, guide a new user through the steps of creating a new presentation using the AutoContent Wizard. Have the user develop a presentation by using a template. Finally, have the user print the presentations as both slides and outlines.

Keep PowerPoint open if you plan to complete additional exercises.

2. Using the AutoContent Wizard

As Marketing Manager, you just found out that your boss wants you to present your new marketing plan at the upcoming annual company meeting. Because the meeting is only two days away, you decide to use the AutoContent Wizard to quickly create an onscreen presentation. [L2–5, 7–8]

1. Display the New Presentation dialog box. Launch the AutoContent Wizard from this dialog box.

2. Choose the Marketing Plan as the presentation type. Create the presentation for use as an onscreen slide show. Make sure to include complete footer information, including your name, in the footer area. Finally, enter `Top Sales Marketing Plan` as the presentation title. Finish creating the presentation.

3. Replace the text in the subtitle placeholder of the Title Slide with `Super Sports Equipment, Inc.`

4. View the presentation in Outline view, Slide Sorter view, and as an electronic slide show.

5. Save the presentation as `Marketing Plan for the Annual Meeting`.

6. Print the presentation as an outline. Close the presentation. Leave PowerPoint open if you plan to complete additional exercises.

3. Creating a New Presentation

You work for a company that deals in computer ergonomic products—products designed to help people work more comfortably and effectively at the computer. You want to create a presentation to promote your products for a sales meeting. You decide to use the AutoContent Wizard to create the basic framework and suggested slide content. [L2, 4–5, 7–8]

1. Launch the AutoContent Wizard. In the Wizard, choose Product/Services Overview as the presentation type. Develop the presentation as an onscreen slide show.

2. Use `Ergonomic Products` as the presentation title, but don't include any footer information. Finish creating the presentation and display it in Normal view.

3. On Slide 2, Overview, replace the bulleted points with the following text:
   - `Workstations`
   - `Keyboards`
   - `Monitors`
   - `Chairs`

4. View the presentation as an onscreen slide show. Display the Slide Show Help dialog box to view the list of keyboard shortcuts available in a slide show. Clear the dialog box and practice using several of the shortcuts listed. When you finish, end the slide show.

5. Display the presentation in Normal view. Practice moving among slides in the presentation by using information in Lesson 4 as a guide.

6. Save the presentation as **Company Products** and print the presentation as an outline. When you finish, save any changes and close the presentation. Keep PowerPoint open if you plan to complete additional exercises.

4. Creating a Presentation Based on a Template

You're planning a birthday party for a friend. To create the invitations in a snap, you decide to use a template. After you initially create the presentation, you print it in both color and black and white. [L1, 7–8]

1. Display the Design Templates page of the New Presentation dialog box. Preview each of the templates listed.

2. Create a title slide based on the Neon Frame template. Then enter **Rebecca's Birthday Party!** in the title placeholder. In the subtitle placeholder, type **March 24, 1999**, and then press ⏎**Enter**. On the second line in the subtitle placeholder, type **3:00 p.m.** On the third line in the subtitle placeholder, type **Raccoon Creek Park**.

3. After looking over your announcement, you decide that you want to use a different template. Instead of re-creating the entire slide, you decide to just apply a different template to this slide. Choose F̲ormat, App̲ly Design Template to display the Apply Design Template dialog box. Click the Azure template, and then click App̲ly. (If you want to, practice applying other templates. When you've finished experimenting, be sure to reapply the Azure template.)

4. Print your presentation slide in black and white. First, use your ScreenTips to locate the Grayscale Preview button on the Standard toolbar and click it. Choose F̲ile, Print. Make sure that the G̲rayscale box is checked and that **Slides** is selected in the Print w̲hat text box. Click OK to print the slide.

5. If you have a color printer available, print your presentation slide in color. First, click the Grayscale Preview button to change the display back to color. Choose F̲ile, Print. In the Print dialog box, uncheck the G̲rayscale box. Click OK.

6. Save the presentation as **Birthday Party**. Close the presentation. Keep PowerPoint open if you plan to complete additional exercises.

5. Creating a New Presentation

You're a college student who loves working with computers and software. Unfortunately, you spent too much time playing around on the World Wide Web this term and your grades have suffered. To communicate this news to your parents, you decide to develop a presentation for them. (Because you're scared to face them in person, you plan to email them the presentation before you go home!) [L2–3, 5, 7–8]

1. In PowerPoint, display the Presentations page of the New Presentation dialog box.

2. Click the Communicating Bad News presentation and choose OK.

3. View the presentation as a slide show to see what content is already included. Then add `By Your Loving Child` in the subtitle placeholder of the Title Slide.

4. Switch the presentation to Outline view. Replace the sample content with the following information:

`Slide 2, My Situation`

- `I'm failing classes this term`
- `I'll be on probation next term`

`Slide 3, How Did This Happen?`

- `I love working with computers`
- `I spent too much time in the computer lab (but I did learn a lot there!)`

`Slide 4, Alternatives Considered`

- `I've talked with my advisor and professors`
- `Two professors will give me incomplete grades instead of Fs`
- `I can attend summer school`

5. Display the first presentation slide, and then run the presentation as a slide show.

6. Print the presentation as an outline. Save the presentation as `I promise to do better`. Leave the presentation open if you plan to complete the next Challenge exercise; otherwise, close it. (Keep PowerPoint open if you plan to complete additional exercises.)

6. Moving Among Slides in Normal and Slide Show Views

To practice working with your presentation, you decide to experiment by switching between views and moving among slides. [L4–5]

1. Display the `I promise to do better` presentation that you created in the last exercise in Normal view.

2. Practice using keyboard shortcuts to move between slides in Normal view. (If you need a refresher on the keyboard shortcuts, refer to Lesson 4.)

3. Practice using the mouse to move between slides in Normal view.

4. Switch to Outline view. Explore ways to move between slides in this view. Make sure to use keyboard shortcuts as well as the mouse. If necessary, use Help to research the methods available.

5. Switch to Notes Page view. Experiment to learn ways to move between slides in this view. Compare the methods used in Notes Page view to those used in other PowerPoint views.

6. Run your presentation as an electronic slide show. Display the Slide Show Help dialog box. Clear the dialog box and practice various ways to move around the slide show. Make sure to use the Slide Navigator as well as the keyboard shortcuts. Also practice blackening and unblackening the screen.

7. Develop a table that outlines the methods you can use to move between slides in each of PowerPoint's views. (If you develop this table in Word, print it out.) Close the presentation. Keep PowerPoint open if you plan to complete additional exercises.

Discovery Zone

Discovery Zone exercises require advanced knowledge of topics presented in Essentials lessons, application of skills from multiple lessons, or self-directed learning of new skills.

1. Researching Printing Problems

You've just been hired by the Information Technology Department at a local manufacturing company. Your department supports over 100 users, and your main job is to help them work through problems they encounter when working with software programs (such as PowerPoint). Lately, your users have had a high percentage of printing problems while printing in PowerPoint. To find out possible reasons for the problems, you tap into PowerPoint's Help.

Using the Microsoft PowerPoint Help window, troubleshoot the printing problems. Then, so that you have a handy reference list of the possible problems, develop a table of them. In the left column of your table, enter the printing problem. In the right column, write the causes and possible solutions. (If you are familiar with Word, you might want to develop the table in that program and print it.)

Keep PowerPoint open if you plan to complete additional exercises. [L8]

2. Creating Presentations

You're the secretary of the University Bicycling Club. To get ready for an upcoming meeting, you develop several presentations.

- A one-slide flyer that announces the meeting time and location. (*Hint*: Use a template for this flyer.)
- A presentation that introduces a speaker for the meeting. (*Hint*: Use the AutoContent Wizard.)
- A presentation to motivate your team of club members. (*Hint*: Use the AutoContent Wizard.)

Enter appropriate information in each of the presentations. Print the announcement flyer as a slide in color and in black and white (grayscale). Print the other two presentations as outlines.

Unless instructed otherwise by your teacher, close the presentations without saving them. Keep PowerPoint open if you plan to complete additional exercises. [L1–2, 8]

3. Developing a New Presentation

One of the requirements for your business class is to give a speech on a software program. Because you are familiar with PowerPoint 2000, you decide to create a PowerPoint presentation to supplement your talk.

Use the AutoContent Wizard and the Training presentation type to develop your talk. Research information on PowerPoint's main features (perhaps by using the Table of Contents of your student workbook as a guide or by using Help). Replace the sample content supplied by the AutoContent Wizard with your information.

View your presentation as an electronic slide show. If possible, share the presentation with at least one other user. Print the presentation as an outline. Then, unless instructed otherwise by your teacher, close the presentation without saving it. [L2, 5]

4. Creating a Certificate

You're an assistant to a boss who likes to encourage and motivate her team of employees. She wants you to develop some certificates to show appreciation for employees who have worked extra hard on projects. To create these certificates quickly, you decide to use a predesigned presentation in PowerPoint.

First, display the Presentations page of the New Presentation dialog box. Double-click Certificate to create your presentation.

Replace the sample content so that your certificate matches the one shown in Figure 2.26.

Figure 2.26
You can easily create certificates in PowerPoint.

Create at least five additional certificates for other employees and/or projects. Print each of the certificates. (If possible, print the certificates in both color and in grayscale.) Unless instructed otherwise by your teacher, close the presentation without saving it. [L2, 8]

Modifying Presentations

Objectives

In this project, you learn how to

➤ **Open an Existing Presentation**

➤ **Add and Delete Slides**

➤ **Change Slide Order**

➤ **Add, Demote, and Promote Text**

➤ **Select and Move Text**

➤ **Create Speaker Notes**

➤ **Print Speaker Notes and Handouts**

Key terms introduced in this project include

- Clipboard
- demote
- drag-and-drop
- frame
- handouts
- notes box
- promote
- reverse video
- slide image
- speaker notes

Why Would I Do This?

Creating the framework of a presentation, as you did in the previous two projects, is a good start on the road to success with PowerPoint. However, any presentation that you create with the AutoContent Wizard (or a template) is really just a springboard for further revisions. As you develop your thoughts, you'll want the flexibility of adding (or removing) other slides and text.

Fortunately, it's easy to modify an existing presentation—and in this project we'll show you how! First, you learn how to open an existing presentation. You focus on quick methods of adding and deleting slides, changing slide order, and revising your text. Finally, you learn how to create and print speaker notes and handouts.

Visual Summary

In this project, you learn proven methods of modifying a presentation. First, you see how to locate a presentation quickly by using the Open dialog box. You also find out how to save the presentation with a new name.

Figure 3.1
The Open dialog box helps you locate and preview presentations before opening them.

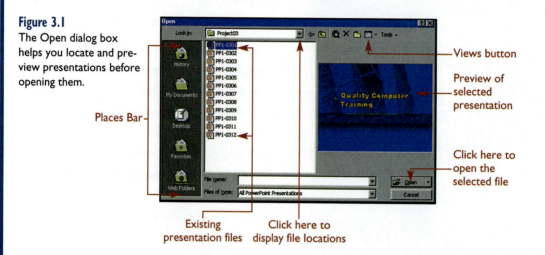

Views button

Preview of selected presentation

Click here to open the selected file

Places Bar

Existing presentation files

Click here to display file locations

You also learn how to modify your presentation by adding and deleting slides. You switch to Outline view so that you can easily change text in the Outline pane and use buttons on the Outlining toolbar (see Figure 3.2). Finally, you see how to add speaker notes in the Notes pane and print them.

When you finish, you'll have modified a presentation so that it looks similar to that shown in Figure 3.3. Try opening and modifying presentations now.

Outlining Promote   Demote
toolbar   button   button   Outline pane

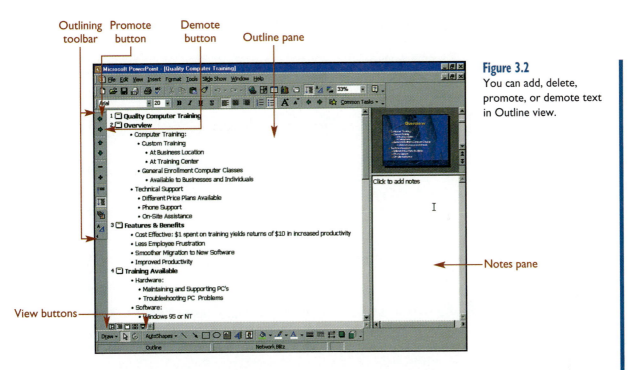

Figure 3.2
You can add, delete, promote, or demote text in Outline view.

Notes pane

View buttons

Figure 3.3
Modify existing presentations to customize them for your needs.

Lesson 1: Opening an Existing Presentation

When you want to work with a paper file in your office, you probably get it from a file cabinet, make a copy, and then put it on your desk so that you can work on it. In the same way, opening an existing presentation in PowerPoint simply creates a copy from one of the computer's storage areas and places it in memory so that you can work with it.

This is handy because it allows you to revise existing presentations instead of having to create new ones from scratch. Think of how time-consuming it would be to re-create every presentation you want to use!

After you open a file, it's also sometimes advantageous to immediately create a "clone" of the file by saving it with a new name. When you do this, you can work with the copy but still keep the original file intact. You will use this method for the tutorials in this book.

Now try opening an existing presentation.

To Open an Existing Presentation

① **Start PowerPoint, if necessary, and clear the Startup dialog box.**

ⓘ Opening Presentations
You can open an existing presentation directly from the Startup dialog box. To do this, choose the Open an existing presentation option button, and then click OK to display the Open dialog box. However, if PowerPoint is already open, you'll probably use the File, Open command instead.

② **Choose File, Open. (Alternatively, you can click the Open button on the Standard toolbar or press Ctrl+O from the keyboard.)**
The Open dialog box displays, as shown in Figure 3.4. This dialog box shows the folders and files on your computer. And, just as a folder in your office might contain several documents, an electronic folder might contain several presentations.

Figure 3.4
PowerPoint makes it easy to find and open presentations.

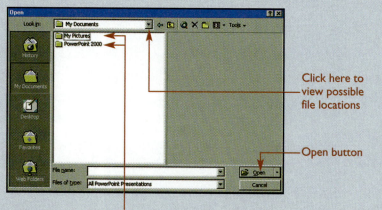

Click here to view possible file locations

Open button

File and folder list

✕ If the list of folders on your system doesn't match that shown in Figure 3.4, don't worry. Because the folders on each computer can be set up to match your work habits, it's unlikely that you'd have exactly the same ones as those shown in the book. However, the My Documents folder is designated (by Microsoft) as the central location to save all your work.

③ **Insert the student data file CD-ROM that accompanies this book into the CD-ROM drive (usually drive D), click the Look in drop-down list arrow, and select the CD-ROM drive (D:).**
A list of folders on the floppy disk displays (see Figure 3.5). The student folder includes subfolder (by project) with student data files you will use to complete the tutorials in this book.

4 **Double-click the student folder, and then double-click the Project03 folder to display the data files.**

A list of files previously saved on the CD-ROM displays (see Figure 3.5). This listing includes the data files you'll use to complete the tutorials in this book.

Selected presentation

Figure 3.5
You can list the files on your CD-ROM drive.

Views button

Preview of selected presentation

5 **Click to select PP1-0301, if necessary.**

PP1-0301 displays in *reverse video*, so that you can tell that it is the file you're working with. Reverse video is simply the computer's method of highlighting text on the display so that dark text is shown as bright characters on a dark background. Once this is selected, you can display information about the file.

6 **Click the Views button's drop-down list arrow; then choose List.**

Only the presentation's filenames are shown. Because of this, the List view enables you to see more files or folders in the dialog box than the other views.

7 **Click the Views button's drop-down list arrow, and then choose Details.**

The size, type, and modification date of the files are shown in addition to the filename.

8 **Click the Views button's drop-down list arrow and choose Properties.**

Pertinent information related to the selected file is shown, including its title, author, number of slides, last modification date, and so on. You can also click the vertical scrollbar's down arrow to view more information (see Figure 3.6).

You can also preview the first slide in a presentation to quickly determine whether a presentation is the one you want to open.

9 **Click the Views button's drop-down list arrow; then choose Preview.**

The title slide for the selected presentation is shown in miniature, which helps you identify the correct file. After you locate the file you want, make sure it's selected, and then click Open.

continues ▶

To Open an Existing Presentation (continued)

Figure 3.6
You can click Properties on the Views list to display valuable information about a file.

Location of the selected file

Selected file

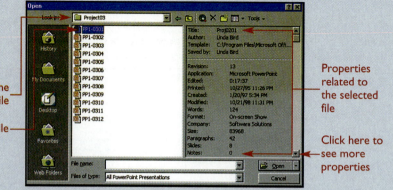

Properties related to the selected file

Click here to see more properties

🔟 **With PP1-0301 still selected, click the Open button.**
PowerPoint opens the selected file and displays it in Normal view. To help you quickly identify which presentation is open, PowerPoint displays the presentation's name in the Title bar.

Now that the file is opened in memory, you can use the Save As dialog box to copy and rename the file. This keeps the original file unaltered.

⓫ **With the PP1-0301 presentation onscreen, choose File, Save As.**
The Save As dialog box displays (see Figure 3.7). In the Save As dialog box, you can enter a new name for the file and choose Save. This effectively creates a copy of the original file with a new name.

Figure 3.7
You can save a second copy of a presentation with a new name.

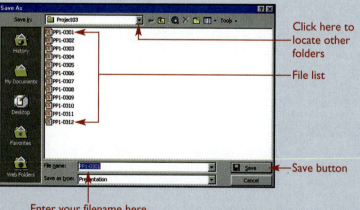

Click here to locate other folders

File list

Save button

Enter your filename here

⓬ **Click the Save in drop-down list arrow and choose 3 1/2 Floppy (A:). In the File name text box, type Quality Computer Training, and then click the Save button.**
The PP1-0301 file is copied and renamed Quality Computer Training simultaneously. Notice that the Title bar displays the new name. You'll work with this presentation in the next lesson, so leave it open.

Using File Extensions

PowerPoint automatically adds a three-character extension (.ppt) to each file to uniquely identify it as a PowerPoint file. Depending on the way your system is set up, however, the extension may or may not display. In general, if the .ppt extension displays, you should type it in when renaming the file. If it doesn't, PowerPoint will add it automatically—even though you won't see it displayed onscreen.

Using the Open Dialog Box

PowerPoint 2000 includes a number of spiffy options in the Open dialog box that help you work more effectively with your presentation. For example, you don't have to use the Look in drop-down list arrow to locate file locations. Instead, you can click the file locations (such as My Documents or Favorites) on the left side of the dialog box.

You can also open a file as read-only or as a copy. To do this, click the Open button's drop-down list arrow, and then choose the option you want on the list.

Finally, you can use the Places Bar, located on the left side of the Open dialog box, to quickly find files on your computer (or even the Web). For example, you can click the History folder to display the files you used most recently.

Lesson 2: Adding and Deleting Slides

Whether you rely on the AutoContent Wizard to create your presentations, use a template, or develop presentations from scratch, you'll want the flexibility of adding and deleting slides. To provide you with a handy reference, the following table lists the methods you can use to add or delete a slide.

Action	Methods
Add a slide	Choose Insert, New Slide from the menu bar.
	Click the New Slide button on the Standard toolbar.
	Press Ctrl+M.
	Click the Common Tasks button's drop-down list arrow, and then choose New Slide.
Delete a slide	In Outline and Slide Sorter views, click to select the slide, and then press Del.
	In Normal and Slide views, choose Edit, Delete Slide.

In this lesson, you add and delete slides in the Normal and Slide Sorter views because it's the easiest way to see the effect on the overall presentation. Try adding and deleting slides now.

To Add and Delete Slides

1 **Display the Quality Computer Training presentation in Normal view, if necessary.**

2 **Click the Outline pane's vertical scrollbar down arrow until you can see Slide 6, Pricing.**

You can instantly select an entire slide by clicking the icon in the Outline pane.

3 **Move the mouse pointer over the icon for Slide 6 until a four-headed arrow displays, and then click.**

Slide 6 is selected, as displayed in Figure 3.8. (If a selected slide contains subpoints, they'll be selected as well.)

Figure 3.8
You can select a slide in the Outline pane by clicking its icon.

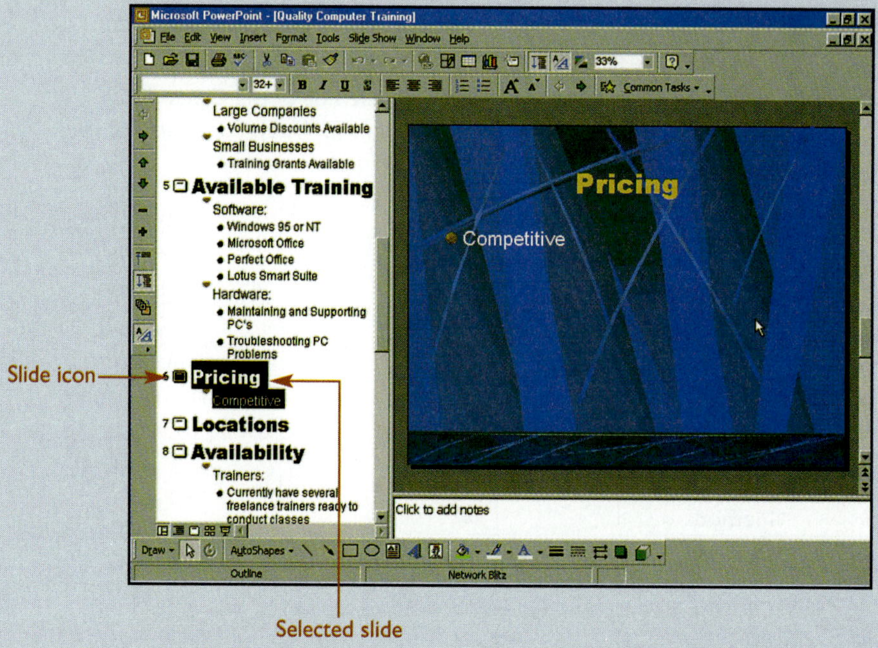

4 **Press Del.**

The selected slide, Slide 6, is deleted from the presentation, and the remaining slides are renumbered. You can reverse this deletion, however, by using a handy feature that PowerPoint provides to cancel your last action—Undo.

5 **Click the Undo button on the Standard toolbar.**
Slide 6 is reinserted into the presentation.

> **ⓘ Using Multiple Undo**
> You can reverse more than one action by clicking the Undo button as many times as is necessary to reverse your action. By default, you can reverse up to 20 actions.

You can also delete slides in Slide Sorter view. This is a good view to use when deleting, adding, or rearranging slides, because you can easily see the effect of your action on the presentation as a whole.

⊞ **6** **Click the Slide Sorter View button, and then click Slide 7, Locations.**
The presentation is shown in Slide Sorter view with a double border surrounding Slide 7. This indicates that it is the selected slide (see Figure 3.9).

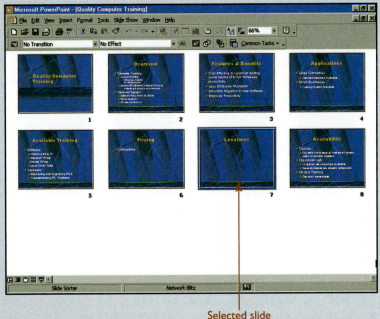

Figure 3.9
You can select a slide in Slide Sorter view.

Selected slide

7 **Press [Del].**
The selected slide is deleted. The black line between slides 6 and 7 indicates that the insertion-point location is between the two slides. This is where you want to add a new slide.

⊟ **8** **Click the New Slide button on the Standard toolbar.**
PowerPoint displays the New Slide dialog box. As you remember from Project 1, you use this dialog box to select which AutoLayout you want to use for your new slide.

9 **Double-click the AutoLayout for Bulleted List (the second layout in the first row).**
A blank bulleted list slide is inserted into your presentation.

▣ **10** **Click the Save button to save your changes.**
Clicking Save updates the changes you made to your presentation. Keep your presentation open for the next lesson, in which you change the slide order.

Adding and Deleting Slides

When you add a slide to a presentation, it is inserted after the slide where the insertion point is currently positioned. You can add slides in any view except the Slide Show view.

In Outline and Slide Sorter views, you can delete several slides simultaneously. Click the first slide you wish to delete, press ⬆Shift, and click the last slide. All the intervening slides are selected. You can also select non-adjacent slides by pressing Ctrl while clicking the slides you want. After you select the slides, press Del to remove them all.

If you accidentally delete a slide, don't panic. Instead, immediately choose <u>U</u>ndo from the <u>E</u>dit menu to reinsert the slide.

 Applying a Slide Layout

You may find that you have a slide already developed, but you want to use a different slide layout. You don't have to re-create the slide from scratch—you can instead apply a slide layout. Here's how: Display the slide, and then choose F<u>o</u>rmat, Slide <u>L</u>ayout. In the Slide Layout dialog box, double-click the AutoLayout you want to use.

Lesson 3: Changing Slide Order

You may need to rearrange the slides in your presentation to create a more logical sequence. The best view to use for reordering slides is Slide Sorter view because you immediately see the move's effect on the presentation. It's easy to move a slide in this view. First, select the slide; then drag it to the new location before releasing the mouse button. This method is sometimes referred to as ***drag-and-drop***. Try moving slides using this technique now.

To Change Slide Order

🔳 ❶ **Make sure that the Quality Computer Training presentation displays in Slide Sorter view.**

This is a good view to use to rearrange slides. Before you move a slide, though, you must first select it.

❷ **Click Slide 4, `Applications`, to select it.**

A double border surrounds Slide 4, indicating that it is selected.

❸ **Move the mouse pointer to the middle of the selected slide, and then drag the line indicator to the space between Slides 5 and 6.**

The new location for the slide is indicated by the inserted line between Slides 5 and 6 (see Figure 3.10).

❹ **Release the mouse button.**

The selected slide is moved to the position between Slides 5 and 6. PowerPoint also renumbers the slides to line up with their new positions.

Figure 3.10
You can drag a selected slide to the new location.

The indicator line shows the new location for the slide

You can also select multiple slides and then move them. To select more than one slide, press ⇧Shift as you click to select (or deselect) the slides. Release ⇧Shift, and then drag the group of slides to the new location. Try moving multiple slides now.

⑤ With Slide 5, Applications, still selected, press ⇧Shift while clicking Slide 4, Available Training.
Double borders encompass both slides, indicating that you successfully selected them. You can move them to a new location by dragging, just as you did earlier in this exercise. If you drag one of the selected slides, both will move. As before, the indicator line shows the new location for the selected slides.

⑥ Move the mouse pointer to the middle of Slide 4, Available Training, and then drag the indicator line between Slides 2 and 3.

⑦ Release the mouse button to "drop" the slides into their new location.
Both slides are moved to the specified location. Notice that PowerPoint also renumbers them.

⑧ Choose Edit, Undo Drag and Drop (or click the Undo button) to reverse the move.
The slides are moved to their previous location.

⑨ Save your changes and keep the presentation open for the next exercise, in which you add, demote, and promote text.

Moving Slides in Outline View
Although it's a bit tricky, you can select and move slides in Outline view as well. In Outline view, click a slide's icon to select it. Move the mouse pointer over the icon until a four-headed arrow displays. Drag the slide to the new location (indicated by a horizontal line), and then release the mouse button.

Lesson 4: Adding, Demoting, and Promoting Text

When you first create a presentation, you have only a framework for adding text and graphics. In the previous two lessons, you focused on changing the basic structure so that your presentation would flow in a more logical manner. You did this by adding, deleting, and rearranging slides. After the framework is in place, however, there are numerous ways to enter and modify the text itself. Being able to manipulate the text in a presentation is an important skill. This lesson focuses on ways to enter, demote, and promote text in the Slide pane of the Normal view. You use the blank slide you inserted in Lesson 2 to do this. Try working with text now.

To Add, Demote, and Promote Text

1 **Select Slide 7 in the Quality Computer Training presentation, and then click the Normal View button.**
The new blank slide is shown with placeholders for a title and a bulleted list (see Figure 3.11). The placeholders that display depend on the AutoLayout you choose. For this slide, you have title and bulleted list areas.

Figure 3.11
You can enter text in the slide's placeholders.

Placeholder for title text

Placeholder for bulleted text

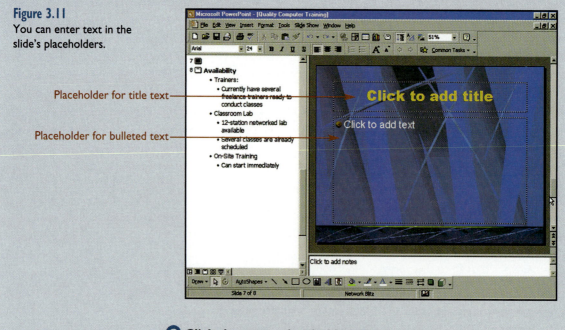

2 **Click the upper placeholder, Click to add title.**
An insertion point replaces the placeholder words, so you can enter text.

3 **Type** `Experienced Trainers`, **and then click the lower placeholder,** `Click to add text`.
The title is fixed in the upper placeholder and the insertion point is moved to the bulleted list area. Because this slide is based on the Bulleted List AutoLayout, you can quickly create a list with bullets. Bulleted lists are generally used when you want to emphasize each subpoint, but the order of the items is not particularly important.

4 **Type** `Rebecca Bell` **as the first bullet point, and then press** ⏎Enter.
`Rebecca Bell` is listed as the first bullet point, and a second bullet is automatically created.

5 **Type** `Sarah Jones` **as the second bullet point and press** ⏎Enter.
`Sarah Jones` is entered as the second point. You can create subpoints that support or enhance your main point. One way to create subpoints is to press Tab⇥ to insert the line. Alternatively, you can click the Demote button on the Formatting toolbar.

6 **Press** Tab⇥, **type** `Ten years corporate training experience`, **and then press** ⏎Enter.
Pressing Tab⇥ will *demote* this line—indenting it to show that it has less importance than the previous one. Additionally, every time you press ⏎Enter, another subpoint is created at the same level.

7 **Type** `Writes books for Prentice Hall` **as the second subpoint, and then press** ⏎Enter.

> ❌ If a red squiggly line appears beneath a word, don't worry. PowerPoint doesn't recognize the word, and thinks that you've either misspelled or mistyped it. You can either ignore the line or right-click on the word to display a spelling shortcut menu. Choose a replacement word (or Ignore All) from the menu.

You can also *promote* a line so that it is indented less. By indenting text less, you indicate its relative importance. You can do this by pressing ⇧Shift+Tab⇥ or clicking the Promote button on the Formatting toolbar.

8 **Press** ⇧Shift+Tab⇥ **to promote the bullet on the current line, and type** `Lonnie Stegall`.
Your slide should now look similar to Figure 3.12.

9 **Save the Quality Computer Training presentation.**
Keep it open for the next lesson, in which you select, copy, and move text.

continues ▶

To Add, Demote, and Promote Text   (continued)

Figure 3.12
You can demote bulleted points by pressing Tab.

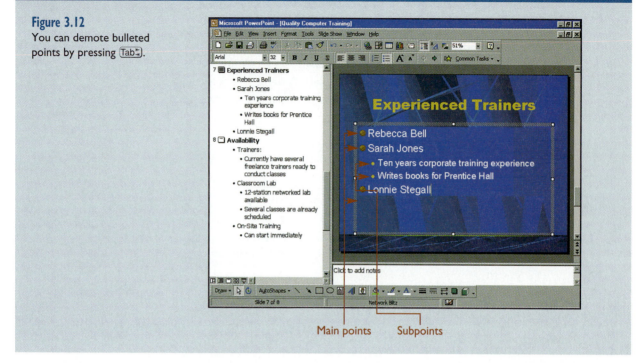

Main points   Subpoints

(i) Editing Text

You delete text in PowerPoint the same way as in a word processing program. Press Del or ◄Backspace to erase one character at a time. You can also drag to select larger sections of text with the mouse, and then press Del. If you accidentally delete too much text, click the Undo button.

You can also enter and edit text in the Outline pane. You position the insertion point on the slide, and then type the text. You can also press Tab or ◄Shift+Tab to demote or promote points—just like in the Slide pane.

Lesson 5: Selecting and Moving Text

In addition to entering text, you can easily change the order of the presentation bullet points. Copying and moving text is facilitated by the **Clipboard**—a temporary area of memory that holds material that is cut or copied to be pasted elsewhere. Before you cut or copy text, however, you must first select it. After the text is selected, you can click the Cut or Copy buttons to move or copy the selected text to the Clipboard. Move the insertion point to where you want to place it, and then click the Paste button. You can also drag selected text to a specified location. You can move text most easily in the Normal or Outline views. For this exercise, you use Outline view.

To Select and Move Text

❶ In the open presentation, click the Outline View button.
The presentation displays in Outline view.

② Use the Outline pane's vertical scrollbar so that you can view Slide 4, Available Training.

You can select a word, a subpoint, or the entire slide contents. The quickest way to select a single word is to double-click it.

③ On Slide 4, double-click the word Available.

The word Available displays in reverse video to indicate that you selected it. You can move this word by cutting it, which sends it to the Clipboard, and then by pasting it at another location. Try this now.

④ Choose Edit, Cut.

The selected word is removed from the screen and sent to the Clipboard. (You can also cut text by clicking the Cut button or pressing Ctrl+X on the keyboard.)

You can position your insertion point where you want to place the text, and then choose Edit, Paste. (Alternatively, you can click the Paste button or press Ctrl+V on the keyboard.)

⑤ Click to set the insertion point to the right of the word Training, and then choose Edit, Paste.

The word is pasted at the location you indicated.

In Outline view, you can also select a subpoint and move it by using the Move Up or Move Down buttons on the Outlining toolbar. First, however, you need to display this toolbar, which includes a number of buttons that you can use to work with your presentation in Outline view.

> **✗** If the Outlining toolbar is already displayed on your system, it just means that another user previously turned it on. If this is the case, proceed to Step 8.

⑥ Right-click either the Standard or Formatting toolbar.

A shortcut menu displays with a list of PowerPoint's toolbars (see Figure 3.13).

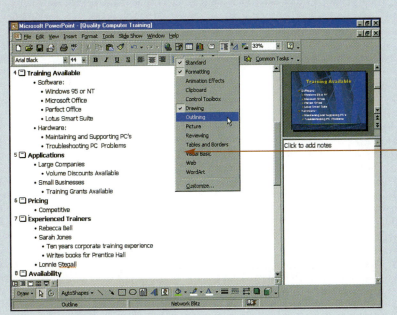

Figure 3.13
PowerPoint's toolbars are only a mouse click away.

Right-click on a visible toolbar to display this shortcut menu

continues ▶

To Select and Move Text   (continued)

7 **Click Outlining on the shortcut menu.**
The Outlining toolbar displays on the left side of the Outline pane (see Figure 3.14). Now try using the Move Up and Move Down buttons to adjust the position of text on your outline.

Figure 3.14
Use the Outlining toolbar buttons to work with your presentation.

Move Up button
Move Down button

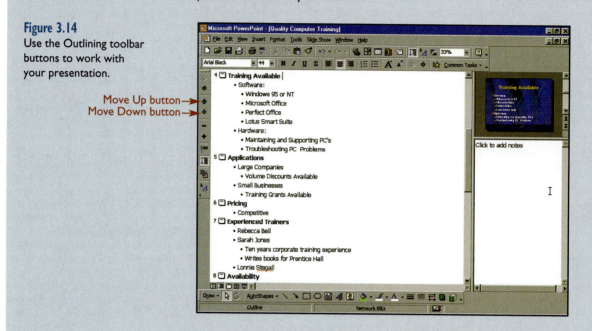

8 **On Slide 4, position the mouse pointer over the bullet for the subpoint Windows 95 or NT until it displays as a four-sided arrow, and then click.**
The entire subpoint is selected (see Figure 3.15). Now you can use the Move Down button to position it where you want it.

Figure 3.15
You can use the Move Up and Move Down buttons in Outline view.

Click here to move the selected text up

Click here to move the selected text down

Click a bullet to select the associated text

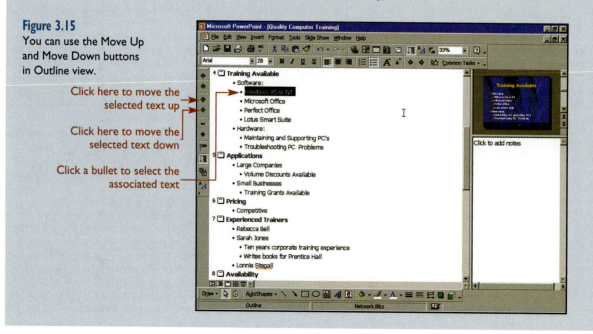

⬇ **9** **With the subpoint still selected, click the Move Down button on the Outlining toolbar.**

The subpoint moves down one line in the presentation. Likewise, you can move it up.

⬆ **10** **Click the Move Up button on the Outlining toolbar.**

The subpoint moves back to its previous location.

You can also select a main point and then move it. When you select a main point, all the subpoints are automatically selected as well.

11 **On Slide 4, click the bullet for Software.**

The main point (Software) and all the related subpoints are selected.

12 **Click the Move Down button three times.**

The information about software programs is moved down three lines. Your slide should appear similar to the one shown in Figure 3.16.

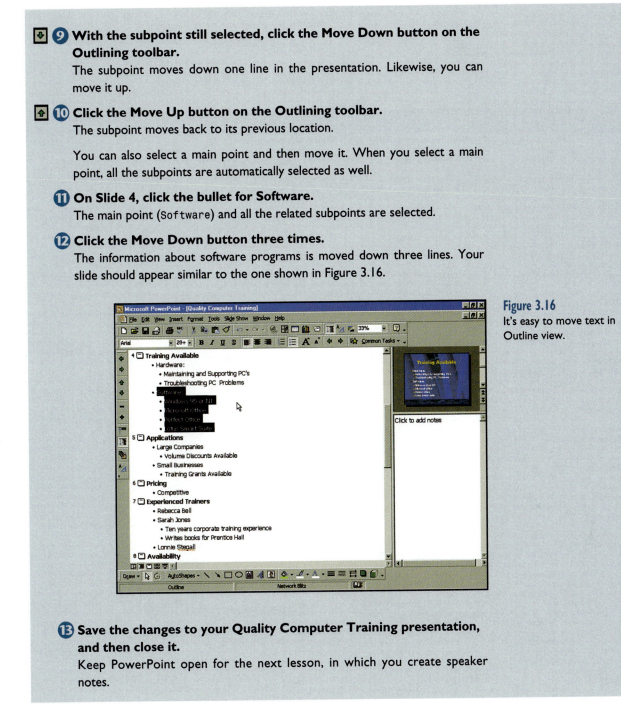

Figure 3.16
It's easy to move text in Outline view.

13 **Save the changes to your Quality Computer Training presentation, and then close it.**

Keep PowerPoint open for the next lesson, in which you create speaker notes.

Lesson 6: Creating Speaker Notes

Have you ever been in the middle of an important presentation, when suddenly your mind went blank? Or been asked a particularly tricky question by someone in your audience? In either case, if you had *speaker notes* to rely on, you probably got through the situation without too much trouble. Speaker notes are just what their name implies—supporting data, quotations, or illustrations that you can use when giving a presentation. Although you may have developed notes in the past by writing on a legal pad, PowerPoint includes a feature that helps you create the electronic equivalent—from right within the program.

This lesson shows you how to quickly create and print speaker notes so that supporting data is right at your fingertips. Each slide can have corresponding notes. You can prepare speaker notes when you initially create your presentation or you can add them later. Additionally, you can use the Notes Page view to add your notes, or use the Notes pane in Normal view. Try using both methods of preparing notes now.

To Create Speaker Notes

1 **In PowerPoint, open PP1-0302 from the CD-ROM and save it to the floppy disk as Safety Report. (If you need a brush-up on opening and saving files, refer to Lesson 1.)**
You can easily add notes to a page by switching to Notes Page view because this view provides a slide image and a notes box area.

2 **Make sure that Slide 1, Safety Report, is displayed, and then choose View, Notes Page.**
The current slide is shown in Notes Page view (see Figure 3.17). This view shows a small-scale version of the slide (called a **slide image**), as well as an area where you can enter your notes—the **notes box**.

Figure 3.17
You can add notes quickly in the Notes Page view.

Slide image for current slide ⎯

Notes box ⎯

Zoom button

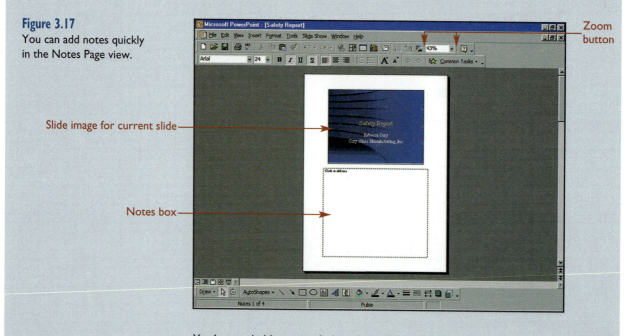

You've probably noticed that the notes box area is too small to reasonably view (or enter) text. Fortunately, you can enlarge the view by using the Zoom button.

 3 **Click the Zoom button's drop-down list arrow and choose 75%.**
The view is enlarged so that you can enter your notes (see Figure 3.18). Because monitor displays may vary a little from one computer to the next, don't be concerned if your screen looks slightly different from that shown in the figure.

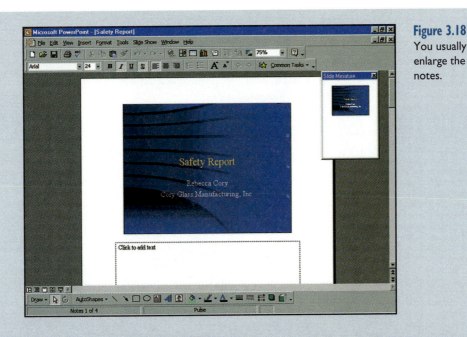

Figure 3.18
You usually need to enlarge the view to enter notes.

> ⊗ By default, a Slide Miniature displays whenever you change the zoom percentage to 65% or greater in Notes Page view. However, if you accidentally close the Slide Miniature, here's how to redisplay it: Choose View, Slide Miniature from the menu. Remember—the Slide Miniature option is available only if you choose a zoom percentage greater than 65%.

Now, create your speaker notes. Remember that these notes are usually used as reminders for yourself—to keep you on track and to make sure you don't forget any critical information during a presentation.

④ Click in the notes box and type the following:

```
(Make sure to play Bach's Brandenburg Concerto #5 as people arrive, and then fade it out.)
```

```
"Welcome! I'm glad to be presenting this safety report to you today. Here at Cory Glass Manufacturing we have some good news about our safety record, as well as some challenges ahead."
```

The text you typed is entered in the notes box and becomes part of the slide. Even when you switch to another view, the notes are still attached to the slide. (Later in this project, you learn how to print the notes.)

Another method of entering notes is to use the Notes pane in either Normal or Outline view. Try using this method now.

⑤ Click the Normal View button, and then press [PgDn] to display Slide 2, Overall Status of Safety Campaign.
This is the slide to which you want to attach some notes. By default, however, the Notes pane is so small that it's hard to see your notes. To make it easier to enter (and view) your notes, it's a good idea to first resize the Notes pane.

continues ▶

To Create Speaker Notes (continued)

⑥ **Move your mouse pointer over the horizontal divider that separates the Notes pane and Slide pane until a two-headed resizing arrow displays (see Figure 3.19).**

Figure 3.19
Display and drag the resizing arrow to change the size of the Notes pane.

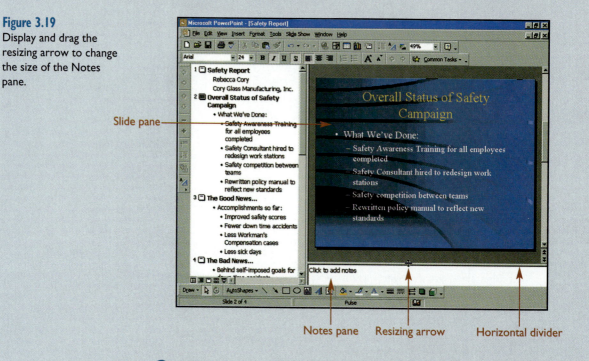

Slide pane

Notes pane   Resizing arrow   Horizontal divider

⑦ **Drag the resizing arrow upward until the screen is evenly split between the Slide and Notes panes, and then release the mouse button.**

The Notes and Slide panes are resized so that you can more easily see notes as you enter them (see Figure 3.20). Now try entering your notes.

Figure 3.20
Resizing the Notes pane helps you more easily see your notes.

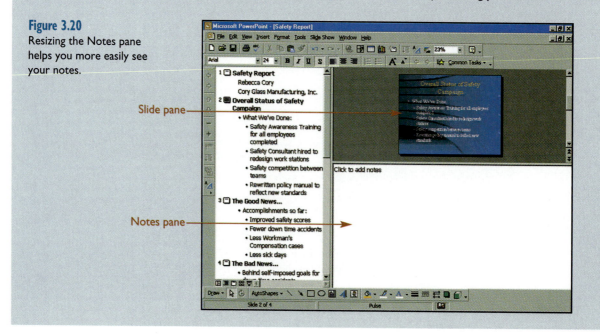

Slide pane

Notes pane

8 **Click in the Notes pane and enter the following text:**

Safety Awareness Training: The 1-hour mandatory program was completed by all 275 employees during the last two months.

Safety Consultant: We used Safety Engineers, Inc. from Columbus, Ohio to work closely with employees and managers. The new workstations were designed with input from our employees, and surpass OSHA, state, and local regulations.

Safety Competition: We want to thank Lauren Clark for this idea! The competition is 2 months long, and measures safety criteria (lost-time accidents, sick days, etc.) for the 3 teams involved. Each member of the winning team will receive an extra 1% salary bonus. The competition is still going on, and will finish at the end of the month.

Now, resize your Slide and Notes panes back to their original sizes.

9 **Drag the horizontal divider between the Slide and Notes pane downward until each pane displays by using its original size, and then release the mouse button.**

The slide appears in Normal view. Notice that the Notes pane has a vertical scrollbar that you can use to scroll through your notes. If you want, practice scrolling through your notes.

In this lesson, you learned two methods of creating speaker notes. Keep the Safety Report presentation open for the next lesson, in which you print the notes.

Entering Notes During a Slide Show

It's most common to enter and view notes in the Normal or Notes Page views. However, you can even view and enter notes during a running slide show. To do this, right-click your mouse to display the Slide Show shortcut menu, and then choose Speaker Notes. View, enter, or modify the text in the Speaker Notes window that displays. When you finish working with the notes, click the Close button.

Lesson 7: Printing Speaker Notes and Handouts

Your speaker notes would be of little value if you couldn't print them for a ready reference during your presentation. Fortunately, printing your notes is straightforward and relatively easy. To print the notes, choose File, Print, and then choose Notes Pages in the Print what area of the Print dialog box.

You can also print **handouts** to give to your audience. By default, PowerPoint includes options to print two, three, four, six, or nine slides per page as handouts. In contrast to the notes pages, handouts include only the slide's contents, not the accompanying notes. You print handouts the same way you print notes—by specifying the type of output you want in the Print what area of the Print dialog box.

Try printing speaker notes and handouts for your presentation now.

To Print Speaker Notes and Handouts

1 **With Slide 2 in the open Safety Report presentation displayed, choose File, Print.**

The Print dialog box displays (see Figure 3.21). You used this dialog box in Project 2 to print slides and outlines. In this lesson, you use it to print notes.

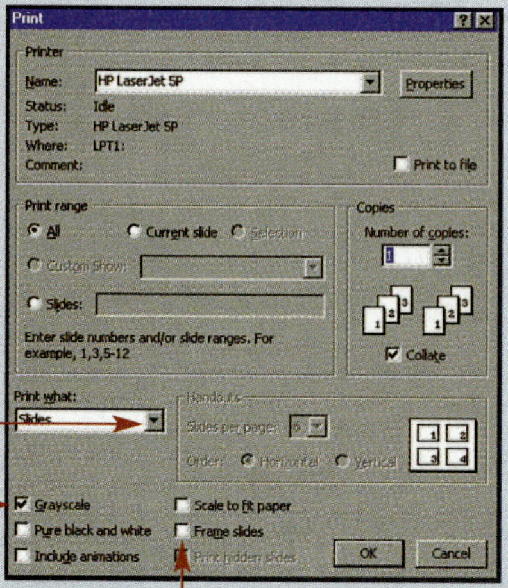

Figure 3.21
The Print dialog box provides ready access to printing options.

Click this arrow and then choose Notes Pages or Handouts

Check this box to print in grayscale

Check this box to add borders

2 **Click the Print what drop-down list arrow and choose Notes Pages from the list.**

This specifies to PowerPoint that you want to print the speaker notes associated with the current presentation.

The notes generally print with a better appearance if you frame the slide image, notes box, and page. A *frame* is simply a border that surrounds the slide element you choose. You can add frames by checking the Frame slides box.

3 **Check the Frame slides box, if necessary.**

You can print the current slide, print all presentation slides, or pick and choose just that you want. You specify which slides PowerPoint should print in the Print range area of the dialog box.

4 **In the Print range area, choose the Current slide option button.**

After selecting the options you want, you're ready to print.

5 **Make sure that your printer is turned on, and then choose OK.**

The notes for your current slide print. Now, try printing handouts.

6 **Choose File, Print to display the Print dialog box again.**

7 **Click the Print what drop-down list arrow and choose Handouts from the list.**

When you choose Handouts on the list, the Handouts section of the Print dialog box becomes active (see Figure 3.22). You use this section to designate how you want to set up your handouts. For example, you can click the Slides per page drop-down list arrow and choose a different number of slides.

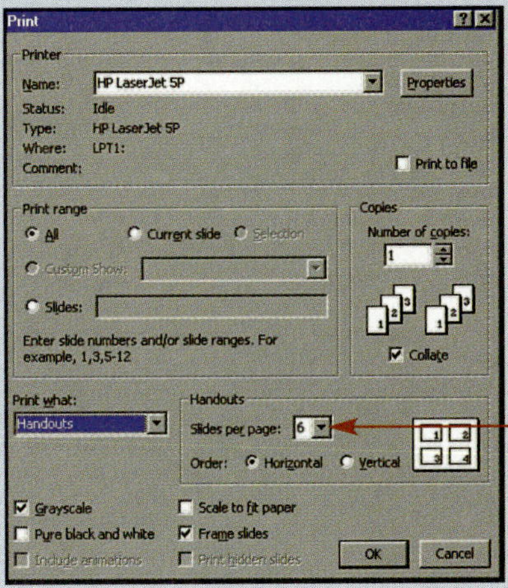

Figure 3.22
You can print handouts to give to your audience.

Choose the number of slide images per page here

8 **Click the Slides per page drop-down list arrow and choose 4.**
This specifies that four slide images will print per page.

9 **Make sure that the Grayscale and Frame slides boxes are checked, and that the Print range is set to All.**

10 **Click OK to print your handouts.**

11 **Save the Safety Report presentation, and then close it.**
Keep PowerPoint open if you plan to complete the Skill Drill, Challenge, and Discovery Zone exercises at the end of this project. Otherwise, make sure to exit PowerPoint and shut down Windows properly before turning off your computer.

Checking Your Spelling
One of the last steps before printing or giving a presentation is to make sure it's error-free. Besides manually proofreading the presentation, you can spell-check it. To do this, click the Spelling button on the Standard toolbar, or choose Tools, Spelling. PowerPoint searches your presentation for typos and misspelled words and displays them in the Spelling dialog box. You can choose Ignore to skip over the word, Change to replace it with another word, or Add to place the word in the dictionary. When PowerPoint is finished spell-checking your presentation, it displays a message box. Click OK to close the message box, and you're on your way to an error-free presentation!

Summary

As you worked through this project, you refined your PowerPoint skills. First, you learned how to modify the overall structure of a presentation by adding, deleting, and reordering slides. Then, you learned how to revise the content of individual slides by adding, demoting, promoting, copying, and moving text. Finally, you developed and printed speaker notes.

To expand on your knowledge, spend a few minutes exploring Help on these topics. Additionally, complete some of the Skill Drill, Challenge, and Discovery Zone exercises.

Checking Concepts and Terms ✓

True/False

For each of the following, check *T* or *F* to indicate whether the statement is true or false.

__T __F   **1.** You can preview presentations before opening them. [L1]

__T __F   **2.** Demote means to decrease the size of your text. [L4]

__T __F   **3.** You typically use speaker notes onscreen during a running slide show because you can't print them out. [L6–7]

__T __F   **4.** Slide Show view is the best view to use when you want to rearrange slides. [L3]

__T __F   **5.** You can add a new slide to a presentation by clicking the Promote button. [L2]

__T __F   **6.** The Details view allows you to see a miniature of the selected presentation in the Open dialog box. [L1]

__T __F   **7.** The extension for PowerPoint files is .ppt, but it may or may not display—depending on how the computer is set up. [L1]

__T __F   **8.** You can drag-and-drop slides to reorder them in Slide Sorter view. [L3]

__T __F   **9.** You promote a bulleted point when you click the Move Up button on the Outlining toolbar. [L4]

__T __F   **10.** You can print handouts as 2, 3, 4, 6, or 9 slides per page. [L7]

Multiple Choice

Circle the letter of the correct answer for each of the following.

1. To promote a point means to _____. [L4]

   a. make the text larger

   b. select a subpoint

   c. indent it less

   d. indent it more

2. You can delete a slide by _____. [L2]

   a. clicking the Move Out button

   b. showing the presentation in Slide Show view, and then pressing Esc

   c. selecting a slide in Slide Sorter view, and then pressing Del

   d. double-clicking a slide in Slide Sorter view

3. To add a slide, _____. [L2]

   a. click the Slide Sorter View button, and then press ↵Enter

   b. press PgDn in Normal view

   c. click the Get a New Slide button on the Slide Sorter toolbar

   d. click the New Slide button on the Standard toolbar

4. The _____ view in the Open dialog box displays information about the selected file, such as revision date, author, and title. [L1]

   a. List

   b. Properties

   c. Preview

   d. Details

5. To display the Open dialog box, _____. [L1]

   a. click the New button on the Standard toolbar

   b. choose File, Open

   c. choose File, Template

   d. choose Tools, AutoContent Wizard

6. When you delete a slide, _____. [L2]

   a. PowerPoint automatically renumbers the remaining presentation slides

   b. PowerPoint prompts you before removing the slide

   c. the presentation automatically displays in Normal view

   d. all of the above

7. You can select more than one slide in Slide Sorter view by pressing _____ as you click the slides. [L3]

   a. `Ctrl`+`⬆Shift`

   b. `Alt`

   c. `Ctrl`+`F1`

   d. `⬆Shift`

8. When a slide is selected in Slide Sorter view, _____. [L3]

   a. it displays in reverse video

   b. its text is highlighted

   c. a double red border surrounds the slide

   d. none of the above

9. Speaker notes _____. [L6–7]

   a. provide supporting data or documentation during a presentation

   b. help you keep on track during a presentation

   c. help you remember quotations or anecdotes

   d. all of the above

10. The two ways to view and add speaker notes to your presentation are _____. [L6]

   a. Notes Page view and the Notes pane

   b. Handout view and Notes Page pane

   c. Speaker Notes window and Handout view

   d. Speaker pane and Normal pane

Screen ID

Identify each of the items shown in Figure 3.23.

Figure 3.23

A. Promote button

B. Zoom button

C. New Slide button

D. Slide image

E. Demote button

F. Notes box

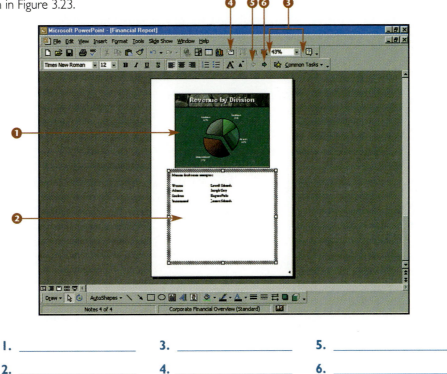

1. _____   3. _____   5. _____

2. _____   4. _____   6. _____

Discussion Questions

1. What are the two main ways to add and view speaker notes? What is an additional method you can use to access speaker notes when viewing your presentation as a slide show?

Which method do you prefer? Why? What are the advantages and disadvantages of each method? [L6]

2. Refer to the information covered in Projects 1-3. What PowerPoint feature impressed you the most? Which feature(s) will you use the most frequently? Why?

3. Outline the sequence of developing a presentation. Include information from the previous three projects in this book. Present this sequence to another user.

Skill Drill

Skill Drill exercises reinforce project skills. Each skill reinforced is the same, or nearly the same, as a skill presented in the project. Detailed instructions are provided in a step-by-step format.

1. Using Help

You help manage a college computer lab, and you're concerned that students will save presentations to multiple locations and you won't be able to properly find or manage the files on all the computers. To find out more about file management (such as opening and deleting presentations) in PowerPoint 2000, you tap into Help. [L1]

1. In PowerPoint, choose Help, Microsoft PowerPoint Help to display the Microsoft PowerPoint Help window.

2. Click the Contents tab to display that page, and then double-click the Opening, Moving, Copying, and Deleting Files icon.

3. Click the icon for each of the following topics. Read the information on each. Take notes so that you can remember the information covered.

- Add a folder or file shortcut to the Favorites folder
- Best place to store files

- Copy a file
- Delete a file
- Move a file
- Open a presentation
- Select multiple files

4. Close the Microsoft PowerPoint Help window.

5. Using your written notes as a guide, practice each of the procedures listed in Step 3. Keep PowerPoint open if you plan to complete additional exercises.

2. Using the Open Dialog Box to Find a Presentation

Your boss is having trouble locating a presentation that she desperately needs to conduct a new employee orientation seminar. Because you're much more familiar with computers (and PowerPoint) than your boss is, she asks you to help. To quickly lay your hands on the correct file, you use the Views button in the Open dialog box. [L1]

1. In PowerPoint, choose File, Open to display the Open dialog box.

2. Use the Look in drop-down list to locate the drive where your data files are located.

3. Make sure that PP1-0301 is selected on the list. Click the Views button's drop-down list arrow, and then choose List.

4. Click the Views button's drop-down list arrow, and then choose Details.

5. Click the Views button's drop-down list arrow, and then choose Properties.

6. Click the Views button's drop-down list arrow, and then choose Preview.

7. Repeat steps 3–6 for each of the other student data files in the folder until you locate the `New Employee Orientation` presentation. Open the presentation and view it as a slide show.

8. Close the presentation without modifying or saving it. Keep PowerPoint open if you plan to complete additional exercises.

3. Modifying a Presentation

You were promoted at your company and are now in charge of new employee orientation. Some of the employee benefits have changed. In preparation for the next orientation session, you decide to modify the overall structure of the presentation, as well as some of the text. [L1, 4–5]

1. Choose File, Open to display the Open dialog box. Display the folder in which your student data files are located; then double-click `PP1-0303` to open it.

2. Choose File, Save As to display the Save As dialog box. In the File name text box, type `New Employee Orientation`. Click Save.

3. Click the Slide Sorter View button to display the presentation in Slide Sorter view. Click Slide 3, `History of Company`, and then press Del. Repeat the process to delete the (new) Slide 3, `Who's Who`.

4. Click Slide 6, `Required Paperwork,` to select it. Drag the slide to between Slide 2 and Slide 3. Release the mouse button.

5. Double-click Slide 4, `Benefits Review,` to display it in Normal view. Make the following changes to the text in either the Slide pane or the Outline pane:

The fitness center has closed down, so it is no longer a benefit. Eliminate the point associated with it.

Change the text to show that you now get 3/4 sick day per month instead of 1/2.

Move the point for the 401(K) plan to just below the point for the two-week vacation benefit.

6. Save your changes; close the presentation. Keep PowerPoint open if you plan to complete additional exercises.

4. Moving Text and Slides

You're a sales manager for a company and you want to present a short pep talk to your sales force about how to work with different types of people. To prepare for the talk, you revise a previously created presentation. [L1–4]

1. Open `PP1-0304` and save it as `People Skills`.

2. Choose View, Slide Sorter to display the presentation in Slide Sorter view.

3. Click Slide 3, `Summary`, and drag the slide to move it between Slide 1 and Slide 2.

4. With the new Slide 2, `Summary`, still selected, press Del to remove the slide from the presentation.

5. Click the Undo button twice to reverse the previous two actions.

6. Double-click Slide 2, `Skills`, to display it in Normal view.

7. Click to set your insertion point in the last line (`Communication Skills`). Click the Promote button on the Formatting toolbar to make the point the same level of importance as the other bulleted points.

8. Move the point for `Communication Skills` so that it is the first bulleted point on Slide 2.

9. Click the point for `The Lion`, and then click the Demote button. Repeat the process for each of the other personality types (`The Beaver`, `The Golden Retriever`, and `The Otter`).

10. Save the `People Skills` presentation; then close it. Keep PowerPoint open if you plan to complete additional exercises.

5. Creating Speaker Notes

You're in charge of converting your company's network from Windows 95 to Windows NT. To present your progress to management in an upcoming meeting, you prepare speaker notes. [L1, 6]

1. Open **PP1-0305** and save it as **Upgrading to Windows NT**.

2. Press (PgDn) twice to display Slide 3, **Progress**. Choose View, Notes Page.

3. Click the Zoom drop-down list arrow and choose **75%** from the list to enlarge the view.

4. Click in the notes box and enter the following text:

   Workstation conversion from Windows 95 to Windows NT began on time in early January. Independent contractors have been hired to help in the conversion.

   The original plan was to have trainers work with each employee within two weeks

after the employee's workstation was converted. At this point, 68% have received training within two weeks, while the remaining 32% have been trained within three weeks.

5. Click the Normal View button. Press (PgDn) twice to display Slide 5, **Costs**.

6. Type the following text in the Notes pane area of Slide 5:

   Make sure to emphasize that no additional cost overruns are anticipated.

7. Save the changes to your Upgrading to Windows NT presentation. Keep the presentation open if you plan to complete the next exercise on printing speaker notes and handouts.

6. Printing Speaker Notes and Handouts

So that you'll have a ready reference when you give your Upgrading to Windows NT presentation, you print your speaker notes. You also print handouts to give to your audience. [L7]

1. In the Upgrading to Windows NT presentation open from the previous exercise, display Slide 3, **Progress**.

2. Choose File, Print to display the Print dialog box. Click the Print what drop-down list arrow and choose Notes Pages.

3. In the Print range section, click Current slide so that you'll only print speaker notes for Slide 3. Click OK to print your speaker notes.

4. Now print your handouts. Choose File, Print to again display the Print dialog box. Click the Print what drop-down list arrow and choose Handouts.

5. In the Handouts section, click the Slides per page drop-down list arrow and choose **4**.

6. Make sure that the Frame slides box is checked. Click OK to print your handouts.

7. Save the changes to your Upgrading to Windows NT presentation; then close it. Keep PowerPoint open if you plan to complete additional exercises.

Challenge

Challenge exercises expand on, or are somewhat related to, skills presented in the lessons. Each exercise provides a brief narrative introduction, followed by instructions in a numbered step format that are not as detailed as those in the Skill Drill section.

1. Researching Ways to Work with Different PowerPoint Versions

You're the head of the Information Technology Department. In your organization, you have a mixed platform of software programs. In fact, you have so many versions of Office floating around your organization that users may have PowerPoint 4.0, PowerPoint 95, PowerPoint 97, or PowerPoint 2000. You need to find out how (and if) users can share their presentations. To do so, you use Help.

1. In PowerPoint, choose <u>H</u>elp, Microsoft PowerPoint <u>H</u>elp. Click the Show button, if necessary, to split the dialog box into two panes.

2. Click the <u>C</u>ontents tab. Double-click the Sharing Information with Other Users and Programs icon. Double-click the Sharing Presentations with Others subtopic.

3. Use each of the hyperlinks listed to find out more about sharing information between versions.

4. Develop a chart or list that outlines how to share presentations between the different versions. (If you know how to use Word, you may want to use Word's table feature for this step.)

5. Close the Microsoft PowerPoint Help window. Keep PowerPoint open if you plan to complete additional exercises.

2. Creating and Printing Notes

You're in charge of conducting new employee orientation at your company. To prepare for the meeting, you create and print speaker notes. [L6–7]

1. Open **PP1-0306** and save it as **Orientation Meeting.**

2. Add the following speaker note to Slide 1:

   `Make sure to welcome them enthusiastically and make them feel part of the team.`

3. Add the following notes to Slide 3, **History of Company**:

   `Company was founded in 1990 to provide ergonomic computer equipment.`

   `Company has grown at a rate of 10% (average) per year.`

   `With increased interest in ergonomic workstation design, we antici-pate continued growth.`

   `Our motto: "To make working at a computer as comfortable as it is productive."`

4. Run your presentation as a slide show, starting with Slide 1. In the slide show, view your notes for both Slide 1 and Slide 3. (*Hint:* Use the Slide Show shortcut menu.)

5. Print speaker notes for your presentation and print handouts (6 slides per page).

6. Save the changes to your **Orientation Meeting** presentation; then close it. Keep PowerPoint open if you plan to complete additional exercises.

3. Creating and Formatting Speaker Notes

As sales manager of your company, you conduct training for the sales team. To motivate your salespeople, you develop a presentation for an upcoming training session. To help you remember information, you add speaker notes to the presentation. [L6–7]

1. Open **PP1-0307** and save it as **Sales Team Training Session.**

2. Add the following speaker note to Slide 1, **Motivating a Team**:

   `Make sure to have the sales awards displayed at the front of the room and to have upbeat music playing.`

3. Add the following speaker note to Slide 2, **Deliver an Inspirational Opening**:

   `"People tend to support what they help create." Betsy Hudson`

4. Format your notes. First, display Slide 2, `Deliver an Inspirational Opening`, in Notes Page view. Zoom to **75%** to enlarge the notes box area.

5. Select the quotation, and then click the Bold button on the Formatting toolbar.

6. Select the name (`Betsy Hudson`) in the notes box, and then click the Italic button on the Formatting toolbar. Switch your presentation to Normal view.

7. Print your speaker notes. Print handouts of your presentation (3 slides per page).

8. Save your `Sales Team Training Session` presentation, and then close it. Keep PowerPoint open if you plan to complete additional exercises.

4. Revising an Existing Presentation

As president of the University Biking Club, you must present information to prospective members. You decide to revise an existing presentation in order to do this effectively. [L1, 3–4]

1. In PowerPoint, open `PP1-0308` and save it as `Biking Club`.

2. Display the presentation in Slide Sorter view. Move Slide 3, `Officers`, to between Slide 1 and Slide 2.

3. Switch to Normal view. Move the bulleted subpoint on Slide 3, `Trip to watch Virginia Race of Champions`, up two lines. (*Hint:* It should display immediately beneath the `Coming Events` main point.)

4. Add a new slide after Slide 3. Choose the Bulleted List AutoLayout for your new slide.

5. Add the following text on the newly inserted slide:

   Title placeholder: `How to Join`

   Text placeholder: `Fill out membership form`

   `Fill out proof of insurance form`

   `Pay dues to David Reams (Treasurer)`

6. Print an outline of your presentation. Save and close your presentation. Keep PowerPoint open if you plan to complete additional exercises.

5. Modifying a Presentation

As the events coordinator of the College Horseback Riding Club, you're in charge of an upcoming horse show. To publicize the event, you decide to revise an existing presentation to show during the next club meeting. [L1, 3–4, 6–7]

1. Open `PP1-0309` and save it as `Horseback Riding Club`.

2. Make the following changes to Slide 2:
   - Demote the three points listed beneath `Classes`.
   - Move the location (`Indoor Arena`) to the first line in the text placeholder so that it is the first bullet on the slide.

3. Add a slide at the end of the presentation using the Bulleted List AutoLayout. Enter the following information:

   Title placeholder: `How to enter:`

   Text placeholder: `Bring proof of club membership`

```
Sign up for classes at entry stand
Pay club treasurer
```

4. Add the following notes to Slide 3: `Remind members that classes are $5 each.`

5. Print your presentation as handouts (2 slides per page). Print the speaker notes associated with the presentation.

6. Save and close your presentation. Keep PowerPoint open if you plan to complete additional exercises.

6. Working with Presentation Text

As part of one of your business classes, you're required to give a speech on a software program. Because you know PowerPoint 2000, you decide to give your talk on it. Last week, you created the basics of the presentation; today, you finish it by revising the existing presentation's text. [L1–4, 8]

1. Open **PP1-0310** and save it as `Business Class Speech`.

2. Using the following outline as a guide, revise the presentation by adding, demoting, and promoting text. You also need to reorder and delete slides. Use whichever PowerPoint view (Outline, Normal, or Slide Sorter) is appropriate for the action you perform. (See Figure 3.24.)

Figure 3.24
Use this outline as a guide.

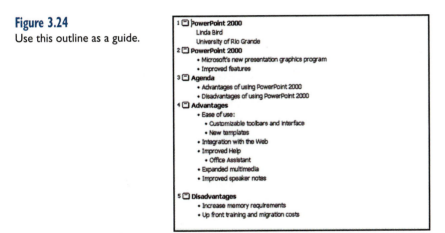

3. Print your presentation as handouts (6 slides per page). Save the presentation; then close it.

Discovery Zone

Discovery Zone exercises require advanced knowledge of topics presented in Essentials lessons, application of skills from multiple lessons, or self-directed learning of new skills.

1. Finding Out More About Notes

As production manager for a manufacturing plant, you develop and give lots of presentations. To help you more effectively prepare your speaker notes, you decide to use Help to research better ways to create your notes.

Using the Microsoft PowerPoint Help window, find ways to use notes more efficiently. (*Hint:* Look for a topic on the <u>C</u>ontents page of the Help window that deals with notes.) Write down at least three things you learn and try out the techniques. Finally, share what you learn with another person.

Keep PowerPoint open if you plan to complete additional exercises. [L6–7]

2. Working with the Notes Master

You're an old hand at creating and printing speaker notes. However, a friend recently told you that you could change how your notes are printed by modifying the notes master.

To find out more about using and modifying the notes master, use PowerPoint's Help. Specifically, find out the answers to the following questions:

- What is the notes master?
- What items are on the notes master?
- How can you delete, move, or resize the items on the notes master?
- Can I add a logo or other picture to a notes master?

Write down the answers to your questions. Open a presentation for which you've already developed speaker notes and modify the notes master. Print your speaker notes. Unless your instructor specifies otherwise, don't save the presentation.

Keep PowerPoint open if you plan to complete additional exercises. [L6]

3. Creating and Formatting Speaker Notes

To document a recruitment talk that you are presenting to prospective members for the University Biking Club, you add speaker notes to a presentation. (If you forget how to perform any of the actions, refer to PowerPoint's Help.)

Open `PP1-0311` and save it as `Prospective Members.` Add the following notes to the presentation:

- Slide 2: `Mention that officers are elected every September.`
- Slide 3: `Mention that Greg Schmidt, famous bicyclist, will be at the Race of Champions.`

Format the speaker note on Slide 3 as follows:

- Enlarge the font to `14` points.
- Add bold to `Greg Schmidt`.
- Italicize `Race of Champions`.

Print the speaker notes for Slide 3. Save the presentation; then close it. [L6–7]

4. Using Speaker Notes

You're putting the finishing touches on the financial report that you will present at your company's annual meeting. As part of your final preparations for giving the presentation, you create and format speaker notes.

Open **PP1-0312** and save it as **Financial Report**. Add the following speaker notes to your presentation:

- Slide 3: **Make sure to point out the increase in each category over the previous three years.**
- Slide 4: **Mention the division managers:**

Western	Lowell Schmidt
Atlantic	Joseph Cory
Southern	Eugene Parks
International	Lonnie Smith

Print the speaker notes for your presentation. Save, and then close your presentation. [L6–7]

Formatting Text and Bullets

Objectives

In this project, you learn how to

➤ **Change Text Appearance**

➤ **Use the Format Painter**

➤ **Change Alignment**

➤ **Adjust Paragraph Spacing**

➤ **Add and Remove Bullets**

➤ **Modify Bullets**

Key terms introduced in this project include

- bullets
- character attributes
- font
- formatting
- horizontal text alignment
- palette
- points

Project

4

Why Would I Do This?

I n the last two projects, you created and revised presentations. Most of the modifications you did involved changing the overall structure, such as changing slide order, or adding and deleting text. Still other changes involved demoting or promoting text.

Now you're ready to add some pizzazz to your presentation. One way to spiff up slides is to change *formatting*, which is the way that your presentation (including text, alignment, bullets, margins, and so on) is set up to display. For example, you can change your text color, size, or overall appearance. After you get the text formatting just the way you want it, you can quickly copy your formatting to other text by using the Format Painter.

Another way to make your slides more visually appealing is to change text alignment and paragraph spacing. No discussion of formatting would be complete without talking about how to use *bullets*, the markers that help delineate your ideas. Fortunately, most of the commands you need to format text and bullets are at your fingertips in the form of the Formatting toolbar. So come along and learn how to add some spice to your presentations!

Visual Summary

To use formatting commands effectively, you should become familiar with the buttons on PowerPoint's Formatting toolbar. This toolbar provides quick and easy access to the most commonly used formatting commands (see Figure 4.1). Additionally, for more specific control over formatting, you can use commands from the Format menu.

Figure 4.1
The Formatting toolbar provides quick access to formatting commands.

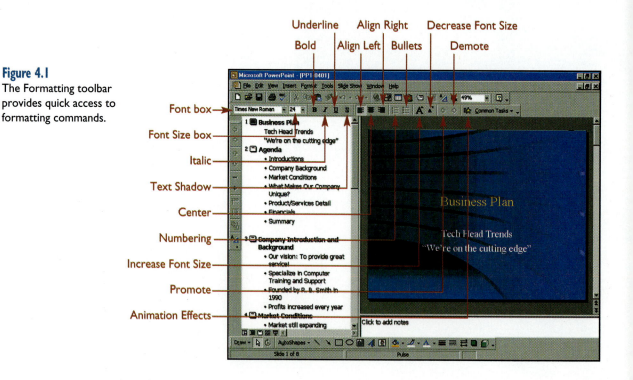

In this project, you also learn how to add or remove bullets and how to change their appearance. To modify bullets, you'll rely on the Bullets and Numbering dialog box, shown in Figure 4.2.

Figure 4.2
You can use this dialog box to change the appearance of your bullets.

Choose a bullet style here

Click here to choose a different bullet color

Change the bullet size here

When you finish working with text and bullets in this project, you'll have a slide in your presentation that is similar to that shown in Figure 4.3. Try working with these features now.

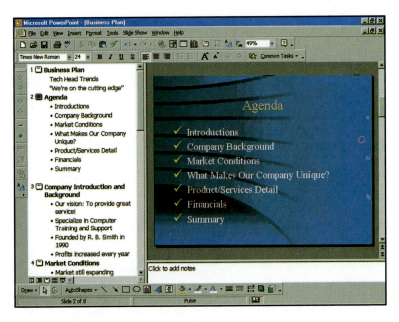

Figure 4.3
You can format text and bullets for a more pleasing appearance.

Lesson 1: Changing Text Appearance

The font that displays on a slide depends on the template you used to create it and the placeholder. A **font** is a collection of characters (letters, numbers, and special symbols) that have a specific appearance. Other terms for font are *typeface* and *font face*.

This font is only a basis for the formatting you add, however. You can add **character attributes**, such as bold, italic, or underline, to emphasize information. You can also change the font size or color.

To change the way text appears, you must first select it. You can select text by clicking in the appropriate placeholder, and then dragging over the text with the mouse. You can also double-click to select a word, or click a bullet to select all the text associated with it. Once it is selected, you apply formatting by clicking buttons on the Formatting toolbar. Try enhancing a presentation by changing its text now.

To Change Text Appearance

1 **Start PowerPoint, if necessary, and then open** PP1-0401 **and save it as** Business Plan.

2 **Display the first slide of the Business Plan presentation in Normal view.**

3 **Double-click the word** cutting.
This selects the word so that you can change the formatting.

4 **Click the Bold, Italic, and Underline buttons on the Formatting toolbar.**
Bold, italic, and underline effects are added to the selected word.

> ### ⓘ Using Keyboard Shortcuts
> You can also add character effects by using keyboard shortcuts. For example, you can press Ctrl+B for bold, Ctrl+I for italic, and Ctrl+U for underline.

5 **Select the text in the title placeholder,** Business Plan.
Notice that the Font and Font Size boxes on the Formatting toolbar indicate that this text is currently Times New Roman, 44 points, shown in Figure 4.4.

Figure 4.4
You can view the current font settings on the Formatting toolbar.

Font of selected text

Click here to choose another font

Font size of selected text

Click here to choose another font size

Selected text

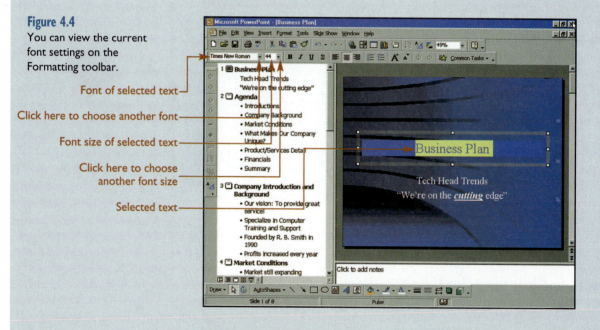

The Formatting toolbar is handy not only for viewing the current font settings, but also for changing them. The easiest way to do this is to click the drop-down list arrows associated with the Font and Font Size boxes.

6 **Click the drop-down arrow to the right of the Font Size box on the Formatting toolbar, and then click** 66 **to select it as the new point size.**
The selected text changes to the larger point size. Font size is measured in *points*, which is a unit of measurement used to designate character height.

The larger the point size, the larger the text. Most slide text should be at least 18 points (or 1/4") to be readable—especially if you plan to produce transparencies or show the presentation by using an LCD panel or an overhead projector.

Changing Font Size

If you're in a hurry, you can change font size quickly by selecting text, and then clicking the Increase Font Size or Decrease Font Size buttons one or more times.

Now try changing the font.

7 With the title text still selected, click the Font box drop-down arrow.

A graphical listing of fonts displays, which you can use for your presentation (see Figure 4.5). Don't panic if the fonts on your system don't match those shown in Figure 4.5. The exact fonts available depend on which programs (and printers) are installed on your system.

Times New Roman ▾

8 Click Comic Sans MS on the list (if Comic Sans MS is not available, select another font).

The selected text is shown, using the new font.

You can also change the font color for selected text. An easy way to do this is to use the Font dialog box.

Click here to display a list of fonts

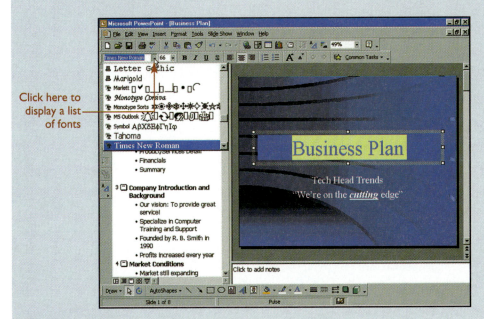

Figure 4.5
PowerPoint shows you how a font looks before you select it.

9 Select the entire line, Tech Head Trends, and then choose Format, Font.

The Font dialog box displays. This dialog box includes a number of ways to format text (see Figure 4.6). Notice that some of the formatting options (such as those listed in the Effects area) are not available on the Formatting toolbar. Because of this, it's handy to know how to use this dialog box.

continues ▶

To Change Text Appearance   (continued)

Figure 4.6
You can change text color
in the Font dialog box.

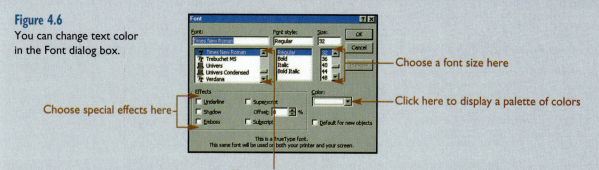

Choose a font size here

Click here to display a palette of colors

Choose special effects here

Choose a font here

10 **Click the Color drop-down list arrow.**

PowerPoint displays eight colors on a color *palette* (see Figure 4.7). The colors displayed are those most compatible with your particular template's color scheme. Just as an artist uses a palette to paint, you can pick and choose which colors you think will dress up your presentation.

Figure 4.7
You can choose a
compatible color from
the list.

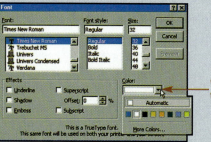

Click here to display
the color palette

11 **Click orange from the color palette (the fifth from the left); then choose OK to close the Font dialog box.**

Don't be surprised if the text doesn't look orange when it's selected. When text is shown in reverse video, the colors don't look the same as they do when the text isn't selected. You can easily see the color change just by deselecting the text.

12 **Click anywhere else in the Slide pane to deselect the text.**

When the text is deselected, you should be able to see the new font color.

13 **Click the Save button to save your changes to the Business Plan presentation.**

Now you know how to wield the basic tools for text formatting. To find out about additional ways to format text, use PowerPoint's Help.

In the next lesson, you learn how to copy formatting by using the Format Painter, so keep the Business Plan presentation open.

(i) **Using Font Colors**
You can rest your mouse pointer over any color box on the <u>C</u>olor drop-down list palette to display a ScreenTip. This ScreenTip identifies which element on the slide (such as the text) is typically formatted with the color. Additionally, if you don't see the color you want on the palette, you can click <u>M</u>ore Colors to display the Colors dialog box. Click the color you want, and then choose OK in both the Colors and Font dialog boxes.

Finally, if you don't want to use the Font dialog box to change text color, you can instead click the Font Color button on the Drawing toolbar.

Lesson 2: Using the Format Painter

Imagine that you worked long and hard to create just the visual effect you want for some text, and you then decide that you want to use the same formatting for text throughout the slide. You may expect that you'd have to spend a great deal of time re-creating the same combination of font, size, and color for the text.

Instead of having to repeatedly create the effect from scratch, however, you can just copy the formatting (including font, point size, and color) to other sections of text. This is an efficient method of formatting text because you can create the font and color combination you want once, and then copy it.

How do you actually "paint" formatting? By using the Format Painter! Think of the text with the formatting you want to copy as a paint can. When you click the Format Painter button, you dip your paintbrush into the can. You then "paint" the formatting to other text by dragging over it—just as you paint a wall by dragging a paint brush over it.

Try using this timesaving feature now.

To Use the Format Painter

❶ In your open presentation, select the `Business Plan` text (in the title placeholder of Slide 1).
It's crucial to select the text from which you want to copy formatting by selecting it *before* you click the Format Painter button. Don't forget this step!

❷ Click the Format Painter button on the Standard toolbar.
The mouse pointer changes to the Format Painter I-beam pointer. This pointer appears (interestingly enough) as a miniature paintbrush, as shown in Figure 4.8. Now you can apply the formatting to other text.

❸ Click and drag the pointer over the text for `Tech Head Trends`.
The formatting styles associated with `Business Plan` are applied to `Tech Head Trends`. However, the Format Painter button is automatically turned off as soon as you paint the format to the new text section. To keep this feature active so that you can format multiple text sections, you can double-click the Format Painter button.

❹ Select the word `cutting` in the lower placeholder, and then double-click the Format Painter button.
The Format Painter is activated so you can copy formatting to several sections.

continues ▶

To Use the Format Painter   (continued)

Figure 4.8
You can copy formats quickly with the Format Painter.

Format Painter button

Format Painter pointer

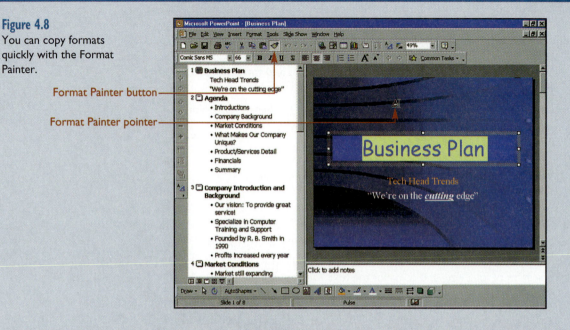

⑤ **Drag over** We're **in the lower placeholder, including the quotation marks immediately before the word.**
The formatting is copied to the selected word and the Format Painter is still active.

⑥ **Drag over the word** edge **(including the quotation marks immediately after the word) in the lower placeholder.**
The formatting is applied to the word. To turn off the Format Painter, you can click its button a second time or press Esc.

⑦ **Click the Format Painter button.**
The Format Painter is turned off.

⑧ **To see the formatting better, click outside the lower placeholder.**
Your slide should now look similar to Figure 4.9.

⑨ **Save your changes to the Business Plan presentation.**
Keep the presentation open for the next lesson, in which you change text alignment.

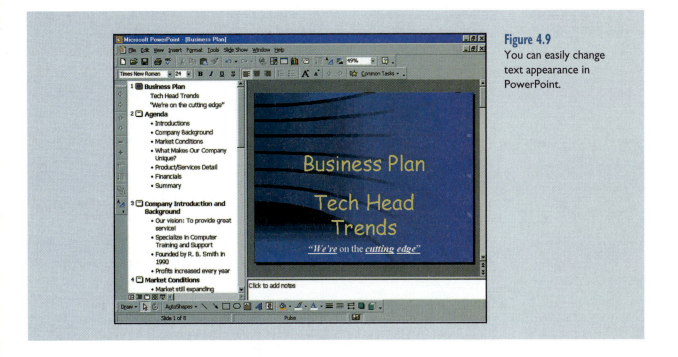

Figure 4.9
You can easily change text appearance in PowerPoint.

ⓘ Copying Formatting to Another Slide

You may be wondering if you can copy formatting to a slide other than the one that contains the original formatting. Fortunately, you can if you know the trick: Select the original text formatting that you want to copy and click the Format Painter button. Then, use the vertical scrollbar (or press a keyboard shortcut such as ⒫ⒼⒹⓃ or ⒫ⒼⓊⓅ) to move to another slide before applying your formatting.

❌ Make sure that the text containing the formatting you want to copy is selected before you click the Format Painter button. If you don't indicate the text formatting to copy, PowerPoint won't copy any formatting!

Lesson 3: Changing Alignment

In addition to changing the text appearance on slides, you can change ***horizontal text alignment***, which is simply the way the text displays horizontally in the placeholder. The way that the text displays in a placeholder—left-justified, centered, or right-justified—depends on the template you use. Most commonly, title and subtitle text are centered; bulleted list text is usually left-justified.

You can easily change text in *any* placeholder to left, center, or right alignment. The easiest way to do this is to use the alignment buttons on the Formatting toolbar. Now try changing the alignment of text in the Business Plan presentation.

To Change Alignment

1 **Display the first slide of the Business Plan presentation in Normal view, if necessary.**

2 **Click in the first line on the slide, `Business Plan`.**
Notice that the Center button on the Formatting toolbar is pushed in, indicating that it is turned on. When you choose another alignment, center alignment will be turned off.

3 **Click the Align Left button on the Formatting toolbar.**
The first line of the slide becomes left-justified and the Align Left button is pushed in.

4 **Press `PgDn` twice.**
Slide 3, `Company Introduction and Background`, now displays. This is a slide that has both title and bulleted list placeholders. You can use this slide to practice changing alignment for more than one line in a placeholder. Remember, however, that you must first select all the lines you want to format before applying a different formatting (such as alignment).

5 **Starting at the beginning of the first bulleted line, drag over all the bulleted text in the lower placeholder on Slide 3 to select it.**

6 **Click the Center button on the Formatting toolbar.**
All the lines you selected are centered (see Figure 4.10).

Figure 4.10
You can align text within a placeholder.

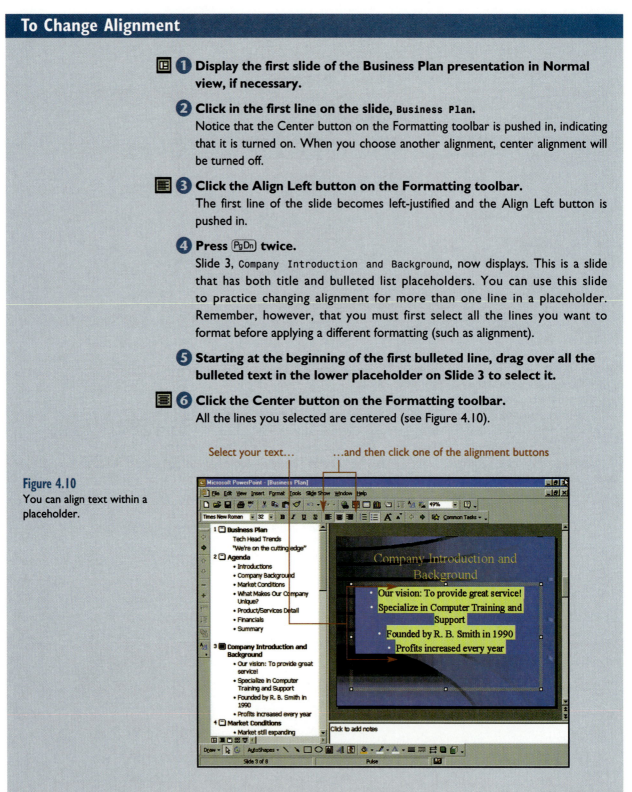

Select your text... ...and then click one of the alignment buttons

Leave the text selected and the presentation open for the next tutorial, in which you change paragraph spacing.

Aligning Text

You can also use the Format menu to change alignment. Choose Format, Alignment; then choose Align Left, Center, Align Right, or Justify from the submenu. (The Justify command aligns text to the right and left sides of the placeholder.)

Setting Tabs

Setting tabs in PowerPoint is similar to doing the same process in Word. Display the presentation in Normal view, and then choose View, Ruler. Click the tab type button at the left end of the horizontal ruler until you see the type of tab you want, and then click the ruler where you'd like the tab. To clear a tab stop, drag the tab off the ruler.

Lesson 4: Adjusting Paragraph Spacing

You probably realize that slides with very few bulleted points are more attractive and readable if the lines are spread out evenly within the text placeholder. PowerPoint includes a feature that helps you expand or compress the space in or between paragraphs (such as bulleted list items). To use this feature, you first select the paragraphs you want to space, and then use the Format, Line Spacing command to indicate how far apart you want the lines to appear.

Try adjusting paragraph spacing on your slide now.

To Adjust Paragraph Spacing

1 In the open **Business Plan** presentation, select the bulleted points on Slide 3 (if necessary).

2 Choose F**o**rmat, Line **S**pacing.
The Line Spacing dialog box displays, as seen in Figure 4.11. You use this dialog box to change spacing within or between paragraphs.

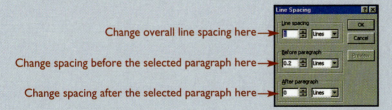

Change overall line spacing here →

Change spacing before the selected paragraph here →

Change spacing after the selected paragraph here →

Figure 4.11
You can use the Line Spacing dialog box to change spacing.

Try increasing the spacing between all the selected lines—both within and between paragraphs.

3 Type **1.5** in the **L**ine spacing text box; then click OK.
The lines of text are spread out within the placeholder (see Figure 4.12), but the effect may not be what you really had in mind! That's because this command spaces out all the lines in the placeholder. In general, however, a slide is

continues ▶

To Adjust Paragraph Spacing   (continued)

more readable if all the lines within a paragraph are single-spaced, but there's space between the paragraphs. Try setting your line-spacing options for this effect now.

Figure 4.12
Increasing line spacing affects all selected lines.

Spacing between paragraphs
Spacing within a paragraph

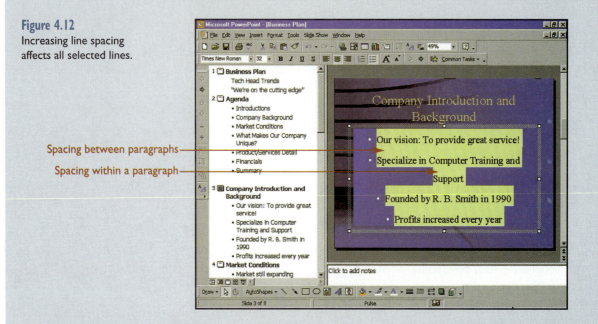

④ **Make sure that all the text in the lower placeholder is still selected, and then choose F̲ormat, Line S̲pacing to display the Line Spacing dialog box.**

⑤ **Enter 1 in the L̲ine spacing text box.**
This resets the line spacing back to single spacing for all selected lines so that lines within a paragraph are together. Now change the spacing between paragraphs. You can change the amount of spacing before each paragraph, after each paragraph, or both. Notice that this slide already has spacing of 0.2 lines before each paragraph. Now increase the spacing after each paragraph as well.

⑥ **Enter .25 in the A̲fter paragraph text box.**
When you finish setting options, they should match those shown in Figure 4.13.

Figure 4.13
You can exert exact control over the way your lines are spaced.

Use single spacing within paragraphs…

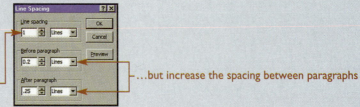

…but increase the spacing between paragraphs

⑦ **Click OK to close the dialog box, and then click in the Slide pane (outside the selection) to deselect your text.**
Your completed slide should look similar to Figure 4.14. Notice that the lines in the second paragraph are single-spaced, but that the space between paragraphs is expanded.

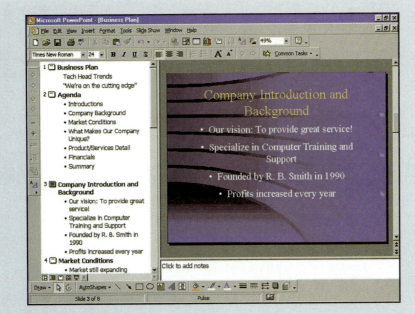

Figure 4.14
Your completed slide is
visually more attractive
and readable.

 Save your Business Plan presentation.

Keep the presentation open for the next lesson, in which you add and remove bullets.

 Previewing Changes to Line Spacing

You can preview any changes you make in the Line Spacing dialog box. Simply make your changes, and then click the Preview button. Most likely, you'll also need to move the Line Spacing dialog box (by dragging its title bar) so that you can see the revisions onscreen. If you're satisfied, click OK to accept the changes.

Using the AutoFit Text Feature

If you have extra text that doesn't fit in a placeholder, you can rely on PowerPoint 2000's AutoFit Text feature. This feature automatically adjusts the size of text to fit within the placeholder.

Lesson 5: Adding and Removing Bullets

In PowerPoint, *bullets* are markers that make a list of items more readable. A bullet is an object, such as a circle or a square, which is used to set off items in a list. PowerPoint displays bullets as circles, diamonds, squares, and so on. Bullets are also usually combined with indentation so that the related text wraps properly.

PowerPoint makes it easy to add bullets to a slide because it automatically includes them as part of any text placeholder that has a bulleted list. To use the existing bullets, just click in this type of placeholder and begin typing. When you finish typing a line, press ⏎Enter to create a new bulleted paragraph.

There may also be times when you want to remove bullets from your slide. To do this, click in the line from which you want to remove the bullet, and then click the Bullets button on the Formatting toolbar. If you want to remove bullets from several paragraphs simultaneously, first select the paragraphs, and then click the Bullets button. You use the same button to add bullets to text again—just select the text, and then click the button a second time.

Because it's easiest to make changes to bulleted items in Normal view, you'll use that view for this lesson. Try working with bullets now.

To Add or Remove Bullets

❶ In the open Business Plan presentation, display Slide 2, Agenda, in Normal view.
This slide contains a text placeholder with bullets. You can remove the bullets easily by selecting the associated text, and then clicking the Bullets button.

❷ Position your insertion point at the beginning of the bulleted list, press ⬆Shift, and then click at the end of the list.
All the bulleted text is selected. Now you can remove the bullets.

❸ Click the Bullets button.
Bullets are removed from all the paragraphs you selected. You can also add bullets by clicking the Bullets button again.

❹ With the paragraphs still selected, click the Bullets button again.
Bullets are added to the selected paragraphs.

Now try changing the bullets to numbering. You generally use numbers instead of bullets when you want to emphasize the order or sequence of the items listed. For example, it's appropriate to use numbers if you want to show the steps involved in placing an order, maintaining a machine, or sending email. Luckily, PowerPoint makes it easy to change a bulleted list to a numbered list (or vice-versa). Just select the paragraphs, and then click the Numbering button.

❺ With the paragraphs in the text placeholder still selected, click the Numbering button.
The bullets are replaced by numbering (see Figure 4.15).

Now try reapplying bullets to your list.

❻ With the text still selected, click the Bullets button.
The sequential numbers are replaced by bullets.

❼ Save your Business Plan presentation.
Keep the presentation open for the next exercise, in which you modify the appearance of bullets.

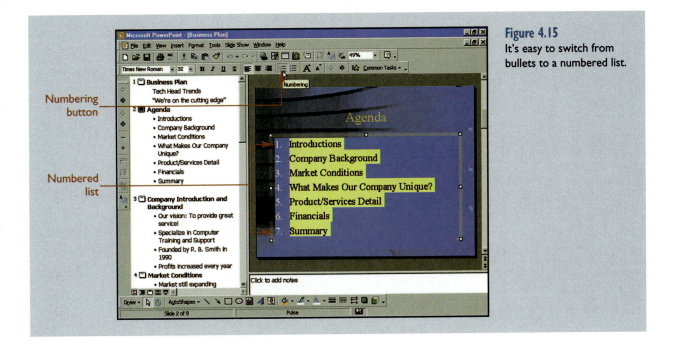

Figure 4.15
It's easy to switch from bullets to a numbered list.

⚠️ **Creating Numbered Lists**
You can also start a numbered list when you initially create a new slide. Click in the text placeholder and then click the Numbering button before you start entering text. Every time you press the ↵Enter key, you create a new numbered line.

There are also times when you want to move down to the next line without creating a new paragraph. To start a new line within a paragraph without a bullet (or number), press ⬆Shift+↵Enter.

Lesson 6: Modifying Bullets

The bullet's appearance is determined by each presentation's template. If you don't like the bullet's predesigned look, however, you can always change it. First, select the paragraphs with the bullets you want to change, and then choose Format, Bullets and Numbering from the menu bar to display the Bullets and Numbering dialog box. You can use this dialog box to change the color, size, or appearance for your bullets.

Try modifying some bullets now.

To Modify Bullets

❶ **In the Business Plan presentation, select the bulleted list on Slide 2, if necessary.**

continues ▶

To Modify Bullets   (continued)

2 Choose F̲ormat, B̲ullets and Numbering; then click the Bulleted tab if necessary.
The Bullets and Numbering dialog box displays (see Figure 4.16). You use this dialog box to change the way your bullets (or numbers) appear.

Figure 4.16
PowerPoint offers you many ways to modify your bullets.

Currently selected bullet ——

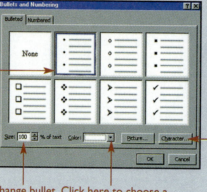

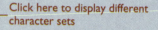
Click here to display different character sets

Change bullet   Click here to choose a
size here   color for your bullet

First, change bullet color. To do this, click the C̲olor drop-down arrow to display a palette of colors that coordinate with your template. If you're good at combining colors (or simply adventurous), you can click More Colors on the palette, and then select a color from the Colors dialog box that displays.

3 In the Bullets and Numbering dialog box, click the C̲olor drop-down arrow to display the color palette (see Figure 4.17), and then choose yellow (the last box from the right).

Figure 4.17
You can change bullet color to jazz up your presentation.

Click here to display the palette... ——

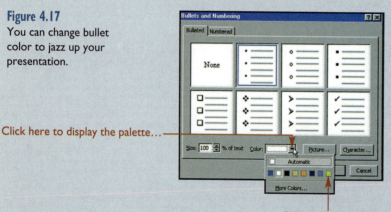

...and then choose this color

You can also use the Bullets and Numbering dialog box to change the size of your bullet relative to text. Type the bullet's percentage of the text (from 25–400%) in the Size text box, or use the spinner arrows to change the percentage in 5% increments. Try changing the bullet size now.

4 In the Bullets and Numbering dialog box, double-click in the S̲ize text box.
The current percentage (100) is selected. Once information in a text box is selected, you can simply type to replace it.

5 **Type 125, and then choose OK to close the dialog box.**

The slide displays your changes (see Figure 4.18). Notice that the text is still selected and displays in reverse video.

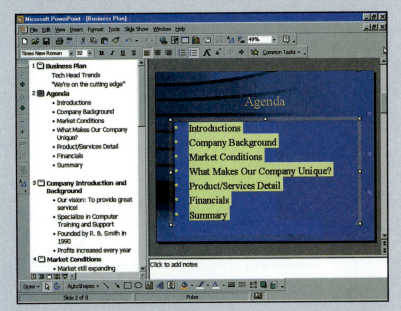

Figure 4.18
You can change bullet size and color.

You can also use a wide variety of symbols for bullets. The Bullets and Numbering dialog box includes a number of font and character sets from which you can choose bullet symbols. Try changing the bullet symbols now.

6 **With the bulleted list still selected, right-click in the list to display a shortcut menu (see Figure 4.19).**

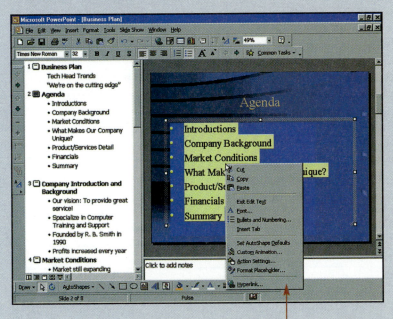

Figure 4.19
You can use the shortcut menu to open the Bullets and Numbering dialog box.

Right-click in the selected text to display this shortcut menu

continues ▶

To Modify Bullets   (continued)

7 **Left-click on Bullets and Numbering from the shortcut menu.**
The Bullets and Numbering dialog box displays.

8 **Click the check mark symbol (the fourth symbol on the second line), and then click OK.**
The default bullets are replaced by the check mark symbol you choose, as shown in Figure 4.20. Customizing bullets this way helps to spice up your presentation for greater impact. Remember—the only lines for which the bullets are changed are those that you select before displaying the Bullets and Numbering dialog box.

Figure 4.20
Tired of the default bullets for a slide? Choose another symbol!

New bullet symbols

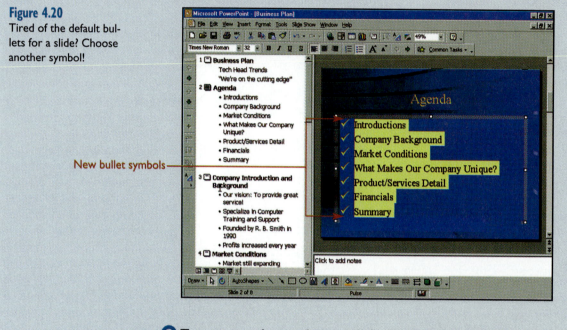

9 **To see your changes better, click outside the placeholders.**

 10 **Save and close the Business Plan presentation.**
When you finish your work session, exit PowerPoint and shut down Windows before turning off your computer.

Modifying Numbered Lists
You can also change the type of numbered list you use by using the Bullets and Numbering dialog box. After selecting the paragraphs, choose Format, Bullets and Numbering; then click the Numbered tab. Click the type of numbered list you want and click OK.

 Finding More Bullet Symbols
If you want a bigger selection of bullet symbols to use, you're in luck. On the Bulleted page of the Bullets and Numbering dialog box, click Character to display the Bullet dialog box. Click Bullets from the drop-down list arrow, choose a character set, and then double-click the symbol you want to use.

Summary

In this project, you learned how to spice up your presentation by changing text appearance such as font, font size, and color. You gained efficiency by using the Format Painter to quickly apply existing formats to other sections of text. You adjusted paragraph spacing and alignment for better appearance. Finally, you learned how to add, remove, and modify bullets and numbers.

To expand on your knowledge, spend a few minutes exploring Help on these topics. Additionally, complete some of the Skill Drill, Challenge, and Discovery Zone exercises.

Checking Concepts and Terms ✓

True/False

For each of the following, check *T* or *F* to indicate whether the statement is true or false.

__T __F   **1.** You can toggle bullets on and off by clicking the Bullets button. [L5]

__T __F   **2.** PowerPoint provides a variety of symbols you can use for bullets. [L6]

__T __F   **3.** You can double-click the Format Painter button to keep it active. [L2]

__T __F   **4.** In general, the larger the point size, the smaller the font. [L1]

__T __F   **5.** You increase point size automatically when you increase paragraph spacing. [L4]

Multiple Choice

Circle the letter of the correct answer for each of the following.

1. You can change character attributes, such as bold, italic, and underline, _____. [L1]

   a. by using the Font dialog box

   b. by clicking toolbar buttons

   c. by pressing keyboard shortcuts, such as Ctrl+B for bold

   d. all of the above

2. A point is _____. [L1]

   a. a method of quickly applying formatting from one text section to another

   b. the unit of measurement typically used to designate character height

   c. a button used to promote and demote text

   d. a button used to change text alignment

3. The way text appears on a slide is determined by _____. [L1]

   a. the underlying template

   b. the placeholder

   c. formatting changes you apply

   d. all of the above

4. Which of the following is true about the Format Painter? [L2]

   a. You must first select the text that contains the formatting you want to copy.

   b. You can change text appearance only for a text placeholder (not a title placeholder).

   c. Changes are made to the underlying template.

   d. all of the above

5. Which of the following is true about bullets? [L5-6]

   a. They are usually combined with indentation so that the related text wraps properly.

   b. They can be added or removed.

   c. They can be formatted.

   d. all of the above

Screen ID

Identify each of the items shown in Figure 4.21.

Figure 4.21

A. Font Size box

B. Bullets

C. Text Shadow button

D. Italic button

E. Increase Font Size button

F. Font box

G. Underline button

H. Center button

I. Align Left button

J. Bold button

K. Align Right button

L. Numbering button

M. Decrease Font Size button

N. Bullets button

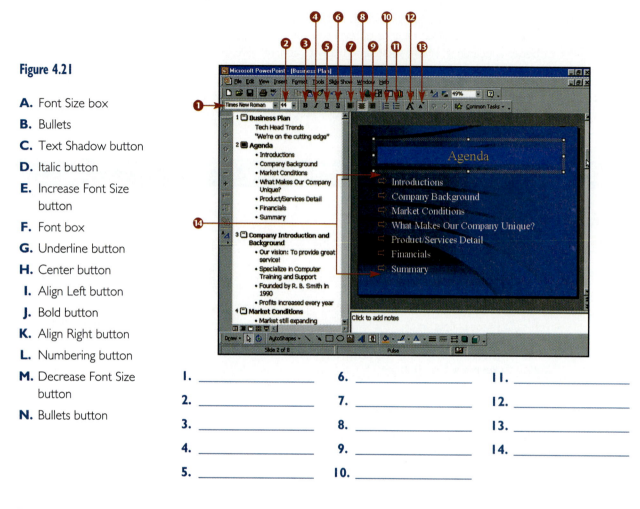

1. _____

2. _____

3. _____

4. _____

5. _____

6. _____

7. _____

8. _____

9. _____

10. _____

11. _____

12. _____

13. _____

14. _____

Discussion Questions

1. Name the ways to change text appearance. How can each effect help improve a presentation? [L1–2]

2. In general, bullets and numbers are used for different types of lists. Describe two examples when bullets are more appropriate to use, and then describe two examples when numbers should be used instead of bullets. [L5–6]

3. Explore the various character sets available in the Bullet dialog box. Which character sets include the best symbols to use for bullets? Why? [L6]

Skill Drill

Skill Drill exercises reinforce project skills. Each skill reinforced is the same, or nearly the same, as a skill presented in the project. Detailed instructions are provided in a step-by-step format.

⑦ 1. Using Help

Although you're amazed that using bullets and numbers is so easy in PowerPoint, you want to find out more about using (and modifying) the existing bullets and numbers. To research other ways to use bullets and numbers, you use Help. [L5–6]

1. In PowerPoint, choose Help, Microsoft PowerPoint Help to display the Microsoft PowerPoint Help window. Click the Show button, if necessary, to display both panes.

2. Click the Contents tab. Double-click the Bullets and Numbering icon to display a list of related subtopics.

3. Click the first subtopic on the list and read the associated information. Repeat the process for each of the other subpoints. Remember to take notes on what you learn.

4. Close the Microsoft PowerPoint Help window. Practice working with Bullets and Numbers by using information from your written notes. Keep PowerPoint open if you plan to complete additional exercises.

2. Changing Text Appearance

You work for a company that conducts seminars. One of your most popular seminars is "How to Give Exciting Presentations," but you think that the publicity materials used for this seminar are not very exciting. To jazz them up, you decide to use PowerPoint's formatting features. [L1–2]

1. Open PP1-0402 and save it as ABC Training. Display Slide 1 of the presentation in Normal view.

2. Select the text in the title placeholder for Slide 1.

3. Click the Font drop-down list arrow and choose Impact from the list. (If this font isn't available on your system, choose another font.)

4. With the text still selected. click the Font Size drop-down list arrow and choose 48 from the list.

5. Press Ctrl+B and Ctrl+I to add bold and italic to the title text.

6. Choose Format, Font to display the Font dialog box. Click the Color drop-down list arrow and choose the red color (the second color box from the right). Click OK.

7. Click in the Slide pane to deselect your text and view your changes.

8. Double-click the word How in the subtitle placeholder to select it, and then click the Bold and Italic buttons on the Formatting toolbar.

9. With the word How still selected, double-click the Format Painter button. Drag over the remaining text in the subtitle placeholder to apply the formatting to the text.

10. Press Esc to turn off the Format Painter.

11. Save the ABC Training presentation. Keep it open for the next exercise.

3. Working with Bullets

To further modify your ABC Training presentation, you change the bullets in the presentation. Because you're not sure which bullet appearance you want, you experiment by using different bullet symbols before you finally settle on one. [L5–6]

1. Make sure that the ABC Training presentation you worked with in the previous exercise is displayed in Normal view.

2. Display Slide 2. Select the bulleted text in the lower placeholder.

3. Click the Bullets button to remove the bullets from the slide. Then click the Bullets button again to add bullets.

4. Choose Format, Bullets and Numbering to display the Bullets and Numbering dialog box. Click the open circular bullets (the third bullet symbol on the first line), and then click OK.

5. Repeat Step 4 to apply each of the different bullet symbols shown in the Bullets and Numbering dialog box.

6. With the text in the lower placeholder still selected, display the Bullets and Numbering dialog box. Choose the square bullet symbol (the first bullet symbol on the second line).

7. In the Bullets and Numbering dialog box, click the Color drop-down list arrow and choose the red color box (the second box from the right). Choose OK.

8. Click in the Slide pane to deselect your text and view your bullets.

9. Print Slide 2 as a slide.

10. Save and close the ABC Training presentation. Keep PowerPoint open if you plan to complete additional exercises.

4. Changing Paragraph Alignment and Spacing

You represent a small text company that specializes in children's clothing. To present an overview of your company to potential investors, you develop a presentation. You decide to change the paragraph alignment and spacing for a better appearance and greater readability. [L3–4]

1. Open **PP1-0403** and save it as **Creative Kids**.

2. Show the presentation in Normal view, and then move to Slide 2, **Our Goals**.

3. In the Slide pane, select the bulleted text in the lower placeholder. (Leave the text selected for Steps 4–6.)

4. Click the Center button to center the bulleted points.

5. Click the Font Size drop-down list arrow and choose **32**.

6. Choose Format, Line Spacing to display the Line Spacing dialog box. In the After paragraph text box, enter **.25**. Click OK.

7. Print Slide 2 of the presentation as a slide.

8. Save the Creative Kids presentation, and then close it. Keep PowerPoint open if you plan to complete additional exercises.

5. Formatting Text and Bullets

You work for Hickory Hill Nurseries. To spice up a presentation and make your points more effective, you add bullets to an existing presentation. You also modify the bullets by changing their color, size, and appearance. [L1, 5–6]

1. Open **PP1-0404** and save it as **Hickory Hill Nurseries**.

2. Display Slide 2, **Our Objectives**, in Normal view.

3. Select all the text in the lower placeholder. Click the Bullets button to add bullets to the text.

4. With the text still selected, choose Format, Line Spacing.

5. In the Line spacing text box, enter **1.5**, and then click OK.

6. With the text still selected, choose Format, Bullets and Numbering.

7. In the Bullets and Numbering dialog box, click the Color drop-down list arrow and choose the red color box (the second box from the right). Click the third bulleted symbol from the left on the second row. Choose OK.

8. Press PgUp to display Slide 1, **Hickory Hill Nurseries**.

9. Select the text in the title placeholder (**Hickory Hill Nurseries**). Choose Format, Font to display the Font dialog box. Click the Color drop-down list arrow, and then choose the red color box. Click OK.

10. Deselect your text. View your presentation as a slide show and print it as slides. Save and close the Hickory Hill presentation. Keep PowerPoint open if you plan to complete additional exercises.

6. Modifying Bullets and Changing Alignment

You work part-time in a sports store near campus. To help recruit quality workers, you've put together a presentation that shows the company's commitment to their employees. To add interest to the presentation, you decide to modify bullets. You also decide to space and align the bulleted points so that they are more readable. [L3, 6]

1. Open PP1-0405 and save it as Sports Store.

2. Display Slide 2, Our Commitment to Employees, in Normal view. Select the text in the lower placeholder.

3. Choose Format, Line Spacing to display the Line Spacing dialog box. Enter .35 in the Before paragraph text box, and then click OK.

4. With the text still selected, click the Center button on the Formatting toolbar.

5. With the text still selected, choose Format, Bullets and Numbering. Click the check mark symbol (the last symbol on the second row).

6. Click the Color drop-down list arrow. Choose More Colors from the palette to display the Colors dialog box. Click a turquoise color in the dialog box, and then click OK to close the Colors dialog box.

7. Click OK to close the Bullets and Numbering dialog box, and then click in the Slide pane to deselect the text.

8. Save the Sports Store presentation; then close it. Keep PowerPoint open if you plan to complete additional exercises.

Challenge

Challenge exercises expand on, or are somewhat related to, skills presented in the lessons. Each exercise provides a brief narrative introduction, followed by instructions in a numbered-step format that are not as detailed as those in the Skill Drill section.

1. Researching Formatting Features

You're intent on becoming the "PowerPoint guru" at your office. In order to do so, you spend a few minutes each day researching ways to use PowerPoint more effectively. Today's topic is formatting text. [L1]

1. In PowerPoint, choose Help, Microsoft PowerPoint Help. Click the Show button, if necessary, to split the dialog box into two panes.

2. Click the Contents tab, and then double-click the Working with Text icon.

3. Click each of the subtopics associated with the main topic (Working with Text).

4. Develop a chart or list that outlines the various ways to work with text in PowerPoint. (If you know how to use Word, you may want to use Word's table feature for this step.) Share the information with at least one other user.

5. Close the Microsoft PowerPoint Help window. Keep PowerPoint open if you plan to complete additional exercises.

2. Using Formatting Features

You previously created a presentation to promote your company, which sells ergonomic products. To enhance it, you use some of the formatting features PowerPoint provides. [L1–3]

1. Open PP1-0406 and save it as Ergonomics.

2. Display Slide 1 in Normal view, and then format the word Ergonomics with italic, bold, and text shadow features. Increase the point size for Ergonomics to 60 points and change the text color to orange.

3. Use the Format Painter to apply the formatting from `Ergonomics` to the word `healthy` on Slide 1.

4. Display Slide 2 and select all the bulleted text. Center the text horizontally, and then increase paragraph spacing so that the text fills up the text placeholder.

5. Save and close the Ergonomics presentation. Keep PowerPoint open if you plan to complete additional exercises.

3. Using the Format Painter

For your speech class, you develop a short presentation on the advantages and disadvantages of Windows 95. You want to jazz up the formatting, but your class starts in five minutes. To change text appearance efficiently, use the Formatting toolbar buttons. To quickly apply the formatting to other areas of text, you use the Format Painter. [L2]

1. Open `PP1-0407` and save it as `Speech Class`.

2. On the first presentation slide, change the title, `Windows 95`, to a blue color. Also make it bold and increase the font size to `72` points.

3. On Slide 2, change the title, `Advantages`, to red and `36` points.

4. Using the Format Painter, apply the formatting from the word `Advantages` to the following text on the same slide:

`Friendly User Interface`

`Support for 32-bit software`

`Multitasking/Multithreading`

5. Increase the size of the title text (`Advantages`) to `48` points. Apply the formatting from the word `Advantages` to the word `Disadvantages` on Slide 3. (*Hint*: Double-click the Format Painter to keep it active.)

6. Save the `Speech Class` presentation, and then close it. Keep PowerPoint open if you plan to complete additional exercises.

4. Formatting a Presentation

Because you learned PowerPoint so well, you freelance by revising presentations for various businesses. You're currently working on a production report for one of your clients. You decide to spice it up by using PowerPoint's formatting features. [L1–2, 4, 6]

1. Open `PP1-0408` and save it as `Production Report`.

2. Improve the appearance of the title on Slide 1 by changing it to another color (such as pink) and font. Also increase the font size for the title to at least `54` points. Using the Format Painter, copy the formatting from Slide 1 (`Production Report`) to the titles on Slides 2–4. (*Hint*: Double-click the Format Painter to keep it active.)

3. Add italic to the subtitle text on Slide 1.

4. Change the bullet color on Slide 2 to match that of the slide title, and then change the bullets to right-pointing triangles.

5. Increase the spacing between the bullets on Slide 2 for better readability and appearance.

6. Using Slide 2 as an example, change the bullets on Slides 3–4. Increase the spacing between paragraphs, if necessary.

7. View your presentation as a slide show to see how it looks, and then print the presentation as slides and as an outline.

8. Save the Production Report presentation, and then close it. Keep PowerPoint open if you plan to complete additional exercises.

5. Using Numbering and Bullets

You're about to graduate from college, and you are handing over the responsibilities of running the student council and the Sports Club to other students. To train them in leadership skills (including giving presentations), you develop a talk. Because numbers are more appropriate to use than bullets on some of the slides, you revise your presentation to include numbers. [L5–6]

1. Open `PP1-0409` and save it as `Presentation Guidelines`. Revise the presentation as follows:

- Remove the bullet from Slide 3.
- Change the bullets on Slide 4, `Key Topic`, to numbers. (If you wish, choose a different numbering type in the Bullets and Numbering dialog box.)
- Change the color for the numbers to dark blue. (*Hint*: Use the Numbered page of the Bullets and Numbering dialog box.)
- Change the bullets on Slide 5, `Goals and Problems`, to drop shadow square symbols.
- Change the bullets on Slide 6, `Solutions and Opportunities`, to a bullet of your choice.
- Change the bullets on Slide 8, `Close`, to numbered steps. Change the color to dark blue and make the size 75% of text. (*Hint*: Use the Bullets and Numbering dialog box.)

2. Save your presentation, and then close it. Keep PowerPoint open if you plan to complete additional exercises.

Discovery Zone

Discovery Zone exercises require advanced knowledge of topics presented in Essentials lessons, application of skills from multiple lessons, or self-directed learning of new skills.

1. Finding Out More

As Information System manager for a manufacturing plant, you support 75 users. A group of managers has recently asked that you present a short seminar on ways to format bullets, numbers, and text in PowerPoint.

Using the Microsoft PowerPoint Help window, find out ways to work with bullets, numbers, and text. Develop an outline to help you present this information to others. Enter the information in a new PowerPoint presentation. Use numbers and bullets where appropriate in the presentation.

Run the presentation as a slide show to make sure that you're covering all the information necessary. Make sure the presentation contains the content in a logical manner. Print a copy of your presentation as an outline. Save and close the presentation. Keep PowerPoint open if you plan to complete additional exercises. [L1, 5–6]

2. Changing Alignment and Spacing

You're the head of the research and development department in your company. Because you are experienced at giving presentations, your boss has asked you to give a short talk to share your tips and tricks with other employees. In order to enhance the presentation, you change text alignment and paragraph spacing.

Open **PP1-0410** and save it as **Presenting a Technical Report**. Make the following changes to the report:

- Left-align the bulleted text on each slide.
- Remove Slide 2, **Introduction**.
- Adjust paragraph spacing for the bulleted text on each slide so that the points display evenly in the placeholders.
- Change the bullets on Slide 5, **Close**, to numbers.
- Change the bullets on Slides 2–4 to one of the check marks from the Monotype Sorts character set. (If this character set is not available on your computer, choose another character set.)
- View the presentation as a slide show. Print the presentation as slides and as an outline.

Save and close the presentation. Keep PowerPoint open if you plan to complete additional exercises. [L3–4]

3. Formatting Text and Bullets

As the outgoing president of the University Biking Club, you develop a presentation to help the new club officers learn how to facilitate meetings. In order to make the presentation more appealing, you change bullet and text appearance by using PowerPoint's formatting features.

Open **PP1-0411** and save it as **Facilitating a Meeting**. Make the following changes to the presentation, using what you know about PowerPoint:

- Change the font for the Slide 1 title to **Comic Sans MS, 48** point text. Add shadow to the text and change the color to turquoise. Using the Format Painter, copy this formatting to the titles of the other slides in the presentation.
- On Slide 3, **Opening**, change the bullet's symbol for the four subpoints to check marks.
- Increase the spacing between paragraphs for the bulleted text on Slide 4. Change the bullets themselves to check marks.
- Modify Slide 5 and Slide 6 so that the bulleted points display similarly to the bullets on Slide 4.

View the presentation as a slide show. Print the presentation as slides and as an outline. Save and close the presentation. [L1–2, 4, 6]

Working with Charts

Objectives

In this project, you learn how to

➤ **Select an Appropriate Chart Type**

➤ **Create a Data Chart**

➤ **Edit Chart Data**

➤ **Resize, Move, and Change Chart Types**

➤ **Choose a Chart Sub-type and Format a Chart**

➤ **Create an Organization Chart**

➤ **Modify an Organization Chart**

Key terms introduced in this project include

- cell
- cell pointer
- chart
- chart sub-types
- data charts
- data series
- datasheet
- embedded object
- icon bar
- object
- organization charts
- parent box
- peripheral program

Why Would I Do This?

ave you ever longed for a way to convey complicated data in a clear, concise manner to business clients, stockholders, or colleagues? One of the best ways to do this is to present your data as a PowerPoint chart, or graph. A **chart** is simply a pictorial representation of data.

Charts are powerful tools in a presentation. Remember that people are usually more convinced by a well-presented chart than by endless words or explanations. Business users want to know the bottom line—so use PowerPoint's capability to create pictorial charts to your advantage. For example, Figure 5.1 shows information as text. Figure 5.2 shows the same information graphically as a data chart. By the end of this project, you'll learn how to change dull, hard-to-understand statistics into colorful, appealing charts such as that in Figure 5.2.

Figure 5.1
Dull text?

Figure 5.2
Use a chart!

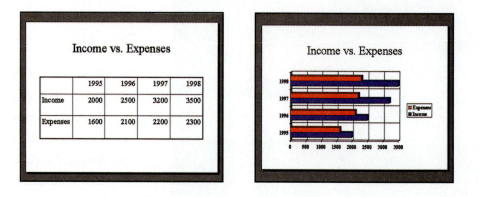

Fortunately, it's relatively easy to create and modify splashy charts in PowerPoint—charts that capture people's attention and emphasize your ideas. After you learn the basics of creating charts, you'll be able to spiff up any presentation!

Visual Summary

In this project, you see the basics of creating and formatting **data charts**. Data charts show numerical data in a pictorial manner, much like the chart in Figure 5.3. You can revise the information in the data chart using the **datasheet**. You can also modify the chart using buttons on Microsoft Graph's toolbar.

You also learn how to create and revise **organization charts**, which show the structure of an organization (see Figure 5.4).

Before you begin, however, it's important to know which type of chart to use for your data. You explore the chart types and learn when to use each.

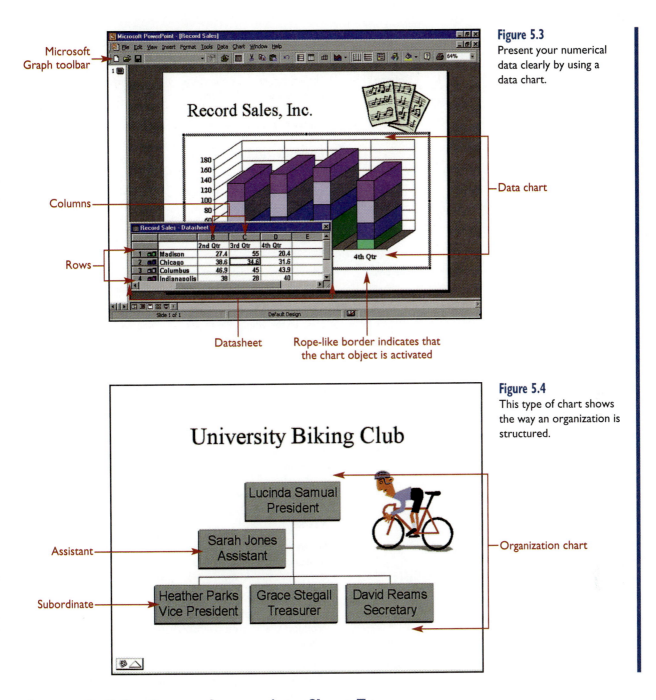

Figure 5.3
Present your numerical data clearly by using a data chart.

Microsoft Graph toolbar

Columns

Rows

Data chart

Datasheet

Rope-like border indicates that the chart object is activated

Figure 5.4
This type of chart shows the way an organization is structured.

Assistant

Subordinate

Organization chart

Lesson 1: Selecting an Appropriate Chart Type

You can select from several standard chart types to present your data clearly and effectively. Additionally, each chart type includes several **chart sub-types**—variations on the main chart types. As you develop your presentation, make sure that you set up your data by using the best chart type for the information you're trying to convey. Because the most commonly used chart types are line, bar, column, pie, and organization, you learn how to use these. Table 5.1 lists all of the chart types used in PowerPoint, so you'll have a handy reference as you expand your charting skills.

Table 5.1 PowerPoint Chart Types

Button	Chart Type	Main Use	Example
	Column chart	Shows data changes over time or illustrates a comparison of items. The values are organized vertically, and categories are shown horizontally to emphasize variation over time.	Sales by quarter for the year.
	Bar chart	Shows comparison of individual items. Categories are arranged vertically and values are arranged horizontally, placing more emphasis on categories than values.	Sales by region, with region on the vertical axis and sales on the horizontal axis.
	Line chart	Shows trends in data at equal intervals.	Monthly production over a twelve-month period.
	Pie chart	Illustrates the relationship of parts to the whole. Pie charts can show only one data series.	Market share held by your company versus the competitor.
	XY (Scatter) chart	Shows the relationship between values in several chart series.	The relationship between quantity and price.
	Area chart	Shows the magnitude of change over time.	Cumulative sales from several divisions.
	Doughnut chart	Similar to a pie chart because it shows the relationship of parts to the whole. However, it can show more than one data series, each "ring" representing a series.	Expenses broken down by category for several departments.
	Radar chart	Shows frequencies of changes in data relative to each other and to a center point.	Analysis of how well several products did in comparison with each other.
	Surface chart	Shows where the result of combining two sets of data produces the greatest overall value.	A chart showing the greatest combination of cold and wind (wind chill).
	Bubble chart	Shows data similar to a scatter chart, but also shows (by size of the bubble) the result of the data.	A chart showing the effect of temperature and humidity on soda sales.
	Stock chart	Shows high, low, and closing values for stock.	A chart that shows stock performance for your company.
	Cylinder, Cone, and Pyramid charts	Shows data similar to that in bar and column charts, but displays it as cylinders, cones, or pyramids.	A chart using pyramids to graphically show the height of mountains.

In addition to the chart types listed in Table 5.1, PowerPoint has the capability to produce organization charts, which show how your business is structured. You learn how to create an organization chart in Lesson 6.

Lesson 2: Creating a Data Chart

PowerPoint has the capability to create different types of data charts so that you can illustrate your points effectively. Data charts are simply charts that include numerical data (as opposed to organization charts, which show how an organization is set up).

PowerPoint uses Microsoft Graph, a **peripheral program**, to create data charts. Peripheral programs are started every time you access a feature within the main program and place an **object** (such as a chart) on a slide. You can think of the object as being a doorway that leads to the peripheral program, giving you access to its features and commands. PowerPoint shares Microsoft Graph with other Office programs. This makes chart development more uniform and efficient when working with PowerPoint and the various Office products.

There are a couple of different methods you can use to launch Microsoft Graph and insert a chart on a slide. You can use a chart placeholder on an existing or new slide, or you can use the Insert Chart button on the Standard toolbar. After you start Microsoft Graph, a datasheet is displayed so that you can enter your information. A datasheet is a grid of columns and rows that enables you to enter numerical data into a PowerPoint chart. The intersection of a column and row is called a **cell**. Cells are always named by the column heading, followed by the row number (such as A1). If you're familiar with Excel, you'll feel right at home using a datasheet because it is set up like a mini-worksheet.

When you finish entering your data in the datasheet, you close the peripheral program and your chart is embedded as an object on your slide. An **embedded object** is an item that is created by one program, but inserted into a document created by another program. In this case, a chart object (created by Microsoft Graph) is placed on a PowerPoint slide.

Now that you know the essentials and terminology associated with data charts, try creating one.

To Create a Data Chart

1 Start PowerPoint, if necessary, and then open PP1-0501 and save it as Bell Manufacturing.

2 Display Slide 3, Revenue, in Normal view, and then click the New Slide button on the Standard toolbar.
The New Slide dialog box displays. As you probably remember from earlier projects, you can choose one of 24 AutoLayouts to quickly produce a slide with preset formatting. Three of the AutoLayouts include a chart placeholder, which makes it easy to use them to create a chart. For this lesson you'll use the AutoLayout with the largest chart placeholder.

continues ▶

To Create a Data Chart (continued)

3 **Click the Chart AutoLayout (the fourth AutoLayout from the left, on the second row).**

The Chart AutoLayout is selected. This AutoLayout includes placeholders for a title and the chart object (see Figure 5.5).

Figure 5.5
You can use a Chart AutoLayout as the basis for your new slide.

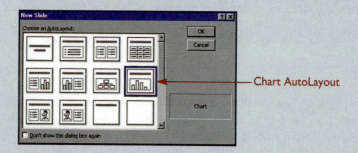

Chart AutoLayout

4 **Choose OK.**

A new slide is inserted into your presentation with placeholders for a title and a chart (see Figure 5.6).

Figure 5.6
The Chart AutoLayout includes a chart placeholder.

Title placeholder —

Chart placeholder —

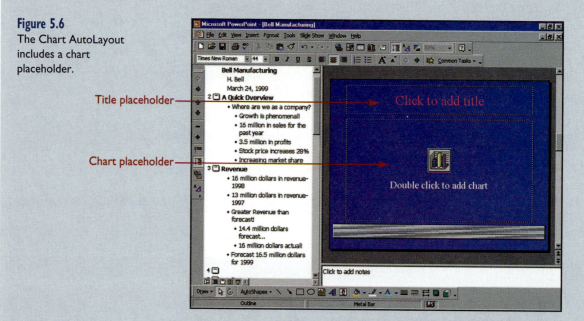

5 **Click in the title placeholder, and then type** Revenues 1997 vs. 1998.

This is the title for the chart. Now you're ready to create the chart itself. To start Microsoft Graph so that you can develop your chart, double-click the chart placeholder.

6 **Double-click the chart placeholder.**

Microsoft Graph starts and a datasheet displays with sample data. Because Microsoft Graph is the active program, the Microsoft Graph Standard and Formatting toolbars are available so that you can use charting commands (see Figure 5.7).

Microsoft Graph
Standard toolbar

Microsoft Graph
Formatting toolbar

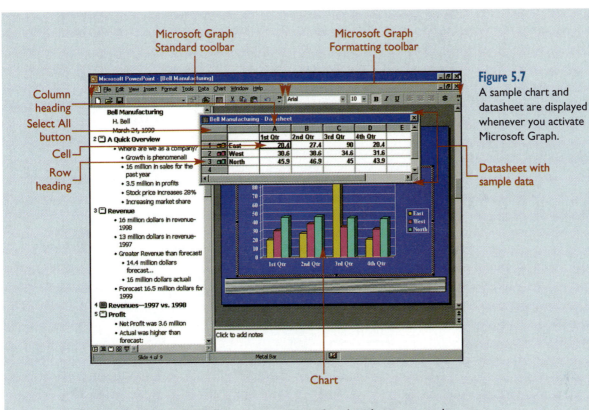

Column heading

Select All button

Cell

Row heading

Chart

Figure 5.7
A sample chart and datasheet are displayed whenever you activate Microsoft Graph.

Datasheet with sample data

The sample data is simply a guide and is easily replaced with your own data. To enter your data, click the cell and type your entry. When you finish, press `⏎Enter` or an arrow key. Try entering some data now.

7 **Click the cell containing the word** East.
A darkened border around the cell, called the **cell pointer**, indicates that this is the active cell—ready for an entry.

8 **Type** 1997 **and press** ⬇.
This enters 1997 in the cell and moves the cell pointer down one cell. (You can also press `⏎Enter` to move the cell pointer down one cell.)

9 **Click in the row 3 heading (**North**).**
The entire row is selected.

10 **Press** `Del`.
The sample data from the entire row 3 is deleted.

11 **Enter the data shown in Figure 5.8 into your datasheet.**

Close button

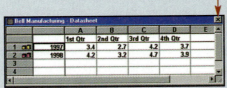

Figure 5.8
You can easily replace sample data with your own.

continues ▶

To Create a Data Chart   (continued)

⓬ **When you finish entering the data, click the Close button in the datasheet's upper-right corner.**

The datasheet closes and you can better see the column chart that is created. This is the *default* chart type, which means that PowerPoint automatically uses this type of chart unless you indicate otherwise. Additionally, the chart is embedded into the slide as an object. Black selection handles encompass the chart, indicating that it's still activated—Microsoft Graph is still active in memory (see Figure 5.9).

Figure 5.9
PowerPoint inserts the graph on your slide as an object.

Microsoft Graph menu bar

Microsoft Graph toolbars

Embedded chart

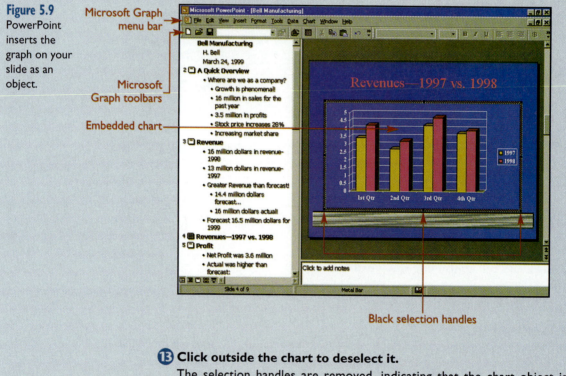

Black selection handles

⓭ **Click outside the chart to deselect it.**

The selection handles are removed, indicating that the chart object is no longer activated (and Microsoft Graph is closed).

Keep the presentation open for the next lesson, in which you learn to edit chart data.

 Entering Information in a Datasheet

It's handy to know some efficient ways to work with information that you enter and edit in your datasheet. For example, you can click a column heading to select an entire column for deletion—just as you selected an entire row for deletion in the previous lesson. In a similar way, you can click the Select All button (at the intersection of the row numbers and column headings) to quickly select the entire datasheet, and then press Del to delete all the sample data at once.

Choosing a Chart AutoLayout as you create a new slide is an easy way to make a chart. However, if you want to place a chart on a slide without a Chart AutoLayout, you can choose Insert, Chart, or click the Insert Chart button on the Standard toolbar.

Lesson 3: Editing Chart Data

After you create a chart, you may want to edit its data. For example, you may want to update sales or production figures as they become available. In this lesson, you learn how to activate Microsoft Graph for an existing chart, as well as ways to edit your data.

Before you make changes to a chart, you must first activate it. There's a difference between *selecting* a chart object and *activating* it, however.

Clicking a chart object one time selects it and places white selection handles around its border. (You use these handles in the next lesson to move and resize the chart.) In contrast, double-clicking the chart activates it and opens Microsoft Graph in memory so that you can again use Microsoft Graph's commands and features. You'll know when the chart is activated because you will see black selection handles and a rope-like border.

Try activating your chart and editing its data now.

To Edit Chart Data

❶ **In the Bell Manufacturing presentation, double-click the chart object you created on Slide 4.**

The chart is activated, as shown by the rope-like border and black selection handles (see Figure 5.10).

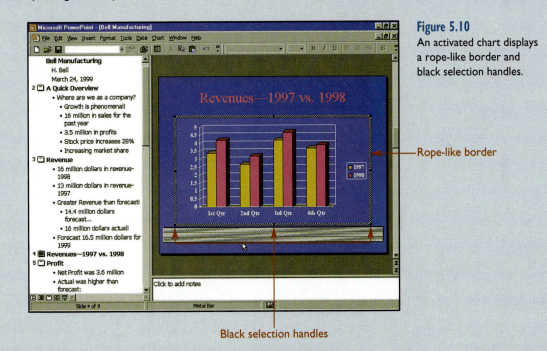

Figure 5.10
An activated chart displays a rope-like border and black selection handles.

Rope-like border

Black selection handles

> ✖ It's sometimes tricky to activate instead of selecting the chart. If your chart doesn't look like the one in Figure 5.10, double-click on the chart again. Make sure to click in fairly rapid succession and to hold the mouse steady between clicks. If you really have trouble activating the chart by double-clicking, you can instead single-click the chart and press ⏎Enter.

continues ▶

To Edit Chart Data   (continued)

2 Click the View Datasheet button on the Standard toolbar.

The datasheet displays, which enables you to revise the data that it contains.

3 Click the Select All button in the upper-left corner of the datasheet.

The entire datasheet is highlighted to show that it's selected (see Figure 5.11).

Figure 5.11
You can select the entire datasheet and then delete its contents.

Click here to select the entire datasheet

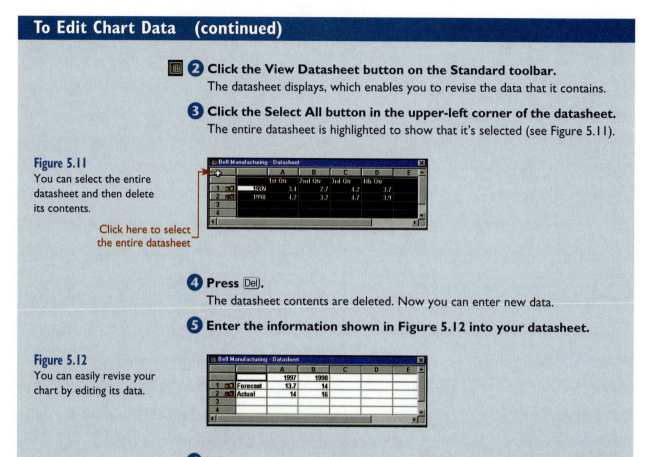

4 Press Del.

The datasheet contents are deleted. Now you can enter new data.

5 Enter the information shown in Figure 5.12 into your datasheet.

Figure 5.12
You can easily revise your chart by editing its data.

6 When you finish entering the data, click the View Datasheet button.

The datasheet closes, but the chart remains active. Keep your Bell Manufacturing presentation open for the next lesson, in which you learn to change the chart type and move and resize your chart.

Lesson 4: Resizing, Moving, and Changing Chart Types

You created a chart and revised its data. You can also move and resize your chart object on the slide, and change the chart type to arrange your data differently. The easiest way to do this is to click the drop-down list arrow next to the Chart Type button. Keep in mind that the underlying data remains the same—the chart types simply display the data differently. Because you don't affect the data when you change the chart type, you can experiment freely to see which chart type best conveys your data.

Now try resizing and moving your chart, as well as changing the chart type.

To Resize, Move, and Change Chart Types

1 In the open Bell Manufacturing presentation, make sure that the chart on Slide 4 is active.

Black selection handles indicate that the chart is still active. (If your chart isn't displayed in this manner, double-click the chart object to activate it.)

Now hide the display of Microsoft Graph's Formatting toolbar. When you do this, you automatically uncover the Standard toolbar's buttons that you need to use.

② Choose View, Toolbars, Formatting.
The Formatting toolbar's display is turned off so that only the Standard toolbar is visible. This toolbar includes the buttons that you use throughout the lesson. One of the most popular buttons is the Chart Type button, which includes a drop-down palette of chart types.

③ On the Microsoft Graph Standard toolbar, click the Chart Type drop-down list arrow.
The types of charts available on your system are displayed on a palette, as shown in Figure 5.13. Notice that some of the charts are simply variations of other types. For example, the palette shows both 2-D and 3-D bar and column charts.

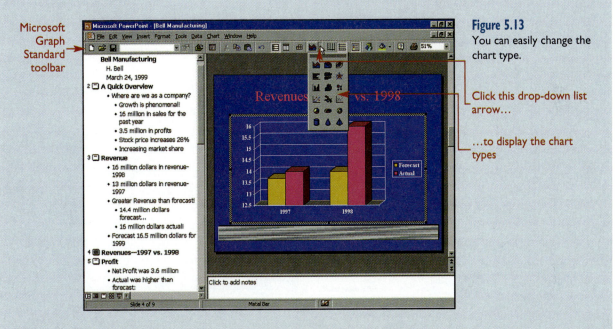

Microsoft Graph Standard toolbar

Figure 5.13
You can easily change the chart type.

Click this drop-down list arrow...

...to display the chart types

④ Rest the mouse pointer momentarily on any chart type on the palette.
A ScreenTip displays and indicates the type of chart (see Figure 5.14). This is a handy feature that you can use to identify chart types.

⑤ Move the mouse pointer to the 3-D Bar Chart button on the palette, and then click to select it.
The chart is displayed as a bar chart (see Figure 5.15). For practice, spend a few minutes changing to other chart types. When you finish experimenting, choose the 3-D Bar Chart before continuing with the lesson.

continues ▶

To Resize, Move, and Change Chart Types   (continued)

Figure 5.14
A ScreenTip displays when you rest your mouse pointer on a button in the palette.

ScreenTip

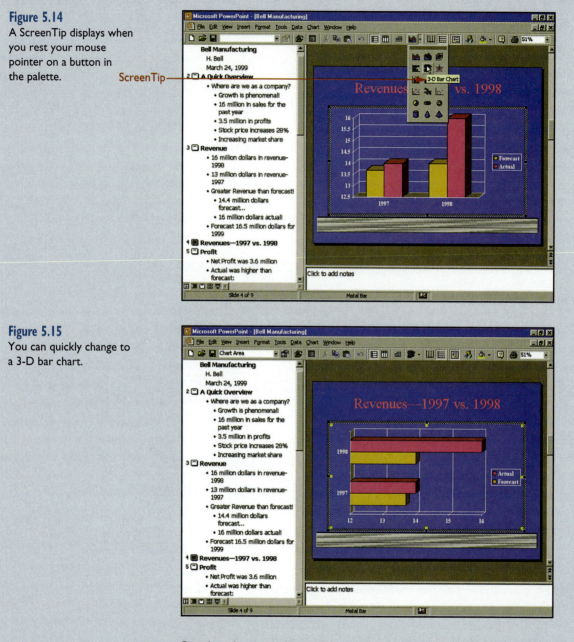

Figure 5.15
You can quickly change to a 3-D bar chart.

Besides changing chart type, you can make other changes to your chart. For example, you may want to resize or move the chart on your slide. Fortunately, PowerPoint makes this task easy.

6 **Click outside the chart to embed it as an object on your slide.**
The selection handles disappear because the chart is not activated. Now select the chart so that you can move it.

7 **Click the chart object one time.**
White selection handles surround the chart object. They indicate that the chart is selected as an object, but that the Microsoft Graph program is not activated.

Now resize the chart object.

8 **Move the mouse pointer to the white selection handle on the upper-right corner of the chart so that the pointer displays as a resizing arrow (see Figure 5.16).**

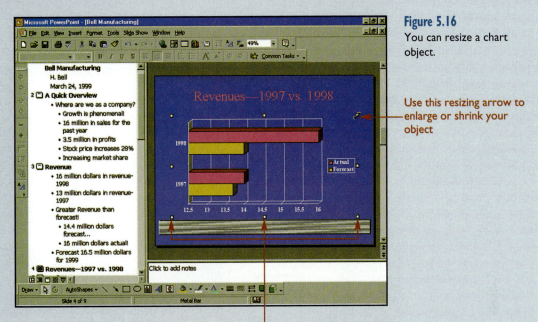

Figure 5.16
You can resize a chart object.

Use this resizing arrow to enlarge or shrink your object

White selection handles indicate that the chart is selected

9 **Drag toward the middle of the chart until the chart is approximately half the original size, and release the mouse button.**
The object is resized on the slide. Now move the object to the middle of the available space.

10 **Move the mouse pointer to the middle of the chart object until a four-headed arrow is displayed (see Figure 5.17).**

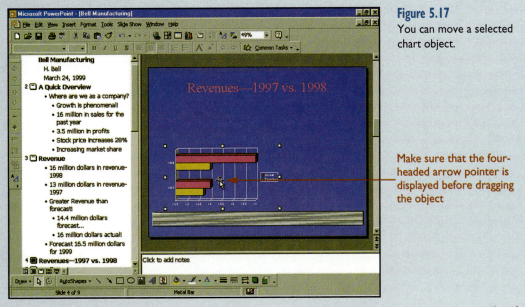

Figure 5.17
You can move a selected chart object.

Make sure that the four-headed arrow pointer is displayed before dragging the object

continues ▶

To Resize, Move, and Change Chart Types   (continued)

11 **Drag the chart object so that it displays in the middle of the slide and release the mouse button.**

12 **Click outside the chart object to deselect it.**
The slide should now look similar to the one shown in Figure 5.18.

Figure 5.18
You can resize and move charts for a better appearance.

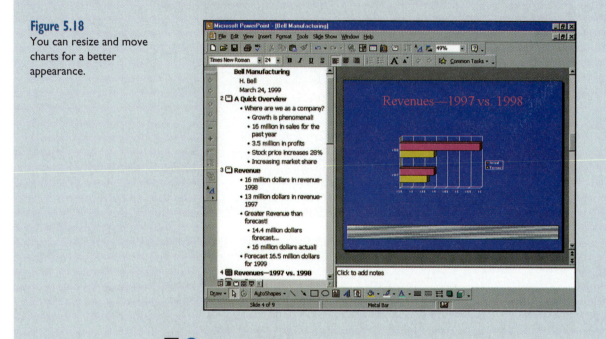

13 **Save your changes and close the Bell Manufacturing presentation.**
Keep PowerPoint open for the next lesson, in which you format charts.

Using Buttons to Modify Your Chart
There are a number of other buttons on Microsoft Graph's Standard toolbar that help you display your data. For example, you can quickly switch the way your data appears by clicking the By Row or By Column buttons. You can also add or remove a legend by clicking the Legend button. To find out more about working with charts, activate a chart, and then choose Help, Microsoft Graph Help from the Microsoft Graph menu bar.

Lesson 5: Choosing a Chart Sub-type and Formatting a Chart

So far in this project, you have learned how to create charts and make some revisions. PowerPoint provides a number of tools you can use to make your charts more readable and understandable, and in this lesson, you learn how to wield them! For example, you learn how to choose a chart sub-type and how to change a chart's text and color. You work with a safety campaign presentation that includes a column chart. Try using some formatting options on this chart now.

To Choose a Chart Sub-type

1 **Open** PP1-0502 **and save it as** Safety.

2 **Double-click the existing chart on Slide 4,** Total sick days per facility, **and close the datasheet.**
Microsoft Graph is activated, as shown by the black handles around the chart. The chart is currently a column chart. For this presentation, however, you want to view the information in a stacked column chart. To change the chart's format to a different sub-type, you use the Chart Type dialog box.

3 **Choose** **C**hart, Chart **T**ype.
The Chart Type dialog box displays, as shown in Figure 5.19. You can use this dialog box to select a variation, or sub-type, of the main chart type.

> ❌ If you don't see the **C**hart command on the menu bar, you probably didn't properly activate the chart. Just double-click the chart object to activate it.

Click a main chart type on this list——

Choose the Stacked column with a 3-D visual effect here

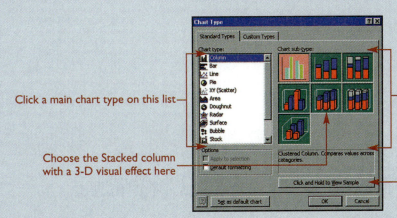

Figure 5.19
You can select and preview chart types in this dialog box.

——Choose a sub-type here

Press the mouse button while pointing here to see your data displayed using the selected chart type

4 **Click on the** Stacked column with a 3-D visual effect **sub-type—the middle chart in the second row.**
A description of the selected sub-type appears below the chart sub-types. You can also preview how your data looks when displayed by the sub-type by using the special preview button that PowerPoint provides.

5 **Move the mouse pointer to the Press and Hold to** **V**iew Sample **button. Click and hold down the mouse button for a few seconds before releasing it.**
PowerPoint displays your data with the selected chart's format. You can select and preview other chart types (and sub-types). When you finish, choose the Stacked column with a 3-D visual effect sub-type before proceeding.

6 **Click OK in the Chart Type dialog box.**
The selected chart type is applied to your chart. Keep your chart activated for the next tutorial, in which you explore some other methods of formatting your chart.

By now, you're familiar with creating a chart, editing data, and changing chart types. Next, you focus on working with individual elements in a chart. A chart is made up of several objects, such as the data series, graph walls, legend, and so on. You can format or delete any of these elements, but first you must select the object. The easiest way to select a chart object is to use the Chart Objects drop-down list on the Standard toolbar. Try selecting, formatting, and deleting chart objects now.

To Format a Chart

| Chart Area ▾ | ❶ **In the activated chart, click the drop-down list arrow to the right of the Chart Objects box.**
A list of the items in your chart displays. You can select an item by clicking it on the list.

❷ **On the list, choose Series "Danville".**
The *data series* that represents the Danville factory is selected. In fact, if you look carefully, you can see selected handles displayed around the series to help you identify your selection. A data series is a collection of values that pertain to a single subject. Now format the data series.

❸ **Choose Fo̲rmat, S̲elected Data Series from the menu bar.**
The Format Data Series dialog box displays, as shown in Figure 5.20. Notice that PowerPoint includes several formatting categories—such as Patterns and Shape—each on a separate, tabbed page.

Figure 5.20
You can change many formatting features by using the Format Data Series dialog box.

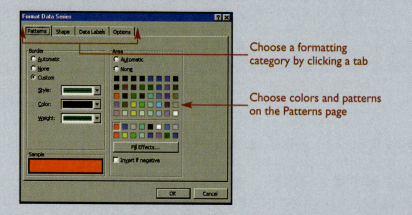

Choose a formatting category by clicking a tab

Choose colors and patterns on the Patterns page

❹ **In the Area section of the Patterns page, click the white color box.**
The Sample box displays the result of your choice. Now change the pattern associated with the data series.

❺ **In the Format Data Series dialog box, click the Fi̲ll Effects button.**
The Fill Effects dialog box displays (see Figure 5.21). You can choose a gradient, pattern, or texture for the data series.

❻ **Click the Texture tab to display its page, and then click several fill textures.**
Each texture you choose is shown in the Sample box. Now view the available patterns.

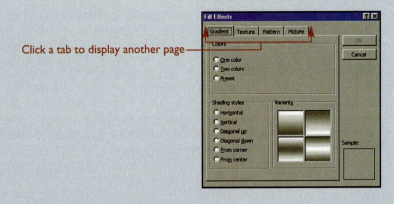

Click a tab to display another page

Figure 5.21
You can choose a variety
of fills for your data.

7 **Click the Pattern tab and choose the second pattern from the left on the fifth row (the black background with white dots).**
Your selected pattern is shown in the Sample box.

8 **Click OK in the Fill Effects dialog box and in the Format Data Series dialog box to accept your changes.**
The color and pattern you chose is applied to the data series. You can format any chart object in a similar way: Use the Chart Objects drop-down list to select an object, and then choose the Selected (*name of object*) command from the Format menu.

You can also double-click a chart object to open an associated Format dialog box. Use this method to change the legend's appearance now.

9 **Double-click the legend to display the Format Legend dialog box.**
You use this dialog box to modify the colors, font, and placement for the legend.

X Make sure that you double-click the legend background, and not one of the legend entries (such as Danville).

10 **In the Area section of the Patterns page, choose red for your legend color, and then click OK.**
The legend's background is formatted with the new color. You can also delete a chart object by selecting it and pressing Del. Delete a data series now.

11 **Click the drop-down list arrow to the right of the Chart Objects box and choose Series "Samville".**
The series is selected so that you can delete it.

12 **Press Del.**
The selected series is removed from the chart. Notice that the legend entry for Samville is deleted simultaneously (see Figure 5.22). Before you close Microsoft Graph, turn the display for the Formatting toolbar back on.

13 **Choose View, Toolbars, Formatting.**
The Microsoft Graph Formatting toolbar is visible again. Now embed the chart on your slide.

continues ▶

To Format a Chart   (continued)

14 **Click outside the chart to embed it on the slide, and then save and close the Safety presentation.**

Leave PowerPoint open for the next lesson, in which you create an organization chart.

Figure 5.22
You can select and then delete a chart object.

The Samville data series is deleted from the chart...

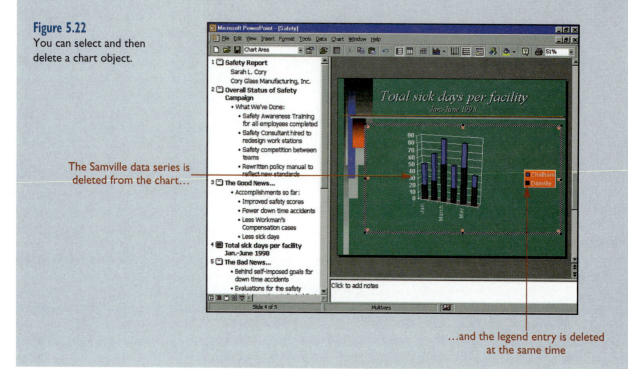

...and the legend entry is deleted at the same time

Lesson 6: Creating an Organization Chart

Organization charts show the structure and relationship between people or functions within an organization. PowerPoint creates organization charts by using a peripheral program, Microsoft Organization Chart. You can start this program and create the chart in two ways. First, choose the Organization Chart AutoLayout in the New Slide dialog box. On the slide, double-click the chart placeholder to start Microsoft Organization Chart. Alternatively, you can choose Insert, Object to display the Insert Object dialog box, and then choose MS Organization Chart from the Object type list. If you use the second method, the chart program is automatically started for you. In either case, Microsoft Organization Chart displays its own menu bar at the top of its window. Additionally, you can use the box tools displayed on the program's icon bar.

In this lesson, you create an organization chart and then enter information in it. In Lesson 7, you change the organization chart structure and format the chart. Try working with an organization chart now.

To Create an Organization Chart

1 Create a new presentation by clicking the New button on the Standard toolbar.

The New Slide dialog box displays with available AutoLayouts. The Organization Chart AutoLayout is on the second row, second from the right.

2 Double-click the Organization Chart AutoLayout.

A new slide is created with a placeholder for the organization chart in the lower portion of the slide (see Figure 5.23).

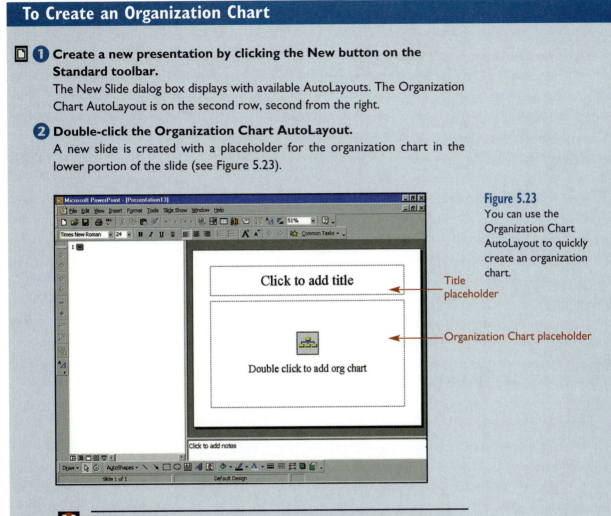

Figure 5.23
You can use the Organization Chart AutoLayout to quickly create an organization chart.

If Microsoft Organization Chart has never run on your computer, PowerPoint displays a message box, telling you that the program isn't installed on your system. This is because PowerPoint 2000 has an *install upon demand* feature. Some features (such as Microsoft Organization Chart) are only installed if and when you need them. Luckily, this doesn't really present a problem. Just make sure that the Office 2000 program CD is inserted in the CD-ROM drive and choose <u>Y</u>es in the message box to install the Microsoft Organization Chart peripheral program. If you need additional assistance, ask your instructor.

3 Click in the title placeholder, type Team Structure, and then double-click the Organization Chart placeholder to activate Microsoft Organization Chart.

The chart program starts and the Microsoft Organization Chart window displays, as shown in Figure 5.24. When you create an organization chart, you actually use a peripheral program that comes with PowerPoint—Microsoft Organization Chart—as an embedded object on a slide. When Microsoft Organization Chart activates, it also displays box tools (on a special bar called the *icon bar*) and its own menu bar so that you can use its commands.

continues ▶

To Create an Organization Chart (continued)

Figure 5.24
Microsoft Organization
Chart displays in its own
window.

Microsoft Organization
Chart menu bar

Microsoft Organization Chart
box tools on the icon bar

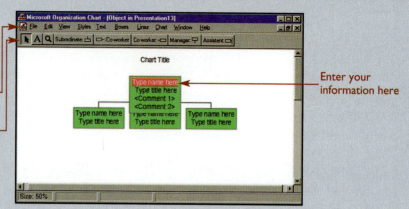

Enter your
information here

When you first open a new chart, the chart template displays with four boxes. The field names, such as name or title, act as placeholders for information that you type. You can enter information as you do in a word processor: by typing and revising text. Just click the box, type data, and then press `Tab↹` or `↵Enter` to move to subsequent fields. Click outside the box when you finish. Try entering information by using these techniques now.

④ **Type** `Lonnie Stegall`, **press** `↵Enter`, **and then type** `President`.
This enters the name and title into the top-level box.

⑤ **Click in the lower level boxes and enter the information shown in Figure 5.25; then click outside the boxes.**

Figure 5.25
Enter the information
shown to create an
organization chart.

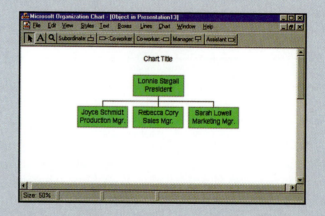

Notice that clicking outside a selected box (either in the background or another box) deselects it.

Now you're ready to format the text you entered in the boxes. You can click a box to select all the text that it contains, or drag over just the characters you want. Choose <u>T</u>ext, <u>F</u>ont, or <u>T</u>ext, C<u>o</u>lor to change the selected text's appearance. Try formatting the text now.

⑥ **Click in the top box, drag over** `Lonnie Stegall` **to select it, and then choose** <u>T</u>ext, <u>F</u>ont **from the Microsoft Organization Chart menu.**
The Font dialog box displays. You can use this dialog box to choose font or point size.

7 **Choose** Impact, **16 points, and then click OK. (If this font isn't available on your system, choose another font.)**
The selected font is formatted with the new font and point size. You can also select a box and then change formatting for all the text included in the box. Try this now.

8 **Click the lower-left box,** Joyce Schmidt, **and choose** T**ext,** C**olor.**
The Color dialog box displays. The color you select will apply to all the text in the selected box.

9 **Click the red color, choose OK, and click outside the box to deselect it.**
The text in the selected box is formatted in red. Leave your presentation open for the next lesson, in which you change the structure of your organization chart.

Selecting and Formatting Multiple Boxes
You can select multiple boxes and apply formatting commands (such as changing text color) to the boxes simultaneously. To select more than one box, press and hold down ⬆Shift while clicking the boxes you want.

Additionally, you can make formatting changes other than text and box color. For example, you can change how the boxes appear by choosing the Shado**w** or **B**order Style commands from the **B**oxes menu. You can modify text alignment by choosing **L**eft, **R**ight, or **C**enter from the **T**ext menu. To find out more about working with organization charts, open Microsoft Organization Chart, and then choose **H**elp, **I**ndex.

Lesson 7: Modifying an Organization Chart

When you initially create an organization chart, PowerPoint automatically sets up the chart with a Manager box and three Subordinate boxes. However, this four-box organization chart is just a starting point. Unless your organization fits perfectly into this default setup, you'll need to make changes to the chart—such as adding, deleting, and generally restructuring the chart. Fortunately, you can add Subordinates, Coworkers, Managers, and Assistants, as needed, by using the box tools on the icon bar.

To add new boxes, click the appropriate box tool, and then click the ***parent box***. The parent box is the existing box to which you want to attach the new one. For example, you can add an assistant to a manager by clicking the Assistant box tool and clicking the Manager box.

Table 5.2 summarizes the tools available on Microsoft Organization Chart's icon bar. You can use this table as a quick reference when working with organization charts.

Table 5.2 Microsoft Organization Chart Icon Bar Tools

Icon Bar Tool	Function
▨	Selects boxes or objects
Ⓐ	Adds a text object to the organization chart
⬛	Zooms the chart to larger or reduced views
Subordinate: ⬚	Adds a box directly below the selected (parent) box
⬚:Co-worker	Adds a box to the left and at the same level as the selected (parent) box
Co-worker: ⬚	Adds a box to the right and at the same level as the selected (parent) box
Manager: ⬚	Adds a box directly above the selected (parent) box
Assistant: ⬚	Adds a box below and to the left of the selected (parent) box

You can also revise your chart by moving, formatting, and deleting boxes. Try modifying your organization chart by using these features now.

To Modify an Organization Chart

[Assistant: ⬚] **1** **In the open organization chart window, click the Assistant box tool, and then click the Manager box (Lonnie Stegall, President).**
An Assistant-level box is added (see Figure 5.26). You enter information in this box as you did in Lesson 6.

Figure 5.26
You can easily add boxes to change your chart's structure.

You can add an Assistant box ────

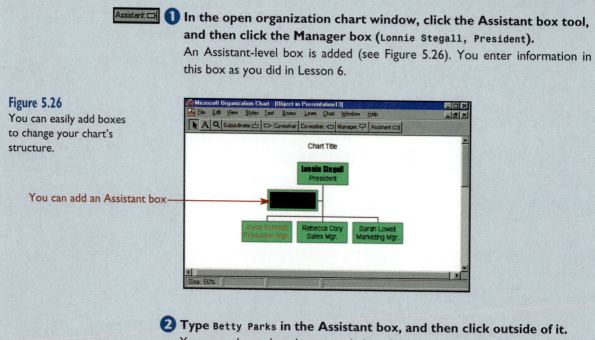

2 **Type Betty Parks in the Assistant box, and then click outside of it.**
You can also select boxes and then format them by choosing Color or Shadow from the Boxes menu. When you finish, you can click in the background area to see the effects of your changes.

Before you apply formatting to your boxes, however, you must first select them. One quick way to select every box in your chart is to choose Edit, Select All. Alternatively, you can press Ctrl+A.

③ Choose Edit, Select All.

Your entire organization chart is selected, as shown in Figure 5.27. The boxes are highlighted and the lines show light gray dashes to indicate that they are also selected. After the boxes are selected, you can format them to highlight information or for greater overall impact.

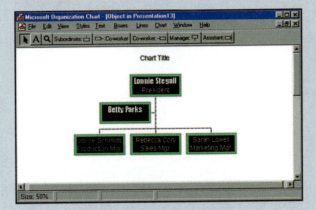

Figure 5.27
You can quickly select an entire organization chart and format it.

④ Choose Boxes, Color on Microsoft Organization Chart's menu bar.

The Color dialog box displays. You can choose a color from this dialog box, and then click OK to apply the color to the selected boxes.

⑤ Click the blue color box (the fourth from the left in the first row) and click OK.

The boxes display in blue, but are still selected. Now try adding a shadow effect to the boxes.

⑥ With all boxes still selected, choose Boxes, Shadow to display a submenu (see Figure 5.28).

Choose this shadow style ⸻

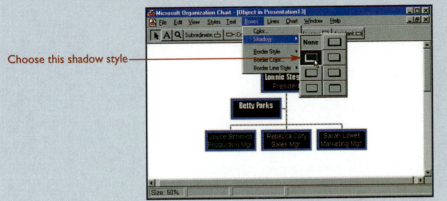

Figure 5.28
You can enhance your chart by adding box shadows.

⑦ Click the shadow style indicated in Figure 5.28, and then click outside the boxes.

The selected shadow is applied to the boxes.

continues ▶

To Modify an Organization Chart (continued)

You can also move a box by dragging it to another location. Select the box you want to move, and then drag its border until it is on top of the box to which you want it attached. You can't simply drop it next to the box, because the program doesn't understand where you want the box placed. Keeping this in mind, move the Assistant box from its current location and attach it to Joyce Schmidt's box now.

8 **Select the Assistant box (`Betty Parks`), and then point to the border of the box until a white selection arrow appears.**
It's important to display this selection arrow before dragging the box. If the I-beam displays instead, you might accidentally place the box in editing mode (and expand it) when you start to drag it.

9 **Drag the Assistant box on top of (but slightly below) the Joyce Schmidt box until you see the special assistant pointer (see Figure 5.29). Release the mouse button.**

Figure 5.29
Modify your organization chart by dragging and dropping boxes to other locations.

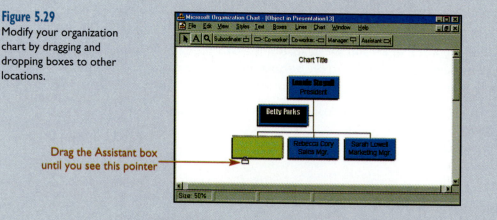

Drag the Assistant box until you see this pointer

The Assistant box attaches to Joyce Schmidt's box.

You can also modify a chart's structure by deleting unwanted boxes. To remove a box, you select it, and then press Del.

10 **Select the Betty Parks box, if necessary, and then press Del.**
The box is removed from your chart. As usual, if you want to reverse the action, you can choose Edit, Undo. For now, you can leave the chart in its present state and close Microsoft Organization Chart to return to the presentation.

11 **In the Microsoft Organization Chart window, choose File, Exit and Return to Presentation.**
A confirmation box prompts you to update the organization chart in the presentation with the changes you made.

12 **Choose Yes to update the chart object, and then click outside the chart.**
Congratulations! You just added an organization chart to the presentation. If you later want to revise the chart, simply double-click the organization chart object to launch the Microsoft Organization Chart program again.

13 **Save the presentation as `My Organization`, and then close it.**
If you finished your work session, exit PowerPoint and shut down Windows before turning off your computer. Otherwise, complete the exercises at the end of this project.

Summary

In this project, you learned the basics of creating charts in your PowerPoint presentations. First, you learned how to select which chart is most appropriate for the data you want to display. You used two peripheral programs—Microsoft Graph and Microsoft Organization Chart—to create and modify these charts. After you initially developed the charts, you explored ways of formatting and revising the charts.

To expand on your knowledge, spend a few minutes exploring Help on these topics. Additionally, complete some of the Skill Drill, Challenge, and Discovery Zone exercises.

Checking Concepts and Terms ✓

True/False

For each of the following, check *T* or *F* to indicate whether the statement is true or false.

__T __F **1.** PowerPoint uses a peripheral program to create data charts. [L1]

__T __F **2.** Before you can change chart data, you must first activate the chart. [L3]

__T __F **3.** You can create an organization chart by using Word, a peripheral program. [L6]

__T __F **4.** You can enter or edit a data chart's information by using a datasheet. [L2–3]

__T __F **5.** After you create a data chart, you cannot change the chart colors. [L5]

__T __F **6.** Charts are embedded as objects on a slide. [L2–7]

__T __F **7.** You cannot modify individual chart objects. [L5]

__T __F **8.** You choose Format, Organization Chart in PowerPoint to modify an organization chart. [L7]

__T __F **9.** You can start Microsoft Graph by double-clicking a chart placeholder. [L2]

__T __F **10.** A chart sub-type is a variation of a main chart type. [L1, 5]

Multiple Choice

Circle the letter of the correct answer for each of the following.

1. The peripheral program that PowerPoint uses to create or revise data charts is called
_____. [L2]

a. Microsoft Datasheet

b. Microsoft Organization Chart

c. Microsoft Graph

d. Microsoft PowerGraph

2. To add an Assistant box to a Manager box,
_____. [L7]

a. click the Manager box tool and drag it to the Assistant box

b. drag the Assistant box from the icon bar to the Manager box in the chart

c. click the Assistant box on the icon bar, and then click the Manager box to which you want to attach the Assistant box

d. choose Boxes, Attach Assistant from the menu bar, and then click the Manager box to which you want to attach the Assistant box

3. Once a data chart is created, you can
_____. [L3–5]

a. change the color of the data series

b. change the chart type

c. change the data itself

d. all of the above

4. To activate Microsoft Graph to edit an existing data chart, _____. [L3]

a. double-click the placeholder object that contains the chart

b. click the Graphing Programs button on the Standard toolbar

c. choose File, Graph from the menu bar

d. none of the above

5. To select more than one box in an organization chart, _____. [L7]

a. press Ctrl while clicking the boxes you want

b. press ◆Shift while clicking the boxes you want

c. double-click each box you want

d. all of the above

6. You can create a(n) _____ with PowerPoint. [L1, 4–5]

a. bar chart

b. line chart

c. area chart

d. all of the above

7. A pie chart is best used for showing
_____. [L1]

a. the relationship of parts to the whole

b. data changes over time

c. trends in data at equal intervals

d. the magnitude of change over time

8. Which of the following is true regarding an organization chart? [L6–7]

a. It is used to show changes over time.

b. It is used to show stock prices in an organization.

c. It shows comparisons of individual items.

d. none of the above

9. To create a data or an organization chart,
_____. [L2, 6]

a. click the Create a New Chart button on the Formatting toolbar

b. choose the appropriate AutoLayout in the New Slide dialog box

c. choose Format, Create Chart from the menu bar

d. none of the above

10. To select cells in a datasheet, _____.
[L3]

a. click the Select All button to select all cells

b. click the column heading to select a column

c. click a row heading to select a row

d. all of the above

Screen ID

Identify each of the items shown in Figure 5.30.

Figure 5.30

A. Cell

B. Datasheet

C. Graph (or chart)

D. Row heading

E. Microsoft Graph toolbars

F. Select All button

G. Column heading

H. Chart Type button

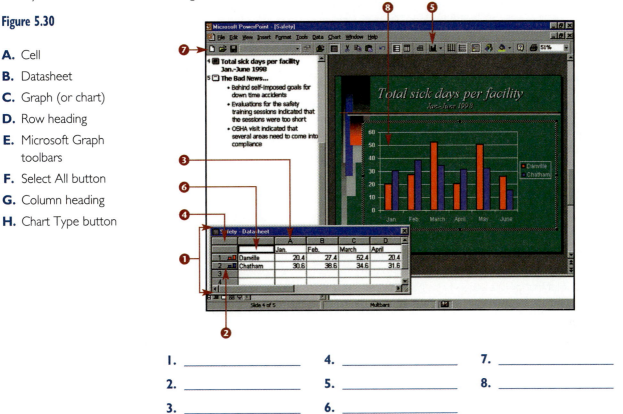

1. _____	4. _____	7. _____
2. _____	5. _____	8. _____
3. _____	6. _____	

Discussion Questions

1. Imagine that you work for a company and need to develop charts for a variety of situations. Which chart type would you use for each of the following?

- A chart that shows your company's market share versus a competitor's market share.
- A chart that shows the structure of your business.
- A chart to show monthly sales amounts for the past year.
- A chart to show your company's stock prices for the last month.
- A chart to show daily production levels for the past month. [L1, 5]

2. Think about how you create, modify, and format data charts and organization charts. How are the processes similar? How are they different? [L2–7]

3. In what ways are pie charts, radar charts, and doughnut charts similar? In what ways are they different? [L1, 5]

4. In what ways are column and bar charts similar? In what ways are they different? [L1, 5]

Skill Drill

Skill Drill exercises reinforce project skills. Each skill reinforced is the same, or nearly the same, as a skill presented in the project. Detailed instructions are provided in a step-by-step format.

1. Using Microsoft Graph's Help

As the production manager for your company, you have to develop charts every month that show production levels. Although you're thrilled that you can use data charts in a PowerPoint presentation to graphically show this information, you'd like to use Microsoft Graph more effectively. To find out more about how to use the peripheral program, you access Help. [L1–7]

1. In PowerPoint, click the New button on the Standard toolbar to quickly create a new presentation.

2. In the New Slide dialog box that automatically displays, click the Chart AutoLayout (the fourth AutoLayout on the second row), and then choose OK.

3. Double-click the chart placeholder to activate Microsoft Graph.

4. In Microsoft Graph, choose Help, Microsoft Graph Help.

5. Research several topics related to creating, modifying, and formatting data charts.

6. Write down what you learn, and close the Microsoft Graph Help window. Keep PowerPoint open if you plan to complete additional exercises.

2. Using Help in the Microsoft Organization Chart Program

As assistant to the president of a large company, you're in charge of developing organization charts for each division. You're pleased that you can use the Microsoft Organization Chart from within PowerPoint, but need to know more about how to use the program more effectively. To do so, you use Help. [L1–5]

1. In PowerPoint, click the New button on the Standard toolbar to quickly create a new presentation.

2. In the New Slide dialog box that automatically displays, click the Organization Chart AutoLayout (the third AutoLayout on the second row), and then choose OK. Double-click the placeholder for the Organization Chart to open Microsoft Organization Chart.

3. On the Microsoft Organization Chart menu bar, choose Help, Index.

4. In the Microsoft Organization Chart Help window, click the first topic represented by a green hyperlink (Creating and updating charts). Click the second subtopic listed (Basic chart operations).

5. Read through the information listed in the Help window, and then click the Back button (below the menu bar).

6. Choose the next subtopic (Opening and closing charts). Read through the information listed, and then click the Back button.

7. Continue to use the hyperlinks and the Back button to explore ways to create organization charts.

8. Click the close button in the upper-right corner of the Microsoft Organization Chart Help window. Keep PowerPoint open if you plan to complete additional exercises.

3. Creating a Line Chart

You need to show your boss that the cost of living is constantly rising, while your wages (adjusted for inflation, of course!) are falling. Create a line chart to emphasize your point. [L2–5]

1. In PowerPoint, click the New button to create a new blank presentation.

2. In the New Slide dialog box, choose the Chart AutoLayout, and then click OK.

3. Click in the title placeholder; enter `I need a raise!` as the title for your slide.

4. Double-click the chart placeholder to activate Microsoft Graph. Enter the following information in the datasheet:

	Jan	Feb	March
Income	2000	1980	1967
Cost of Living	2000	2100	2150

5. Close the datasheet to display the chart as a column chart.

6. Choose Chart, Chart Type to display the Chart Type dialog box.

7. Click Line in the Chart type list. Choose the `Line with markers` sub-type (the first sub-type on the second row). Click OK.

8. Keep the chart activated and your presentation open for the next exercise, in which you format the chart.

4. Formatting a Data Chart

After looking over your data chart, you decide that you need to spiff it up with some formatting. [L5]

1. Double-click the chart object (if necessary) to activate Microsoft Graph. Close the datasheet.

2. Click the Chart Objects drop-down list arrow and choose `Series "Income"` from the list.

3. Choose Format, Selected Data Series from the menu bar. In the Line section, click the Weight drop-down list arrow and choose the thickest line available.

4. In the Format Data Series dialog box, click the Data Labels tab. Choose Show value, and then click OK.

5. Double-click the line that represents `Series "Cost of Living"` to display the Format Data Series dialog box. On the Data Labels page, choose Show value.

6. Click the Patterns page of the Format Data Series dialog box. Click the Weight drop-down list arrow and choose the thickest line. Choose OK to close the Format Data Series dialog box.

7. Click outside the chart to embed it as an object on your slide.

8. Print a copy of your slide.

9. Save the presentation as `Living Expenses`, and then close it. Keep PowerPoint open if you plan to complete additional exercises.

5. Creating an Organization Chart

As secretary for the University Biking Club, you want to show how the club is structured. You decide to use an organization chart to do so. [L6]

1. In PowerPoint, click the New button to create a new blank presentation.

2. In the New Slide dialog box, click the Organization Chart AutoLayout (the third AutoLayout on the second row). Click OK.

3. Click in the title placeholder and type `University Biking Club`.

4. Double-click the organization chart placeholder to activate Microsoft Organization Chart.

5. Enter the following data in the top-level box:

`Lucinda Samual, President`

6. Enter the following data in the three lower-level boxes:

Heather Parks, Vice President

Grace Stegall, Treasurer

David Reams, Secretary

7. Choose File, Update Presentation to save the changes you made (but keep Microsoft Organization Chart open). Keep Microsoft Organization Chart and PowerPoint open for the next exercise, in which you format the chart.

6. Modifying an Organization Chart

After looking over your organization chart, you decide to jazz it up a bit by formatting it. [L7]

1. Make sure that the Microsoft Organization Chart window is open.

2. Add an Assistant box to the President's box. To do this, click the Assistant box tool, and then click the President's box.

3. Enter Sarah Jones, Assistant in the Assistant box, and then click outside of it.

4. Press Ctrl+A to select all boxes and lines.

5. Choose Boxes, Color to display the Color dialog box. Click the gray color (the seventh color on the first row), and then choose OK.

6. Add a shadow effect. With your boxes still selected, choose Boxes, Shadow. From the Shadow submenu, choose the first shadow effect on the third row.

7. Change the text color by choosing Text, Color. In the Color dialog box, choose red (the last color on the first row), and then choose OK.

8. Click outside the boxes to better view your changes.

9. Choose File, Exit and Return to Presentation. Choose Yes in the message box.

10. Click the Print button to print your organization chart.

11. Save your presentation as Club Organization, and then close it. Keep PowerPoint open if you plan to complete additional exercises.

Challenge 💡

Challenge exercises expand on, or are somewhat related to, skills presented in the lessons. Each exercise provides a brief narrative introduction, followed by instructions in a numbered-step format that are not as detailed as those in the Skill Drill section.

[?] 1. Using PowerPoint's Help to Research Charts

You're filling in for a Help Desk employee while he's on vacation. It seems that all the users are interested in working with charts, but they really don't know much about creating them. You decide to spend a few minutes getting more familiar with PowerPoint's Help. [L1–5]

1. In PowerPoint, choose Help, Microsoft PowerPoint Help.

2. Click the Show button, if necessary, to split the Help window into two panes.

3. Click the Contents tab, and then double-click the Working with Equations, Tables, and Charts icon to see a list of related topics.

4. Double-click the Working with Charts icon.

5. Click the first subtopic on the Working with Charts listing. Read the information displayed on the subtopic.

6. Click the Print button at the top of the Help window. In the Print dialog box that displays, choose Print the selected topic, and then choose OK.

7. Repeat the steps outlined in Step 5 for at least five other `Working with Charts` subtopics. Create a table that summarizes your information.

8. Close the Help window. Keep PowerPoint open if you plan to complete additional exercises.

2. Creating a Data Chart

You need to create a presentation that includes sales data for your company. Because PowerPoint excels at creating good-looking charts, you decide to use it to develop the presentation. [L2–3, 5]

1. Create a new blank presentation. For your first slide, create a slide based on the Chart AutoLayout.

2. Create a column chart with the title `Five Year Summary`, using the following data:

	1994	1995	1996	1997	1998
Sales	104	135	125	140	150
Expenses	65	89	67	60	88

3. Change the chart type to at least five other chart types. When you finish, change the chart to a 2-D horizontal bar chart.

4. Change the color for the `Expenses` data series to red. Change the color for the `Sales` data series to blue.

5. Save the presentation as `Sales Summary`.

6. Print one copy of your presentation (as a slide); then close it.

Keep PowerPoint open if you plan to complete additional exercises.

3. Creating and Formatting an Organization Chart

Your boss wants you to create an organization chart to share at an upcoming staff meeting. You decide to use PowerPoint to create this type of chart. [L6–7]

1. Create a new blank presentation. For your first slide, create a slide based on the Organization Chart AutoLayout.

2. Enter `Our Company` in the title placeholder of the slide.

3. Add the following data to your organization chart:

   `Joseph Lowell, President`

   `Ann Luther, Admin. Assistant to the President`

   `Rebecca Cory, Sales Manager`

   `Eugene Stegall, Production Manager`

   `Sarah Jones, Human Resource Manager`

4. Change the box color to white. Format the text in all boxes using Impact, 14-point, red font.

5. Add a shadow effect of your choice to all the boxes.

6. Save the presentation as `Our Company's Structure`.

7. Print a copy of the organization chart, and then close the presentation. Keep PowerPoint open if you plan to complete additional exercises.

4. Setting Up an Organization Chart

You are the communications director for a volunteer organization. To quickly get important information about upcoming meetings and events to those in your group, you create a phone tree using PowerPoint's organization chart feature. [L6–7]

1. Create a new blank presentation. For your first slide, create a slide based on the Organization Chart AutoLayout.

2. Enter `Phone Tree` in the title placeholder of the slide.

3. Add data to your organization chart so that it matches that shown in Figure 5.31.

Figure 5.31
Use this figure as your guide.

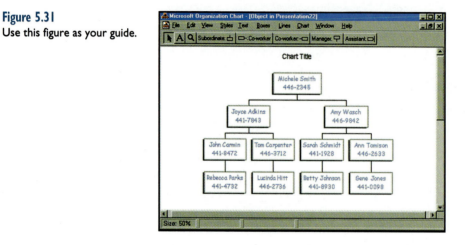

4. Change the box color to white. Format the text in all boxes using Comic Sans, 12-point, blue font.

5. Add a shadow effect of your choice to all the boxes.

6. Save the presentation as `Phone Tree`.

7. Print a copy of the organization chart, and then close the presentation. Keep PowerPoint open if you plan to complete additional exercises.

5. Changing Chart Types

You previously created a stacked column chart that shows expenses as a percentage of income. To spiff up the chart, you decide to change colors and patterns. [L4–5]

1. Open **PP1-0503** and save it as `Income`. Activate Microsoft Graph.

2. Using the Chart Type drop-down list, change the chart to each of the following types:

   - Area Chart
   - 3-D Area Chart
   - 3-D Surface Chart
   - Bar Chart

- 3-D Bar Chart
- Radar Chart
- Column Chart
- 3-D Column Chart
- Line Chart
- 3-D Line Chart
- (XY) Scatter Chart
- 3-D Cylinder Chart
- 3-D Cone Chart
- 3-D Pyramid Chart

3. Change the chart to a 3-D Bar Chart. Display the Chart Type dialog box. Choose the Stacked bar with a 3-D visual effect type, and then click OK.

4. Format the `Income` data series in blue. Choose a Gradient fill effect (*Hint*: Click the Fill Effects button in the Format Data Series dialog box.) Choose a Vertical Shading style.

5. Format the `Expenses` data series in red. Also, apply a Gradient fill effect with the same Vertical Shading style you used for the `Income` data series.

6. Save, print, and close your `Income` presentation. Keep PowerPoint open if you plan to complete additional exercises.

6. Working with a Pie Chart

You created a chart that shows your company's percentage of market share. However, you want to modify the chart to emphasize how well your company is doing. To do so, you rely on Microsoft Graph's features. [L4–5]

1. Open **PP1-0504** and save it as `Market Share.`

2. Activate Microsoft Graph, and then close the datasheet.

3. Change the pie chart to 3-D. Format each of the slices as follows:

   - `Lowell Manufacturing`: format with White marble texture
   - `Cory Manufacturing`: format with Paper bag texture
   - `Hitt Manufacturing`: format with Pink tissue paper texture
   - `Bell Manufacturing`: format with Purple mesh texture

4. Drag the wedge that represents Bell Mfg. away from the rest of the pie chart to emphasize its data.

5. Format the chart's background (Chart Area) in a red that matches the template's color.

6. Format the Legend by using a blue that matches the template's color.

7. Resize and move the chart area so that it takes up approximately 30% less room on the slide.

8. Print a copy of your slide.

9. Save the Market Share presentation, and then close it. Keep PowerPoint open if you plan to complete additional exercises.

Discovery Zone

Discovery Zone exercises require advanced knowledge of topics presented in Essentials lessons, application of skills from multiple lessons, or self-directed learning of new skills.

? 1. Finding Out More About Microsoft Graph

You're a newly hired employee in the Information Systems Department. Charts are extremely popular at your organization. So that you can do a better job of helping those in your company, you decide to research how to use Microsoft Graph more effectively.

Using the Help system in Microsoft Graph, find out the following:

- How can you format data series by using various fill effects?
- What options are available to format a legend?
- What options are available to format a chart's background?
- What options are available to format data walls and gridlines?
- How can you change a column chart to other shapes (such as pyramids)?
- How can you change one data series to a cone shape and another data series (on the same chart) to a cylinder shape?
- What is the purpose of a radar chart?
- How can you use a doughnut chart?
- What similarities are there between doughnut charts and pie charts? What differences are there between them?

Outline the information you find in a logical, easy-to-follow sequence. (If you're familiar with Word, consider entering this information in a Word document.)

Practice by using each of the features that you researched on a chart, and present the information to at least one other user.

? 2. Finding Out More About Microsoft Organization Chart

Several people in your business use organization charts. You decide to research how to use the Microsoft Organization Chart program more effectively.

Using the Help system in Microsoft Organization Chart, find out the following:

- Which options are available to format lines on your chart?
- Which options are available to format boxes on your chart?
- How can you change background color for your chart?
- How do you align text?
- What are different ways of selecting boxes?
- How can you use a different layout, or style, for your chart?
- How can you adjust the view to better see your chart?
- What drawing tools are available in Microsoft Organization Chart? How are they used?
- How can you change the default setup for a new organization chart so that only one box is initially displayed?

Outline the information you find in a logical, easy-to-follow sequence. (If you're familiar with Word, consider entering this information in a Word document.)

Practice by using each of the features that you researched on a chart, and present the information to at least one other user.

3. Developing a Data Chart

Due to rising costs, you need more money for college expenses. To illustrate this to your parents, you prepare a PowerPoint presentation to take with you on your next visit home.

Create a new, blank presentation. Use the Chart AutoLayout for the first (and only) slide in your presentation. Enter `College expenses are increasing!` in the title placeholder. Create a column chart to illustrate the following information:

	1st year	2nd year	3rd year
Tuition	10000	11500	13000
Room/Board	4000	4500	4800
Books	400	450	475
Misc.	300	300	300

View your column chart by row and by column. Add a Data Table and then remove it. Click the By Row button to view your data in that manner.

Display your chart, using each of the chart types and sub-types available in Microsoft Graph. Develop two lists: one that lists which chart types are appropriate for the data, and one that lists which chart types are not appropriate.

Display your data by using the Stacked column with a 3-D visual effect. Format the chart by using either textures or gradient effects. Also change the color for the Books data series to red.

Save the presentation as `Rising College Expenses`. Print your presentation, and then close it. Keep PowerPoint open if you plan to complete the next exercise. [L2–5]

4. Creating and Formatting a Data Chart

As treasurer of the University Biking Club, you track how club dues have been spent over the last two years. Because you want to share this information in an understandable way at your next meeting, you create and format a column chart using PowerPoint.

Create a new blank presentation. Use the Chart AutoLayout for the first (and only) slide in your presentation. Enter `Dues… where do they go?` in the title placeholder. Create a column chart to illustrate the following information:

	1997	1998
Club Activities	1200	1350
Newsletter	350	375
Advertisements	89	125
Contributions	500	500

View your column chart by row and by column. Add a Data Table and then remove it. Click the By Row button to view your data in that manner.

Display your chart, using each of the chart types and sub-types available in Microsoft Graph. Finally, choose the Stacked bar with a 3-D visual effect. Format the chart by using a different texture for each data series.

Save the presentation as **Club Dues**. Print your presentation, and then close it. [L2–5]

Project 6

Changing a Presentation's Overall Appearance

Objectives

In this project, you learn how to

- ➤ **Use Templates**
- ➤ **Work with Color Schemes**
- ➤ **Change the Slide Background**
- ➤ **Work with a Slide Master**
- ➤ **Create Drawn Objects**
- ➤ **Select and Modify Drawn Objects**
- ➤ **Use ClipArt**

Key terms introduced in this project include

- ■ color scheme
- ■ drawn objects
- ■ slide master

Why Would I Do This?

Most people respond more positively to color than they do to black and white. Consider, for example, magazine advertisements. In general, your eye is probably drawn more to a color advertisement than to a black and white one, which is exactly why businesses spend the big bucks to print in color.

You can use the same principle when you create PowerPoint presentations. By adding a splash of color (or a different design), you can strengthen the impact of your presentation. Fortunately, PowerPoint includes various built-in design templates and color schemes that you can use. Another way to use color is to change the slide background for selected (or all) slides in your presentation.

You can also change the appearance of your entire presentation quickly by making changes on the presentation's slide master. You use the slide master to add design elements—such as date, slide number, or company logo—to all slides in your presentation.

Finally, you can spice up a presentation by including drawings and illustrations. PowerPoint comes with a set of electronic pictures, called *clip art*, that you can add to emphasize information in your presentation. Additionally, you can use PowerPoint's drawing tools to create simple or complex illustrations. You can combine these features to quickly and easily produce an impressive presentation.

Visual Summary

In this project, you learn how to dip into PowerPoint's bag of tricks to develop a colorful, eye-catching presentation. For example, you can change templates or color schemes for any presentation (see Figure 6.1). You can also change a slide's background by using a gradient fill, texture, or pattern. To add these effects, you use the Fill Effects dialog box (see Figure 6.2).

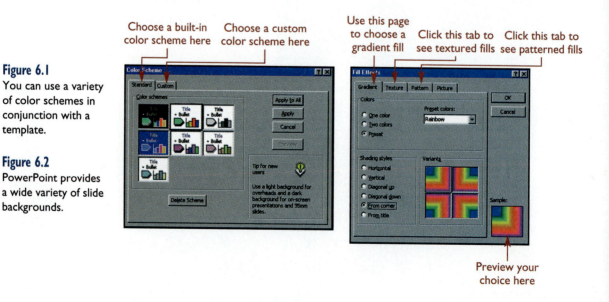

Choose a built-in color scheme here   Choose a custom color scheme here

Use this page to choose a gradient fill   Click this tab to see textured fills   Click this tab to see patterned fills

Figure 6.1
You can use a variety of color schemes in conjunction with a template.

Figure 6.2
PowerPoint provides a wide variety of slide backgrounds.

Preview your choice here

You also learn how to "go behind the scenes" of a slide and modify its design. How? By changing the slide master (see Figure 6.3).

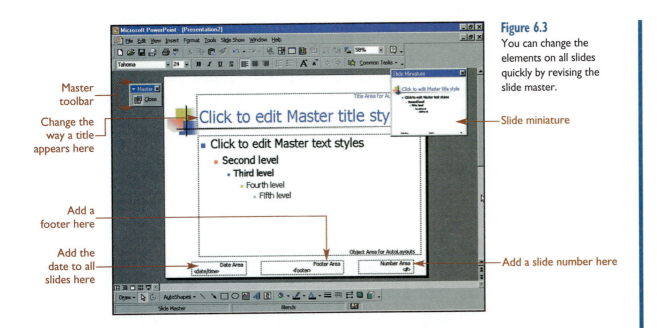

Master toolbar

Change the way a title appears here

Add a footer here

Add the date to all slides here

Figure 6.3
You can change the elements on all slides quickly by revising the slide master.

Slide miniature

Add a slide number here

You also learn how to jazz up any slide quickly by adding clip art. To do this, you access the built-in collection of pictures in the **Clip Gallery** (see Figure 6.4).

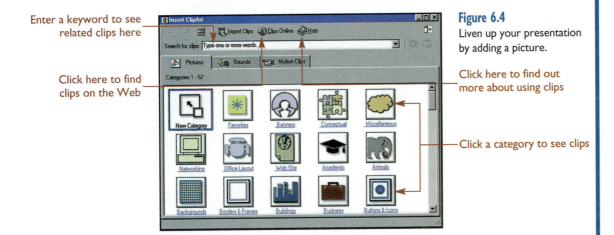

Enter a keyword to see related clips here

Click here to find clips on the Web

Figure 6.4
Liven up your presentation by adding a picture.

Click here to find out more about using clips

Click a category to see clips

When you finish working through the project and combining the features, you'll have a presentation similar to that shown in Figure 6.5.

Figure 6.5
You can change the background and add clip art to enhance your slides.

Try using these features to change your presentation's appearance now.

Lesson 1: Using Templates

PowerPoint provides an extensive group of predesigned *templates* (also called design templates) that you can use for your presentation. A template is a "blueprint" that PowerPoint uses to create slides, including the formatting, color, and graphics necessary to create a particular "look." Because professional graphic artists created these templates, they can help you create a presentation with a consistent, well-designed appearance. Templates allow you to concentrate on content rather than on layout and design.

In Project 2, you learned how to choose a template when you initially created a presentation. In this project, you learn how to change templates for an existing presentation. This is handy if you already developed a presentation but aren't entirely satisfied with the design. You can simply apply different templates until you find one you like. Try working with templates now.

To Use Templates

1 **Start PowerPoint, if necessary, and close the PowerPoint start-up dialog box.**

2 **Choose File, New, and then click the Design Templates tab.**
The Design Templates page of the New Presentation dialog box displays, as shown in Figure 6.6. You can choose a design template on this page.

Figure 6.6
You can choose from a variety of built-in templates.

Choose a design template on this page

Available templates

Large icons button

Details button

List button

Preview area

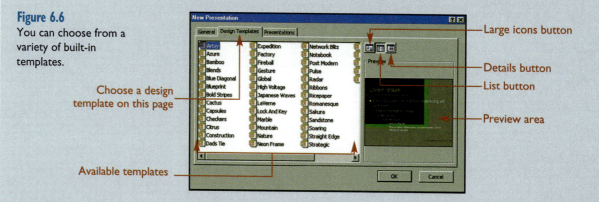

❌ If your templates display differently from that shown in Figure 6.6, don't worry. Your system probably is showing the files in Large Icons or Details view rather than List view. Just click the List button to display the templates as shown.

3 **Click the Checkers template icon.**
The preview area displays an example of the selected template. (If you wish, single-click several templates to preview them, and then proceed with the tutorial.)

4 **Choose the Japanese Waves template, and then click OK.**
The New Slide dialog box displays so that you can select an AutoLayout for your first slide.

5 **Select the Title Slide AutoLayout, if necessary, and then choose OK.**
A title slide using the Japanese Waves template is created. Additionally, all slides you add to this presentation will automatically use the Japanese Waves template.

6 **In the title placeholder, type your company name, and then enter your own name in the subtitle area.**

You created a presentation based on a specific template. However, you can also change templates *after* you initially create the presentation. Try your hand at applying different design templates to your presentation now.

7 **Choose Format, Apply Design Template. (Alternatively, you can right-click on the slide to display a shortcut menu, and then choose Apply Design Template.)**

The Apply Design Template dialog box displays with a list of all available templates (see Figure 6.7). Notice that this is the same list of templates you saw in the New Presentation dialog box. Furthermore, you can preview a template by clicking it, just as you did earlier in this lesson.

Selected template

Figure 6.7
You can change templates at any time.

Views button

Preview of selected template

Click this arrow to scroll through the list

X If your Apply Design Template dialog box doesn't look like the one shown in Figure 6.7, a different view probably displays. Click the Views button drop-down list arrow, and then choose Preview from the list.

8 **Click the Bamboo template.**

The Bamboo template is shown in the Preview area of the dialog box. This gives you a chance to see if you want a particular template.

9 **Choose Apply.**

The new template design is applied to the presentation (see Figure 6.8). Notice that the background, fonts, colors, and text alignment are all affected by the template you choose.

10 **Repeat Steps 7–9 to apply other templates to your presentation. When you finish, close the presentation without saving it.**

Keep PowerPoint open for the next lesson, in which you work with color schemes.

continues ▶

To Use Templates   (continued)

Figure 6.8
You can change design templates for a different appearance.

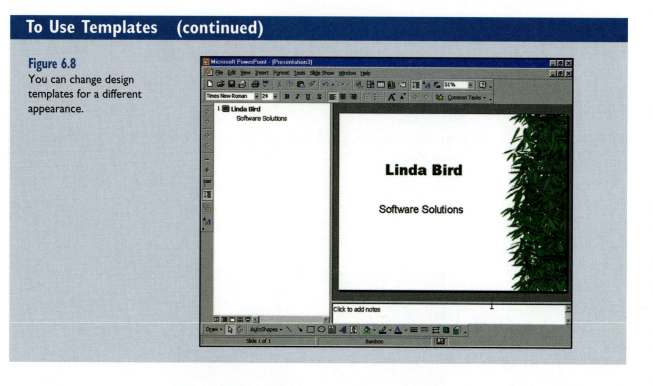

ⓘ **Creating a Custom Template**
If you are artistically inclined (or just want to create a custom look for your presentations), you can also design your own template. To create a custom template, change any feature of a slide—color, font style, or graphics—in a presentation. Choose File, Save As, and then enter a name for your new template. Choose Design Template from the Save as type drop-down list, so that it will be saved as a template and not a file. Click Save, and you have a new, custom-designed template!

Lesson 2: Working with Color Schemes

A **color scheme** is the underlying set of eight coordinated colors for a presentation. Each template you use includes a color scheme to ensure that any new objects you create (or recolor) will match those already in place. Knowing a little about color schemes is useful for three reasons:

- **Text or objects that you recolor will match the underlying scheme.** For example, when you change font color, the colors initially displayed on the palette are from the underlying color scheme.

- **You can change the color scheme for all slides in a presentation.** For example, suppose that you will do a presentation on the road, and the LCD or computer screen doesn't have the same contrast as your office computer. Being able to change the color scheme can create a better contrast and literally save your presentation (or job)!

  You may also have similar presentations, but have added customized slides for different audiences; one set for sales, one for marketing, one for advertising, and so on. By keeping the template the same but changing the color scheme used for each audience, you can tell instantly if you are running the correct version of your presentation.

■ **You can change the color scheme for just one slide to emphasize certain information.** For example, you can highlight a new proposal or agenda. Changing color schemes for the slide that introduces the proposal is a subtle but effective attention-grabber.

Try changing the color scheme of an existing presentation now.

To Work with Color Schemes

1 **Open** PP1-0601 **and save it as** Hickory.

2 **Display the presentation in Slide Sorter view so that the new color schemes are easier to see.**
Color schemes are most commonly applied in Normal view or Slide Sorter view, so that you can quickly see the result.

3 **Choose F_ormat, Slide _Color Scheme.**
The Color Scheme dialog box displays, as shown in Figure 6.9. (When you work in Normal view, you can also open this dialog box by right-clicking in the slide pane and choosing Slide _Color Scheme from the shortcut menu.)

Available color schemes —

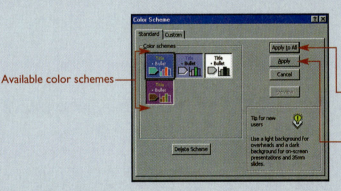

Figure 6.9
You can change color schemes quickly.

Click here to apply a new color scheme to all presentation slides

Click here to apply a new color scheme to the current slide only

In general, you should select a scheme with a light background and dark text for overheads. Select a dark background with light text for onscreen display and 35MM slides. Try selecting a color scheme for onscreen display now.

4 **Select the dark maroon color scheme on the second row, and then choose Apply _to All.**
The presentation is shown with the dark maroon color scheme applied to all slides. If you chose _Apply, the color scheme for only the displayed slide would change. Try changing color scheme for just one slide now.

5 **In Slide Sorter view, click Slide 3,** Our Customer's Needs.
You must select a slide before you can change its color scheme.

6 **Choose F_ormat, Slide _Color Scheme.**
The Color Scheme dialog box redisplays.

7 **In the Color Scheme dialog box, choose the light blue color scheme on the first row, and then choose _Apply.**
The selected color scheme is applied only to the selected slide. Notice that

continues ▶

To Work with Color Schemes   (continued)

the slide elements—such as the graphics and font style—remain consistent on all slides (because they are created by the underlying template), but that the color combinations are different.

 Make sure that you choose Apply rather than Apply to All to change the color scheme for only the current slide.

8 **Save the Hickory presentation, and then close it.**
Keep PowerPoint open for the next exercise, in which you change background color.

Creating Custom Color Schemes
If you like the overall color scheme but want to change color for one color element, click the Custom tab in the Color Scheme dialog box to display the colors that make up the scheme. Click the Scheme color you want to change, and then click the Change Color button. Choose a color in the Color dialog box, and then choose OK. You can choose Apply to use the modified color scheme on the currently displayed slide, or choose Apply to All to use it on all presentation slides.

Lesson 3: Changing the Slide Background

In PowerPoint 2000, you can change the background color and pattern of your slides. By changing the background color, you can add pizzazz to your presentation and capture your audience's attention. You can customize your background by adding shadow effects, textures, and patterns. This differs from changing the entire color scheme of eight colors because you only modify the slide's background. Try changing the background color now.

To Change the Slide Background

1 **Open PP1-0602 and save it as Appalachian Logging Company.**

2 **Display Slide 1, Business Overview, in Normal view, and then choose Format, Background.**
The Background dialog box displays, as shown in Figure 6.10.

Figure 6.10
You can choose a new background for your presentation.

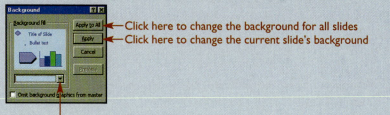

Click here to change the background for all slides
Click here to change the current slide's background

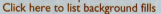

Click here to list background fills

3 **In the Background fill section of the dialog box, click the drop-down list arrow, and then choose Fill Effects.**

The Fill Effects dialog box displays (see Figure 6.11). You can use this dialog box to choose a variety of background styles.

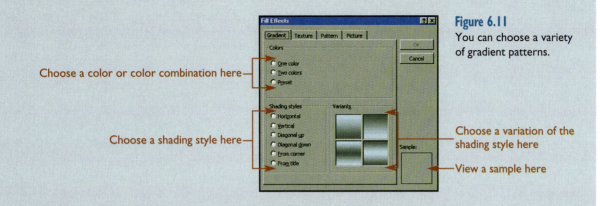

Figure 6.11
You can choose a variety of gradient patterns.

Choose a color or color combination here

Choose a shading style here

Choose a variation of the shading style here

View a sample here

4 **Click the Gradient tab, if necessary, and then click the Preset option button (in the Colors section).**

PowerPoint displays a preset color combination (Early Sunset). Now, explore other preset color combinations you can use for your slide's background.

5 **Click the Preset colors drop-down list arrow, and choose Ocean from the list.**

The Ocean color combination displays in the Sample area (see Figure 6.12). The Sample area gives you an idea of the way the color combination will look when you apply it to your slide's background. You can further modify the color combination by choosing a shading style and variant.

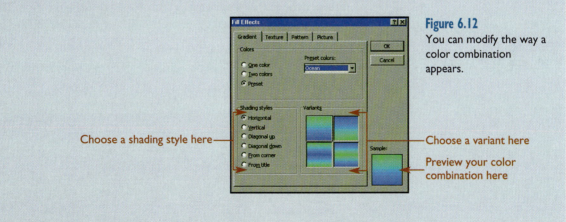

Figure 6.12
You can modify the way a color combination appears.

Choose a shading style here

Choose a variant here

Preview your color combination here

6 **In the Shading styles section, click the From title option button.**

The effect displays in the Sample section of the dialog box. Apply the fill effect to your slide's background.

7 **Choose OK in the Fill Effects dialog box, and then choose Apply to All in the Background dialog box.**

The new background style is applied to your slides.

PowerPoint also provides a number of textures that you can use for a slide's background. Take a look at these textures now.

continues ▶

To Change the Slide Background   (continued)

8 **Right-click in the slide pane area on Slide 1 to display the shortcut menu, then choose Ba_c_kground.**
The Background dialog box displays.

> ☒ Make sure to right-click on the background area of your slide (and not in a placeholder) so that the correct shortcut menu displays.

9 **Choose _F_ill Effects from the drop-down list of available backgrounds.**

10 **In the Fill Effects dialog box, click the Texture tab.**
The Texture page displays with a number of natural-looking backgrounds, such as wood and stone, as shown in Figure 6.13. (If you wish, click several of the textures to preview them before proceeding with the exercise.)

Figure 6.13
You can choose a texture for your slide background.

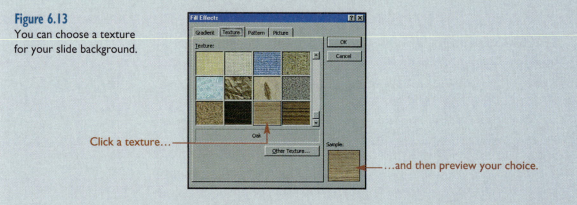

Click a texture...

...and then preview your choice.

11 **Scroll down the list of Textures, choose Oak (the third box in the bottom row), and click OK to close the Fill Effects dialog box.**

12 **Choose Apply _t_o All in the Background dialog box.**
The textured wood background is applied to your presentation slides (see Figure 6.14).

Figure 6.14
When appropriate, you can apply different textures to a slide's background.

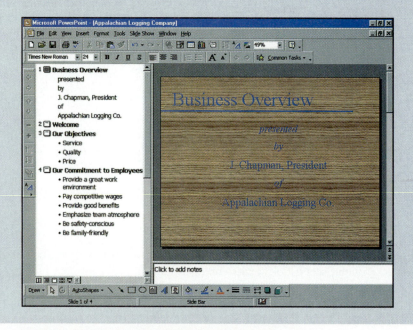

13 **Save the Appalachian Logging Company file, and then close it.**
Keep PowerPoint open for the next exercise, in which you work with Slide Masters.

Lesson 4: Working with a Slide Master

Every presentation you create automatically includes a **slide master**. The slide master is a framework slide that controls the way your presentation slides will look by governing characteristics such as font, background color, shadowing, and bullet style.

You can also use the slide master to automatically place items such as dates, names, page numbers, or logos on each slide. This slide master works behind the scenes, and contains instructions so that the same objects are included on every presentation slide. For example, you can place your company's logo on the slide master so that it appears on all slides in the presentation. When you want to make a global change to all of your slides, you don't have to change each slide individually. Instead, just make the change on the slide master, and PowerPoint automatically updates all existing slides. Furthermore, any new slides you add automatically include the changes.

Try making changes to a slide master now—and watch how it automatically updates all your presentation slides!

To Work with a Slide Master

1 **Open** PP1-0603 **and save it as** Star Manufacturing.

2 **Choose** View, Master, Slide Master.
The master slide for the presentation displays (see Figure 6.15). The master contains a title object and a body object that you can use to specify the default format for the title and body text. You can also add other objects to the slide master (such as the date or a page number) to be included on all slides. Additionally, a Slide Miniature displays so that you can see the effect of changes to the master on one of your presentation slides. Finally, the Master toolbar displays. You can use this toolbar to quickly close the slide master and display the presentation in Normal view again.

> **X** If a Slide Miniature doesn't display automatically, choose View, Slide Miniature. Alternatively, click the Slide Miniature button on the Master toolbar.

3 **Click the object titled** Click to edit Master title style.
The title area is selected, as indicated by the thickened border. The text in this area is currently formatted in italic. Any changes made to this area will affect all title placeholders in your presentation.

_I_ **4** **Click the Italic button in the Formatting toolbar.**
Italic is removed from the title area text. Notice that the italic is also removed

continues ▶

To Work with a Slide Master (continued)

from the title displayed in the Slide Miniature. Because you made the change on the slide master rather than on an individual slide, it affects all the presentation slides.

You can also customize the presentation by including information—such as your name, department, or company name—in the Footer, Date, and Number areas of the slide master. When you enter information on the slide master, it is automatically placed on all slides.

Figure 6.15
You can control which slide elements display by using the slide master.

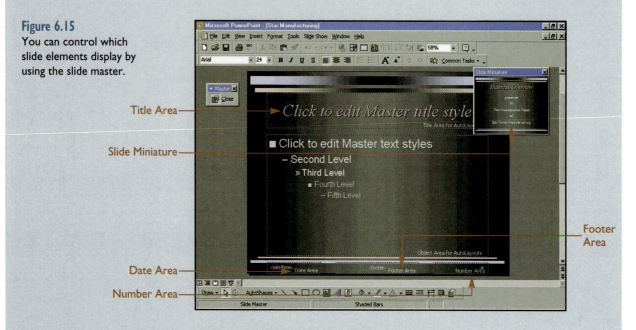

5 **On your slide master, click the Footer Area object.**
The Footer Area is selected (see Figure 6.16). You also see a field for footer text. You can select this field, then enter your own text.

Figure 6.16
You can add text or slide numbers to your presentation.

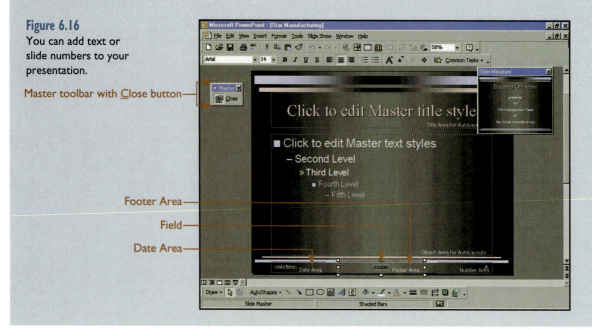

6 In the `<footer>` **field, enter** `Prepared by Sarah Jones.`

The text is inserted in the Footer Area so that it will appear on each presentation slide. Now try adding slide numbers to the Footer Area.

7 **With your insertion point still in the Footer Area, press** ⏎Enter, **and then choose** **I**nsert, **Slide N**umber.

A field for a slide number is entered below the text in the Footer Area. Add the current date to your slides. You do this by clicking the `<date/time>` field within the Date Area box.

8 **Click the** `<date/time>` **field in the Date Area box, and then choose** **Insert, Date and T**ime.

The Date and Time dialog box displays so that you can choose a date format (see Figure 6.17). You can also choose to update the date automatically whenever the presentation is opened, saved, or printed.

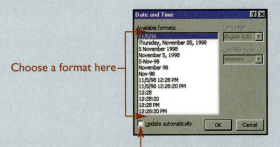

Choose a format here

Check this box to update the date automatically

Figure 6.17
You can easily add a date to your slides.

9 **In the Date and Time dialog box, check the U**pdate automatically **check box, and then click OK.**

The current date is added to the Date Area on your slide master.

Now, switch back to Normal view so that you can see the change on your presentation slides. You can do this by choosing **V**iew, **N**ormal, or by clicking the Normal View button. Alternatively, you can click the **C**lose button on the Master toolbar.

10 **Click the C**lose **button on the Master toolbar (refer to Figure 6.16, if necessary).**

The changes you made on the slide master globally affect all slides (see Figure 6.18). (If you want, press F5 to view your presentation as a slide show to better see your changes.)

11 **Save and close the Star Manufacturing presentation.**

Keep PowerPoint open for the next exercise, in which you create drawn objects.

continues ▶

To Work with a Slide Master (continued)

Figure 6.18
Changes to the slide master affect all the slides.

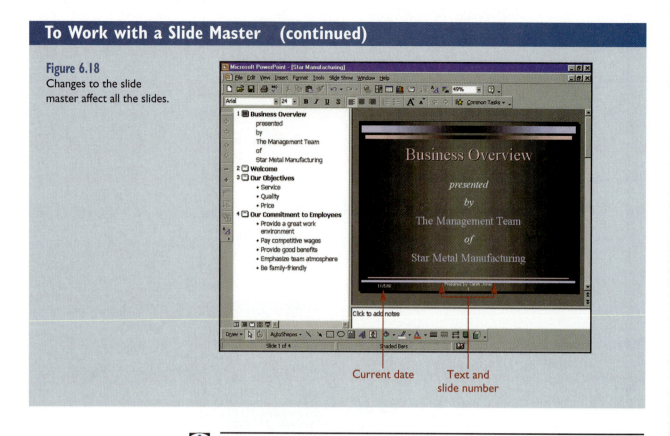

Current date

Text and slide number

ⓘ **Displaying the Slide Master**

To display the slide master quickly, click ⟨⬆Shift⟩ while pointing to the Slide View button. When you finish making changes, click the Slide View (or Normal View) button to close the slide master.

Lesson 5: Creating Drawn Objects

You can jazz up a slide or emphasize specific information by including ***drawn objects*** (such as rectangles, ovals, lines, or arrows) in your presentation. Fortunately, PowerPoint has a variety of drawing tools that enable you to create simple to complex illustrations. These tools are located on the Drawing toolbar at the bottom of the application window.

After you initially create a drawn object, you can move, resize, and otherwise modify the object. By using graphics on your presentation, you make it a cut above the rest and help get your audience's attention (see Figure 6.19).

In this lesson, you learn how to create basic objects using the tools on the Drawing toolbar. Table 6.1 describes these tools. You can use this table as a handy reference when you create and modify drawings.

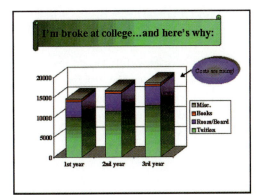

Figure 6.19
You can jazz up a slide with drawn objects.

Table 6.1   PowerPoint's Drawing Tools

Button	Tool	Use this tool to
Draw ▾	Draw	Display drawing commands
	Select Objects	Select drawn objects
	Free Rotate	Rotate a selected object
AutoShapes ▾	AutoShapes	Display menu options for inserting a predesigned shape
	Line	Draw a line
	Arrow	Draw an arrow
	Rectangle	Draw rectangles and squares
	Oval	Draw ellipses and circles
	Text Box	Draw a text box
	Insert WordArt	Start the WordArt program
	Insert Clip Art	Open the Insert ClipArt dialog box so that you can place electronic pictures in your presentation
	Fill Color	Add, remove, or modify the texture, color, or pattern of a selected object
	Line Color	Add, remove, or modify the line color of a selected object
	Font Color	Change the font color of a selected object
	Line Style	Change the line thickness of a selected object
	Dash Style	Change the line appearance
	Arrow Style	Change the arrowhead appearance
	Shadow	Add, remove, or modify the shadow formatting for a selected object
	3-D	Add, remove, or modify the 3-D formatting of a selected object

Try creating drawn objects in your presentation now.

To Create Drawn Objects

1 **Click the New button to create a new blank presentation. Choose the Blank AutoLayout for your first slide, and then click OK.**

To learn to draw objects, you use a blank slide so that you have plenty of room with which to work. It would also help if you switch to Slide view and turn on PowerPoint's horizontal and vertical rulers. These rulers help you place drawn objects accurately. You can turn the ruler on or off by choosing <u>V</u>iew, <u>R</u>uler. When displayed, the rulers appear at the top and left sides of the slide pane of Normal, Slide, Outline, and Notes Page views. The 0" marks on the horizontal and vertical rulers represent the center of the slide. Furthermore, when you draw an object, markers on the rulers show your exact location on the slide.

2 **Click the Slide View button.**

The presentation displays in Slide view. Now you can turn on the rulers.

3 **If the rulers are not already displayed on your screen, choose <u>V</u>iew, <u>R</u>uler.**

The ruler guides display (see Figure 6.20). Now try using PowerPoint's tools to draw an object.

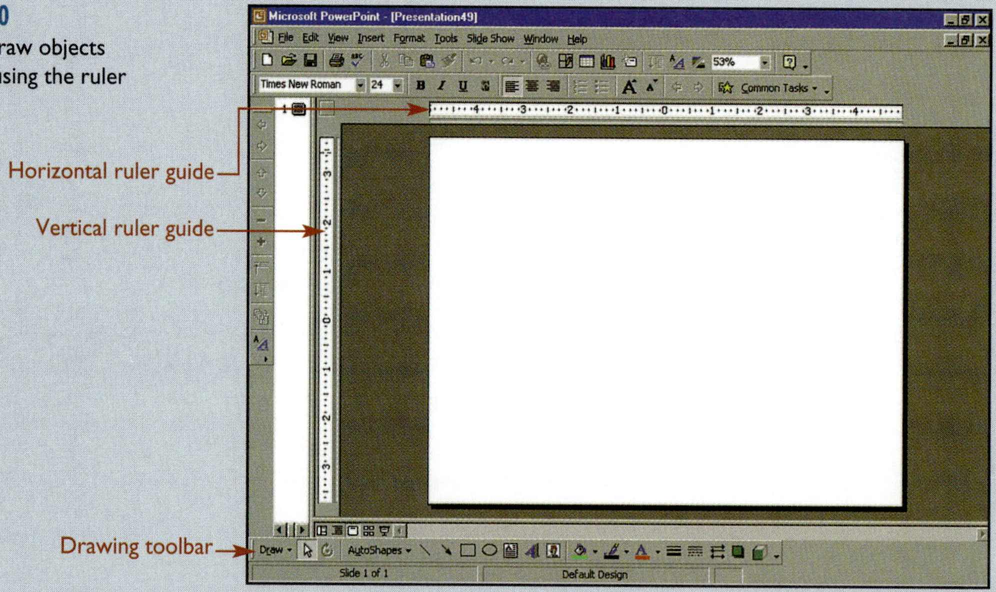

Figure 6.20
You can draw objects precisely using the ruler guides.

Horizontal ruler guide

Vertical ruler guide

Drawing toolbar

4 **Click the Rectangle tool on the Drawing toolbar, and then move the mouse pointer to the slide area.**

The mouse pointer changes to a cross hair, so you can place the drawn object accurately.

X If the Drawing toolbar doesn't display at the bottom of your application window, choose <u>V</u>iew, <u>T</u>oolbars, Drawing from the menu.

5 **Starting with both ruler markers at 0", click and drag downward until the horizontal ruler marker is 3", and the vertical ruler marker is 2", and then release the mouse button.**

A rectangle is added to your presentation (see Figure 6.21). The color and line colors used for the object are determined by the underlying template. (If you're curious about which fill and line colors will be used, take a look at the Fill Color and Line Color buttons on the Drawing toolbar.)

Notice that white selection handles automatically display around the object. When the object is selected, you can make further revisions. When you click on the slide (or draw another object), however, the rectangle is deselected. (You learn more specifically how to select and modify drawn objects in Lesson 6.)

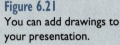

Figure 6.21
You can add drawings to your presentation.

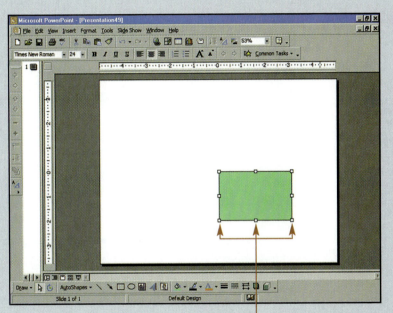

Selection handles

You can use other drawing tools just as you used the Rectangle tool: Click the tool, and then drag to draw the object on the slide. Using this method, try drawing an oval, or ellipse, now.

6 **Click the Oval tool, and then drag to draw an oval in the upper-left corner of the slide.**

An oval is added to your slide. Again, the oval is automatically formatted using the template's default fill and line colors.

You can also make an object symmetrical by pressing ⬆Shift as you draw it. For example, pressing ⬆Shift while drawing a rectangle produces a perfect square; pressing ⬆Shift when you draw an oval creates a perfect circle. Try making a circle now.

7 **Click the Oval tool, and then press ⬆Shift and drag to draw a circle in the lower-left corner of the slide.**

continues ▶

To Create Drawn Objects (continued)

X Make sure that you release the mouse button before the (⬆Shift) key or your object may skew into an oval.

Another popular tool is the Line tool, which (logically) you use to create lines. You can draw the line freehand or press (⬆Shift) while you draw it to make it straight.

8 **Click the Line tool, and then draw a line from the circle to the rectangle (see Figure 6.22).**

Figure 6.22
You can draw lines on your slide.

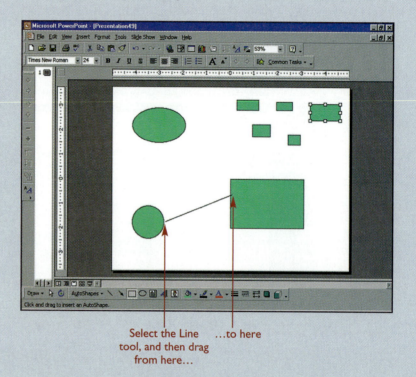

Select the Line   ...to here
tool, and then drag
from here...

Notice that a drawing tool is turned off automatically once you have drawn an object with it. However, you can double-click a tool to keep it active so you can draw multiple objects. When you finish, you turn the tool off by clicking it a second time (or by pressing (Esc)). Try drawing multiple rectangles now by using this technique.

9 **Double-click the Rectangle tool, and then draw several small rectangles (or squares) in the upper-right corner of the slide.**
Your slide should look similar to the one shown in Figure 6.23.

10 **Click the Rectangle tool to turn it off.**
If you want to, practice using the various drawing tools on the slide. When you finish, close your presentation without saving it. Keep PowerPoint open for the next lesson, in which you select and modify objects.

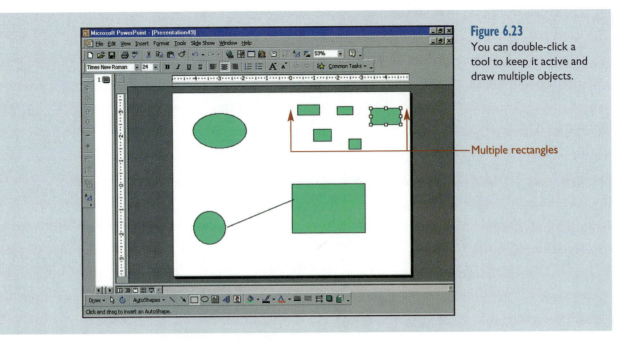

Figure 6.23
You can double-click a
tool to keep it active and
draw multiple objects.

Multiple rectangles

Using AutoShapes

If you're not very artistic, or if you simply want some help when you create drawings, you can use PowerPoint's AutoShapes to create professionally designed shapes. Click the AutoShapes button on the Drawing toolbar to display the AutoShapes menu. Move your mouse pointer to a menu item to display a graphical submenu, and then click the shape you want. You drag to draw the shape on a slide the way you created rectangles, ovals, and lines.

Lesson 6: Selecting and Modifying Drawn Objects

Once they are created, you can modify drawn objects in a number of ways. You can move, resize, recolor, or delete objects. Before you modify an object, you must first select it. You can use Table 6.2 as a handy reference guide for selecting and deselecting objects.

Table 6.2   Methods of Selecting Objects

To	Do This
Select an Object	Click the object.
Select Multiple Objects	Press and hold down ⬆Shift while clicking the objects.
	Using the Select Objects tool, draw a box around all objects.
Deselect One Object	Hold down ⬆Shift, click the object, and then release ⬆Shift.
Deselect All Objects	Click outside selected objects.

In this lesson, you learn how to select drawn objects by using some of the techniques listed in Table 6.2. Once the objects are selected, you can modify them in a number of ways. Try selecting and modifying objects now.

To Select and Modify Drawn Objects

1 Open `PP1-0604` and save it as `Drawing`.

2 Click the diamond object.

The diamond is selected, as indicated by the white selection handles that surround it.

3 Press and hold down `Shift` and click the rectangle object, and then release `Shift`.

The rectangle is selected in addition to the diamond.

4 Click the Select Objects tool on the Drawing toolbar (if necessary), and then drag from the upper-left corner of the slide to the lower-right corner.

A dashed border indicates the area being selected (see Figure 6.24).

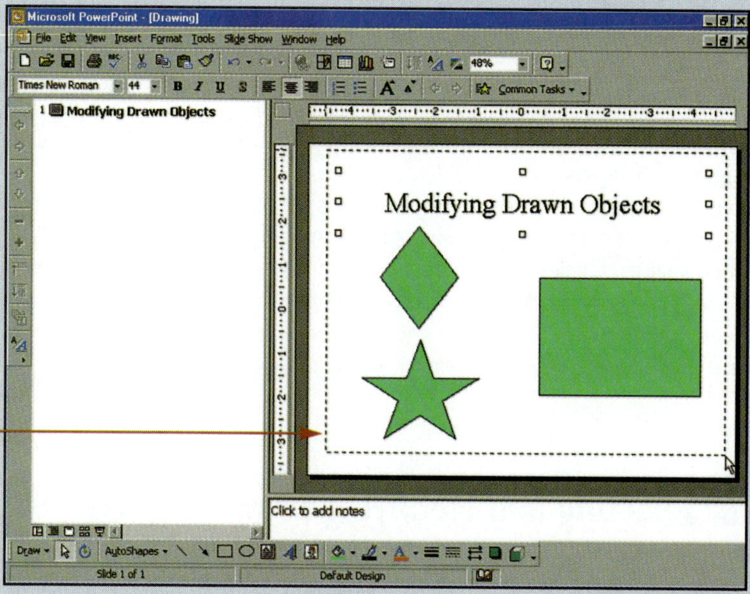

Figure 6.24
You can select multiple objects.

Drag a box around the objects to select them

5 Release the mouse button.

When you release the mouse button, all the objects within the area are selected (indicated by white selection handles).

> ❌ Make sure that you start drawing the selection box above and to the left of all the objects. If you start in the middle of an object, it won't be selected.

6 Click outside the objects.

All objects are deselected.

7 Click the rectangle to select it, and then move the mouse pointer across the top center handle until it becomes a two-sided resizing arrow (see Figure 6.25).

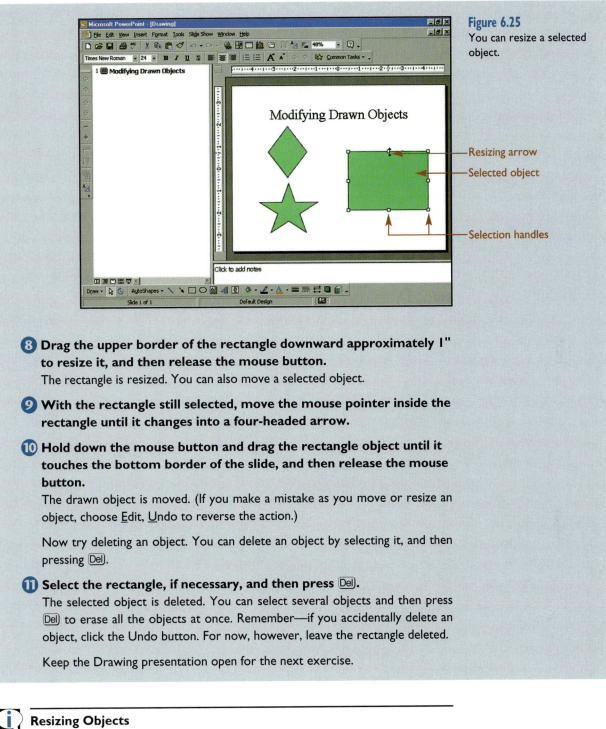

Figure 6.25
You can resize a selected object.

— Resizing arrow
— Selected object

— Selection handles

8 **Drag the upper border of the rectangle downward approximately 1"
to resize it, and then release the mouse button.**
The rectangle is resized. You can also move a selected object.

9 **With the rectangle still selected, move the mouse pointer inside the
rectangle until it changes into a four-headed arrow.**

10 **Hold down the mouse button and drag the rectangle object until it
touches the bottom border of the slide, and then release the mouse
button.**
The drawn object is moved. (If you make a mistake as you move or resize an
object, choose Edit, Undo to reverse the action.)

Now try deleting an object. You can delete an object by selecting it, and then
pressing Del.

11 **Select the rectangle, if necessary, and then press Del.**
The selected object is deleted. You can select several objects and then press
Del to erase all the objects at once. Remember—if you accidentally delete an
object, click the Undo button. For now, however, leave the rectangle deleted.

Keep the Drawing presentation open for the next exercise.

Resizing Objects
If you want to maintain a drawn object's proportions as you resize it, press
Shift while dragging the object's handle.

Once the objects are selected, you can also change the color and lines associated with them.
Changing lines and colors helps to emphasize certain information in your presentation or
create a different "look." Try changing lines and colors now.

To Change a Drawn Object's Lines and Colors

1 In the Drawing presentation that you revised in the previous exercise, click the star object to select it.
As usual, you must first select an object before you can modify it.

2 Click the Fill Color tool's drop-down list arrow.
A color palette displays (see Figure 6.26). You can use this palette to select a coordinating color or a fill effect. Notice that the colors shown on the palette are those of the template's color scheme. Choosing one of these colors ensures that the new color will match the template.

Figure 6.26
You can quickly change fill color or effects.

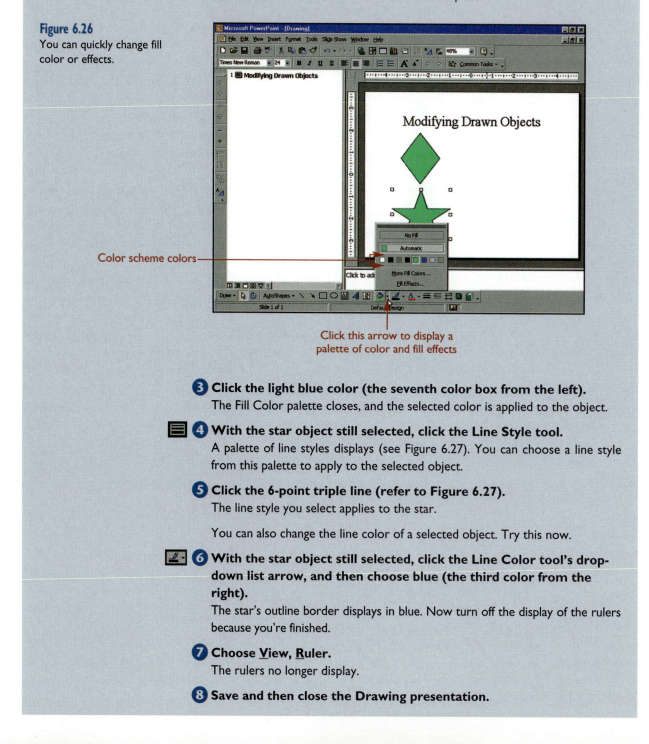

Color scheme colors—

Click this arrow to display a
palette of color and fill effects

3 Click the light blue color (the seventh color box from the left).
The Fill Color palette closes, and the selected color is applied to the object.

4 With the star object still selected, click the Line Style tool.
A palette of line styles displays (see Figure 6.27). You can choose a line style from this palette to apply to the selected object.

5 Click the 6-point triple line (refer to Figure 6.27).
The line style you select applies to the star.

You can also change the line color of a selected object. Try this now.

6 With the star object still selected, click the Line Color tool's drop-down list arrow, and then choose blue (the third color from the right).
The star's outline border displays in blue. Now turn off the display of the rulers because you're finished.

7 Choose View, Ruler.
The rulers no longer display.

8 Save and then close the Drawing presentation.

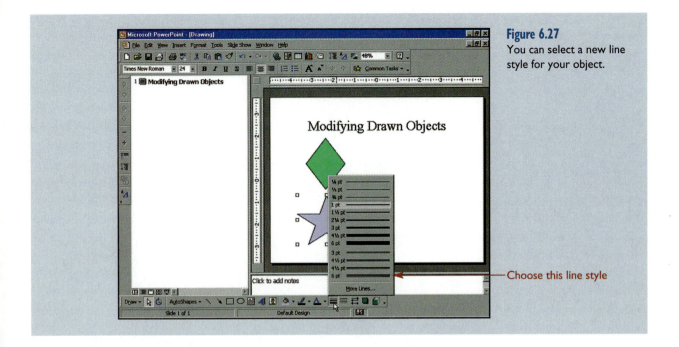

Figure 6.27
You can select a new line style for your object.

Choose this line style

Formatting Multiple Objects
You can apply color and line options to several objects at once by selecting them and then applying the attributes to the entire group.

Lesson 7: Using Clip Art

The PowerPoint program includes a good selection of electronic clip art (electronic pictures) that you can use to enhance your presentation. Including clip art on a slide can help hold an audience's attention or reinforce critical points. PowerPoint includes a variety of pictures for personal and business use. You can also purchase additional clip art if you want more choices, or download clips from the Web.

After clip art is placed on a slide, you can change its location, size, and appearance. Additionally, clip art is actually composed of multiple objects. Because of this, clip art can also be ungrouped into its component parts so that you can work with each part as an individual object. For example, you can recolor parts of a map to highlight data associated with it. Try your hand at using clip art now.

To Use Clip Art

1 **Open PP1-0605 and save it as Financial Services.**
Slide view is a good view to use when you insert clip art because you have more room with which to work.

2 **Click the Slide View button to display the presentation in Slide view.**

3 **Make sure Slide 1 displays, and then click the New Slide button.**

continues ▶

To Use Clip Art (continued)

④ **In the New Slide dialog box, click the Text & Clip Art AutoLayout (the first slide on the third row), and then choose OK.**

A new slide is inserted with a clip art placeholder (see Figure 6.28). You can double-click this placeholder object to display the Clip Gallery and choose a picture.

Figure 6.28
You can use the Clip Art placeholder to access the Clip Gallery.

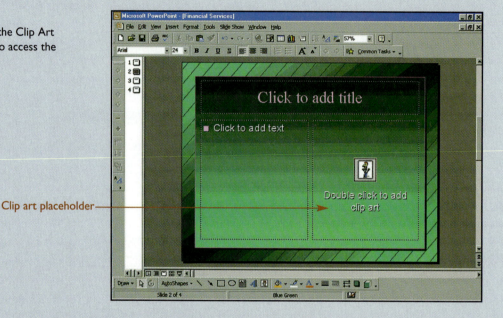

Clip art placeholder

⑤ **Double-click the Clip Art placeholder.**

The Microsoft Clip Gallery dialog box displays with a graphical list of available images (see Figure 6.29). (The Clip Gallery on your computer may list pictures that are different from the one illustrated in this project, depending on what art has been installed.) Once you display the Clip Gallery, you can view all the available clip art or select a specific category to limit the display.

Figure 6.29
You can choose from a wealth of electronic pictures.

Back button

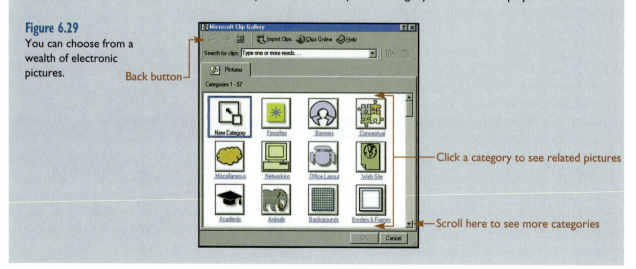

Click a category to see related pictures

Scroll here to see more categories

6 Scroll through the list of categories, if necessary, and then click the Buildings category.

All of the building clips display (see Figure 6.30). You can either insert one of the pictures into your presentation or redisplay all categories by clicking the Back button.

Click the Back button to display the previous screen

Building clips

Figure 6.30
You can choose from a variety of pictures.

7 Click the image indicated in Figure 6.31.

A pop-up menu displays, as shown in Figure 6.31. Each of the items on the menu has a ScreenTip that identifies it when you momentarily rest your mouse pointer over the icon or button.

Selected clip art image

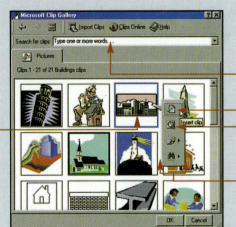

Figure 6.31
You can choose from a variety of clip art images.

Search for clips text box

Insert clip button
Preview clip button

Pop-up menu

8 Click the Insert clip button on the pop-up menu.

The selected image is placed on the slide. The white selection handles indicate that the image can currently be resized, moved, or deleted (as you did in Lesson 6). The Picture toolbar displays so that you can make modifications to the image (see Figure 6.32).

continues ▶

To Use Clip Art   (continued)

X If the Picture toolbar doesn't display on your system, it's probably turned off. To redisplay it, make sure that your clip art object is selected, and then choose <u>V</u>iew, <u>T</u>oolbars, <u>P</u>icture.

Figure 6.32
It's easy to insert clip art on a slide.

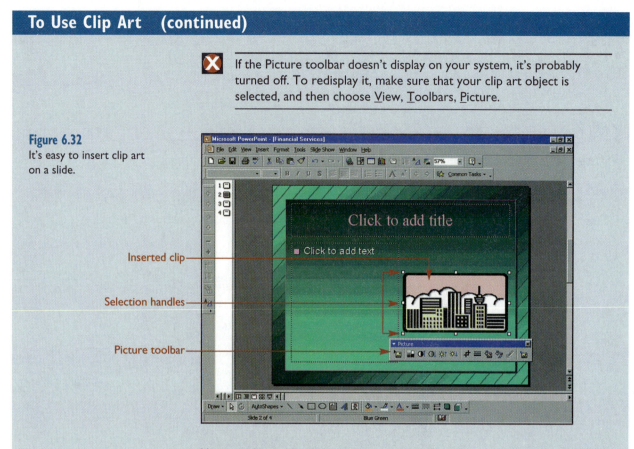

Inserted clip

Selection handles

Picture toolbar

You can also insert clip art on a slide that doesn't have a clip art placeholder by using the Insert Clip Art button. Try this now.

9 **Press** PgUp **to display Slide 1, and then click the Insert Clip Art button on the Drawing toolbar.**
The Insert ClipArt dialog box displays, in which you can choose a picture. This dialog box is similar to the Clip Art Gallery dialog box you used earlier in the lesson.

Earlier in this lesson, you located the clip you wanted by selecting a category. You can also search for the type of clips you want by entering a *keyword* in the Search for clips text box. (A keyword is a topical word that you use to find related clips.)

10 **Type** money **in the Search for clips text box (refer to Figure 6.31), and then press** ↵Enter.
Clips related to the keyword money are displayed.

11 **Click the first clip on the top row, and then choose Insert clip on the pop-up menu.**
The picture is placed on the slide. The Insert ClipArt dialog box remains open so that you can insert additional clips. For now, however, close the dialog box.

12 **Click the Close button in the upper-right corner of the Insert ClipArt dialog box.**
Now you can see the clip on your slide. Notice that the clip isn't the size or location you want.

If you don't like the placement or size of the picture, you can easily move or resize it as you did with drawn objects. Move the object by clicking to select the picture, and then drag it to a new location. Resize the clip art image by dragging the handles.

⑬ Move and resize the picture so that it displays in a blank area of the slide, and then click outside the picture to deselect it.
Your completed slide should look similar to that shown in Figure 6.33.

⊠ Don't be concerned if you had to insert a different clip art image in your presentation from the one shown in Figure 6.32.

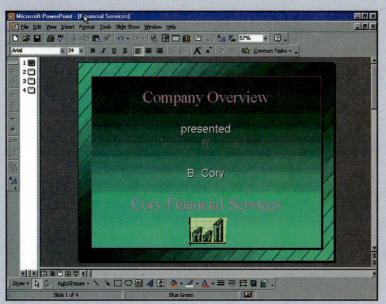

Figure 6.33
You can move and resize a clip art image.

⑭ Save the Financial Services presentation, and then close it.
If you finish your work session, exit PowerPoint and shut down Windows before turning off your computer. Otherwise, complete the exercises at the end of this project.

Summary

In this project, you learned several ways to customize your presentation and change its overall appearance. You learned how to choose a design template when first creating a presentation and how to apply templates to existing presentations. You experimented with various color schemes and slide backgrounds. You changed the slide master so that the same objects display on all presentation slides. You also created and modified drawn objects by using the Drawing toolbar. Finally, you inserted clip art on slides.

To expand on your knowledge, spend a few minutes exploring Help on these topics. Additionally, complete some of the Skill Drill, Challenge, and Discovery Zone exercises.

Checking Concepts and Terms ✓

True/False

For each of the following, circle T or F to indicate whether the statement is true or false.

__T __F **1.** You create drawn objects in your presentation by using the Design toolbar. [L5]

__T __F **2.** Changes to the slide master, such as adding footer text, apply only to the current slide. [L4]

__T __F **3.** The design template is used to draw objects on a slide. [L1]

__T __F **4.** Choosing the template design before building your presentation is usually best because you can't apply another template later. [L1]

__T __F **5.** You can add clip art to a slide, even if it doesn't have a clip art placeholder. [L7]

Multiple Choice

Circle the letter of the correct answer for each of the following.

1. A good reason for changing color schemes is _____. [L2]

 a. to change display contrast when using an LCD projector and overhead projector

 b. to emphasize a particular slide

 c. to keep track of similar, yet slightly different presentations that you created for different audiences

 d. all of the above

2. Design templates _____. [L1]

 a. are the same as a presentation's slide master

 b. are a "blueprint" that PowerPoint uses to determine the overall look of a presentation

 c. can't be changed once selected

 d. none of the above

3. You can select multiple objects and _____. [L6]

 a. apply a color or line style to them simultaneously

 b. apply AutoShapes to them

 c. delete them

 d. a and c

4. You can _____ by using the slide master. [L4]

 a. add Footer Area text

 b. change the font used for a placeholder

 c. add the current date to each slide

 d. all of the above

5. To create a perfect square, _____. [L5]

 a. press ⬆Shift while using the Rectangle tool

 b. press Ctrl while using the Rectangle tool

 c. use the Square tool on the Drawing toolbar

 d. select an existing rectangle, and then choose Format, Square

Screen ID

Identify each of the items shown in Figure 6.34.

Figure 6.34

A. Drawing toolbar

B. Selection handles

C. Select Objects tool

D. Insert Clip Art tool

E. Fill Color tool

F. Clip art placeholder

G. Rectangle tool

H. Line Color tool

I. Oval tool

J. Resizing arrow

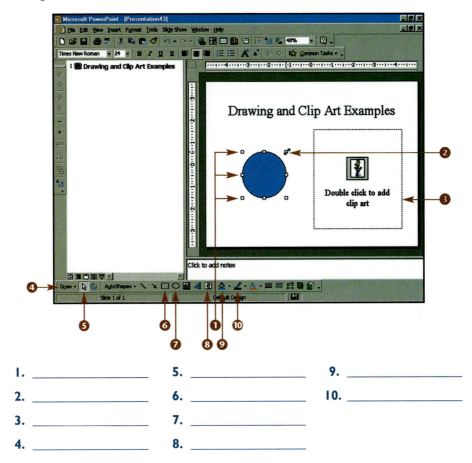

I. _____	5. _____	9. _____
2. _____	6. _____	10. _____
3. _____	7. _____	
4. _____	8. _____	

Discussion Questions

1. What are the differences between the following: slide master, template, slide background, color schemes? In what ways are they similar? [L1–4]

2. What are some items that you can change on a slide master? Give examples of when you might want to change each item. [L4]

3. Which PowerPoint feature would you use for each of the following situations? Why? [L1–2, 4–5]

- You want to display your company's logo on each presentation slide.

- You want to change the overall design and "look" of your presentation.

- You want to use the same design template for your presentation, but need more contrast for an onscreen display.

- You want to create a logo from scratch for an organization.

Skill Drill

Skill Drill exercises reinforce project skills. Each skill reinforced is the same, or nearly the same, as a skill presented in the project. Detailed instructions are provided in a step-by-step format.

? 1. Learning About Color Schemes and Templates

As a middle manager for a company, you frequently give presentations. To learn more about working with color schemes and templates, you use Help. [L1–2]

1. In PowerPoint, choose Help, Microsoft PowerPoint Help. If necessary, click the Show button to split the Help window into two panes.

2. Click the Contents tab, and then double-click Creating the Look of Your Presentation to display a list of subtopics. Double-click the Using Templates icon.

3. Click each of the Using Templates subtopics listed. Take notes on what you learn.

4. Double-click the Working with Color Schemes icon (within the Creating the Look of Your Presentation topic) to display a list of subtopics. Click each of the subtopics listed.

5. With the Working with Color Schemes icon still selected, click the Print button at the top of the Help window. Choose the Print the selected heading and all subtopics option button, and then click OK.

6. Close the Help window. Using your notes and the printed pages as guides, try each of the commands related to working with slide backgrounds and color schemes.

7. Share what you learn with at least one other person. Alternatively, develop a table in Word that outlines ways to use slide backgrounds and color schemes. Keep PowerPoint open if you plan to complete additional exercises.

2. Using Templates, Slide Masters, and Color Schemes to Revise a Presentation

Your boss asked you to revise a presentation that she created. Furthermore, she wants you to add some elements to spiff it up. To do this, you decide to apply a different design template and color scheme. You also add clip art and text to the slide master. [L1, 2–4]

1. Open PP1-0605 and save it as Company Overview. Display Slide 1 of the presentation in Normal view.

2. Choose Format, Apply Design Template to view the Apply Design Template dialog box. See how the presentation looks by clicking the following templates to preview them:

   - Bamboo
   - Blueprint
   - Dad's Tie
   - Expedition
   - Gesture
   - Marble
   - Nature
   - Network Blitz

3. Click the Ribbons template, and then choose Apply.

4. Choose Format, Slide Color Scheme to display the Color Scheme dialog box. Click the first color scheme on the second row (dark blue), and then choose Apply to All.

5. Display the slide master by pressing ◆Shift while clicking the Slide View button. Enter Report developed by B. Cory in the <footer> field.

6. With the slide master still displayed, click the Insert Clip Art button on the Drawing toolbar. In the Insert ClipArt dialog box, click Business. When the Business clips display, click the second clip art image on the second row, and then choose Insert clip.

7. Close the Insert ClipArt dialog box. Resize the clip art image to approximately one-quarter of its original size, and then move it to the upper-left corner of the slide. Click the Close button on the Master toolbar.

8. View your presentation as a slide show to confirm that the changes you made to the slide master display on each slide.

9. Save and then close the presentation. Keep PowerPoint open if you plan to complete additional exercises.

3. Working with Drawn Objects

As the owner of a small company, you develop your own publicity materials. You decide to practice by using PowerPoint's drawing tools, so that you can easily create logos, flyers, and other publicity items. [L5–6]

1. In PowerPoint, click the New button to create a new presentation. In the New Slide dialog box, choose the Blank AutoLayout, and then click OK.

2. Click the Slide View button to display the presentation in Slide view. Click the Rectangle tool on the Drawing toolbar, and then drag to draw a rectangle on your slide. Click the Rectangle tool a second time and press (Shift) as you draw to create a perfect square.

3. With the square selected, click the Fill Color button's drop-down list arrow. Choose the blue color on the palette. Click the Line Style button, and then choose 6 pt from the palette.

4. Double-click the Oval tool, and then drag to draw an ellipse. Press (Shift) while dragging to draw a perfect circle. Click the Oval tool again to turn it off.

5. Select the circle, and then click the Fill Color button's drop-down list arrow. Choose the More Fill Colors option. In the Colors dialog box, click a color of your choice, and then choose OK.

6. With the circle still selected, click the Line Style button, and then choose 4 1/2 pt from the palette.

7. Select the oval, and then press (Del).

8. Resize the rectangle so that it is approximately half the original size.

9. Close your presentation without saving it. Keep PowerPoint open if you plan to complete additional exercises.

4. Selecting and Modifying Drawn Objects

Your boss told you that he wants you to use PowerPoint to develop flowcharts and other diagrams for a training manual. To prepare for the project, you decide to practice selecting and modifying drawn objects. You also experiment with the Shadow and 3-D effects. [L6]

1. Open PP1-0606 and save it as Working with Objects.

2. Practice selecting (and deselecting) objects by performing the following actions:

   - Press (Shift), and then click each of the objects on the slide. Click outside the objects to deselect them.

   - Click the Select Objects tool, if necessary, and then drag to draw a box around all objects.

   - Press (Shift), click the Rectangle to deselect it, and then release the mouse button.

   - Press (Ctrl)+(A) to select all objects on the slide. Click outside the objects to deselect them.

3. Click the Rectangle to select it. Click the Fill Color button's drop-down list arrow and choose Fill Effects. On the Gradient page, choose From center, and then click OK.

4. Click the diamond to select it. Click the Shadow button on the Drawing toolbar to display a palette. Choose the fourth shadow effect on the first row (Shadow Style 4).

5. Click the star to select it. Click the 3-D button on the Drawing toolbar to display the 3-D palette. Choose the first 3-D style on the first row (3-D Style 1).

6. Print a copy of your presentation. Save the Working with Objects presentation, and then close it. Keep PowerPoint open if you plan to complete additional exercises.

5. Using Clip Art and Text Boxes

Your company gives a certificate to employees who successfully complete a computer course. To make the certificate, you decide to insert clip art and a text box on a PowerPoint slide. [L7]

1. In PowerPoint, click the New button to create a new presentation. In the New Slide dialog box, choose the Blank AutoLayout, and then click OK.

2. Click the Slide View button to display the presentation in Slide view.

3. Click the Insert Clip Art button on the Drawing toolbar.

4. Click the Networking category (if you can't locate this category, use another one). Click the second clip art image on the first row (a computer), and then choose Insert clip. Close the Insert ClipArt dialog box.

5. Resize the clip art image so that it takes up most of the slide.

6. On the Drawing toolbar, click the Text Box tool, and then click and drag a rectangle-shaped box beneath the clip art image. Enter `Congratulations!` in the box.

7. Print a copy of your slide. Close the presentation without saving it. Keep PowerPoint open if you plan to complete additional exercises.

6. Working with Design Templates

As president of the University Biking Club, you're preparing for an upcoming meeting. To choose the best design template for your presentation, you preview several before choosing one. You also change the color scheme. [L1–2]

1. Open `PP1-0607` and save it as `Biking Club Meeting`. Display Slide 1 of the presentation in Normal view.

2. Choose F_ormat, Apply _Design Template to view the Apply Design Template dialog box. See how the presentation looks by clicking the following templates to preview them:

   ■ `Blends`

   ■ `Blue Diagonal`

   ■ `Cactus`

   ■ `Checkers`

   ■ `Construction`

   ■ `Global`

   ■ `High Voltage`

   ■ `Japanese Waves`

   ■ `Mountain`

   ■ `Nature`

3. Click the `Pulse` template, and then choose Apply.

4. Choose F_ormat, Slide _Color Scheme to display the Color Scheme dialog box. Click the first color scheme on the first row (light blue), and then choose Apply _to All.

5. Right-click on your slide, and then choose Slide _Color Scheme to redisplay the Color Scheme dialog box. Choose the first color scheme on the second row (maroon), and then choose _Apply.

6. View your presentation as a slide show to see your changes.

7. Save your presentation, and then close it. Keep PowerPoint open if you plan to complete additional exercises.

Challenge 💡

Challenge exercises expand on, or are somewhat related to, skills presented in the lessons. Each exercise provides a brief narrative introduction, followed by instructions in a numbered-step format that are not as detailed as those in the Skill Drill section.

[?] 1. Finding Out About Notes and Slide Masters

Although you know the basics of working with PowerPoint's slide masters, you want to learn more and to make modifications to your presentation's notes masters. To find out how to do so, you use Help. [L4]

1. In PowerPoint, choose _Help, Microsoft PowerPoint _Help. Click the Show button, if necessary, to split the Help window into two panes.

2. Click the Index tab to display the Index page. Enter notes in the Type keywords text box so that notes_master appears, and then click Search.

3. View the items shown on the Choose a Topic list that pertain to the Notes Master and Slide Master.

4. Click the Contents tab to display the Contents page. Double-click the Slide Master icon to display subtopics. Print the topics or take complete notes.

5. Practice creating notes masters and revising slide masters by using the Help information. Keep PowerPoint open if you plan to complete additional exercises.

2. Working with a Slide Master

To make elements appear more uniform on your biking club presentation, you decide to modify the slide master. [L4]

1. Open PP1-0608 and save it as Upcoming Meeting.

2. Display the slide master. Make the title placeholder text italic, 40-point, Comic Sans font. Also make the text red.

3. Add the current date in the Date Area. Indicate that you want the date to be updated automatically.

4. In the <footer> field, add the text May Meeting, and then press ⏎Enter. Add the slide number in the Footer Area below the May Meeting text.

5. Close the slide master to view your changes.

6. Display your presentation in Normal view, and then view the presentation as a slide show to see the changes to each slide.

7. Save the Upcoming Meeting presentation, and then close it. Keep PowerPoint open if you plan to complete additional exercises.

3. Working with Clip Art and WordArt

You work for the Physical Education Department at your college during the summer. In preparation for a sports camp, you develop a flyer in PowerPoint. To make the flyer eye-catching, you use clip art and WordArt. [L7]

1. Create a new blank presentation. Choose the Blank AutoLayout for your slide, and then display the presentation in Slide view.

2. Using Help, research how to use WordArt.

3. On the Drawing toolbar, click the Insert WordArt button to display the WordArt Gallery. Click the fourth WordArt Style on the third row, and then choose OK.

4. In the Edit WordArt Text dialog box, type Sports Camp! and click OK. Move and resize the WordArt object so that it uses the upper one-third of the slide.

5. With the WordArt object still selected, click the 3-D button on the Drawing toolbar. Apply different 3-D effects to the WordArt object to see how they appear. When you finish experimenting, choose the first 3-D style on the fourth row (3-D Style 13). Reposition the WordArt object so that it remains on the slide, if necessary. Click outside the WordArt object to deselect it.

6. Insert a clip art image on your slide. Choose a clip from the `Sports & Leisure` category. Resize and move the clip, as necessary, so that it displays in the lower half of the slide.

7. Save the presentation as `Sports Camp`. Print a copy of the presentation, and then close it. Keep PowerPoint open if you plan to complete additional exercises.

4. Using Clip Art and Changing the Slide Background

You work in the marketing division for a retail computer store. To prepare for a sale, you develop a flyer. [L3, 7]

1. Open `PP1-0609` and save it as `Big Sale`.

2. Use the clip art placeholder to add an image to your slide. (*Hint:* Search for all clips using the keyword `computer`.)

3. Change the background for the slide by using a fill effect. Choose the Rainbow preset color and the From corner Shading style.

4. Print a copy of your slide (preferably on a color printer). Save the presentation, and then close it. Keep PowerPoint open if you plan to complete additional exercises.

5. Using WordArt and Clip Art

You're helping to put on a local horse show. To publicize the event, you create a flyer in PowerPoint. [L7]

1. Open `PP1-0610` and save it as `Horse Show`.

2. Use WordArt to create an object with the text `Horse Show`. Add shadow or 3-D effects to improve the object's appearance, or modify existing effects. Resize and move the object so that it displays in the available space in the upper one-third of the slide.

3. Insert a clip art image of a horse in the lower one-third of the slide.

4. Change the background for the slide to one of the textures.

5. Print a copy of your presentation (preferably on a color printer). Save the presentation, and then close it. Keep PowerPoint open if you plan to complete additional exercises.

6. Revising the Slide Master

You're developing a talk for your company's annual meeting. You modify the slide master so that the elements (such as your company's logo) appear on all slides. [L4]

1. Open `PP1-0611` and save it as `Tech Head Trends`.

2. Move to Slide 2, and then display the slide master. Make the following revisions to the master:

- Change the first-level bullet style to large open squares.
- Format the text in the title placeholder as italic.

- Format the text for the bulleted points without italic.
- Draw a red filled circle in the upper-right corner of the slide master with the initials THT in the middle of the circle. (*Hint*: Use your Oval drawing tools. If necessary, use Help to find out how to add text to drawn objects.)

3. Close the slide master and view your changes. Make any necessary revisions.

4. Print, save, and close your Tech Head Trends presentation. Keep PowerPoint open if you plan to complete additional exercises.

Discovery Zone

Discovery Zone exercises require advanced knowledge of topics presented in Essentials lessons, application of skills from multiple lessons, or self-directed learning of new skills.

1. Finding Out More About Drawing Tools

You work for the marketing department at your company. You develop publicity materials and need to know more about working with drawing tools. To do so, you use Help.]

Using the Help system, find out the following:

- How can you add text to a drawn object?
- How do you use the 3-D Settings and Shadow Settings toolbars?
- What categories does the AutoShapes menu include?
- How can you "tear off" palettes for the AutoShapes?
- What commands are on the Draw menu? How are they used?
- How can you create and modify an arrow?
- How can you work with WordArt?
- How can you format a drawn object with a pattern?

Practice what you learn by developing several flyers, and then guide another user through the process of working with these tools.

Leave PowerPoint open if you plan to complete additional exercises. [L5–6]

2. Finding Out How to Work with Clips

You work for the Human Resources Department and develop several flyers each month. Because people tend to pay more attention to the flyers if they include clip art, you want to find out more about finding and using clips, including clip art, motion clips, and sound clips.

Using the Help system, find out the following:

- How can you download clips from the Web?
- How can you preview a clip before inserting it in your presentation?
- How can you add a clip to another category?
- How can you add a clip to your Favorites folder?
- What are ways to search for a clip?
- How can you insert a Sound or Motion Clip in your presentation?

- What type of file formats can you use in PowerPoint?
- How can you add your own pictures to the Clip Gallery?
- How can you insert a sound file?
- How can you recolor a clip?

Practice what you learn by developing several flyers. Guide another user through the process of working with these tools.

Leave PowerPoint open if you plan to complete additional exercises. [L7]

3. Using WordArt and Clip Art

Using what you know about slide backgrounds, WordArt, and the Clip Gallery, create a flyer similar to that shown in Figure 6.35. Print a copy of the slide. Save the presentation as `This Year's Company Picnic`, and then close it. [L7]

Figure 6.35
Use your knowledge of WordArt and clip art to create a flyer similar to this one.

4. Using Drawing Tools and Clip Art

You need to provide directions to a biking club activity. You decide to create a flyer in PowerPoint, using the program's drawing tools and clip art.

Open `PP1-0612` and save it as `Ride and Picnic`. Using PowerPoint's drawing tools, clip art, and Figure 6.36 as a guide, create a flyer for the upcoming club activity. (*Hints*: Use the Text Box tool to create the text. Use Copy and Paste to copy the clip art image.) Use a texture for the slide's background. Print the presentation as a slide. Save the Ride and Picnic presentation, and then close it and exit PowerPoint. [L5–7]

Figure 6.36
Use drawing tools and clip art to develop this flyer.

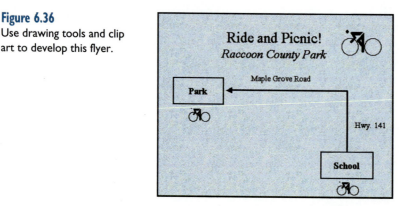

Project 7

Automating Electronic Slide Shows

Objectives

In this project, you learn how to

➤ Use Slide Transitions

➤ Add Text Animation

➤ Time the Slide Show Presentation

➤ Use the Annotation Pen

➤ Use the Meeting Minder

Key terms introduced in this project include

■ action items
■ animate
■ annotate
■ annotation pen
■ multimedia
■ slide transitions

Why Would I Do This?

When you're giving a presentation, you want to make the strongest possible impression. Although your content should be center stage, PowerPoint includes a number of techniques you can use to emphasize the content *and* command your audience's attention at the same time. In this project, you learn a variety of ways to automate your presentation. Each of the techniques can help focus your audience's attention on your ideas.

Visual Summary

One way to keep people's attention is to change the way PowerPoint displays the next slide—the program's **slide transitions**. Another way to create anticipation (and control the flow of information) is to **animate** the text so that your bullet points display one at a time. When you add transitions to your presentation, you can view the slide transition and text animation icons in Slide Sorter view—similar to those shown in Figure 7.1.

Figure 7.1
You can add slide transitions and text-animation effects.

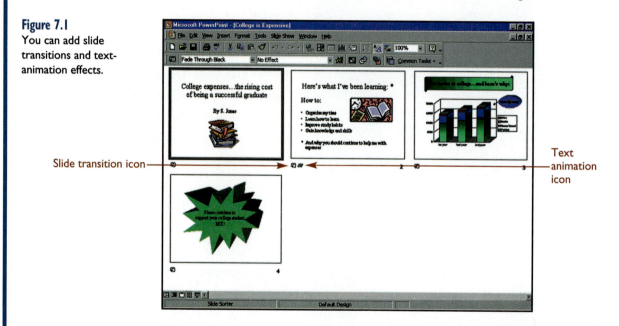

Slide transition icon ———

Text animation icon

You can also use PowerPoint's electronic **annotation pen** to emphasize information—such as the effect you see in Figure 7.2.

Finally, to help you keep track of ideas that pop up during a presentation, you can use the Meeting Minder. You use this feature to develop meeting minutes or **action items** onscreen. For example, when you enter information in the Meeting Minder dialog box, PowerPoint automatically creates a set of action items as a new presentation slide. As a finishing touch for your presentation, you can even print this slide and hand it out to participants as they leave (see Figure 7.3).

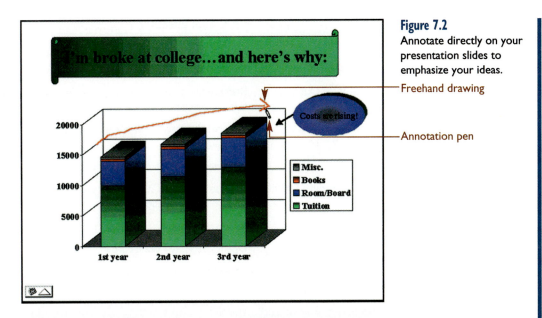

Figure 7.2
Annotate directly on your presentation slides to emphasize your ideas.

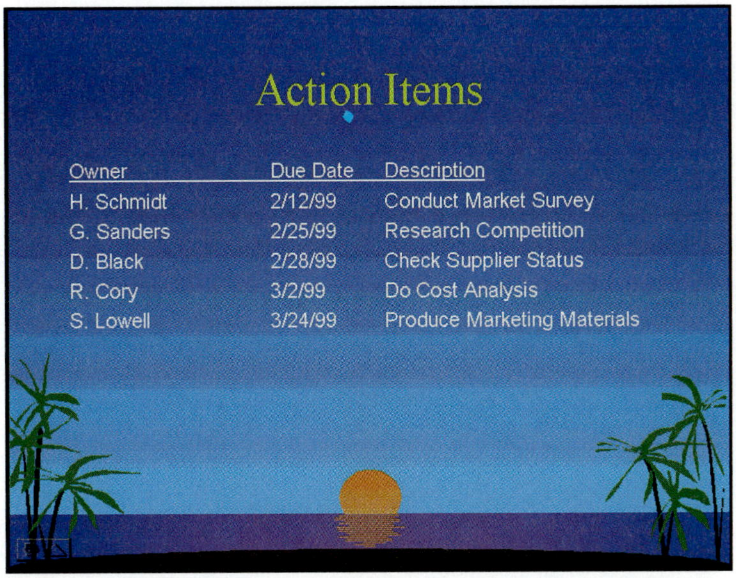

— Freehand drawing

— Annotation pen

Figure 7.3
Create action items "on-the-fly" during a meeting.

To make your presentations more compelling, attention-getting, and professional, take a look at these techniques now.

Lesson 1: Using Slide Transitions

In Project 2, you learned how to move through a presentation in Slide Show view. By now, you have probably run some other slide shows as well. As you ran the slide shows, you probably noticed that each new slide instantly replaced the previous one.

You can change the way that one slide moves to the next by using a slide transition. A slide transition is a visual effect that changes how one slide replaces another. Using PowerPoint's slide transitions helps you make more of an impact during an onscreen presentation. For example, you can set up a slide to fade, wipe, or dissolve into another. Table 7.1 describes some popular transition effects.

Table 7.1 Popular Transitional Effects

Transition Effect	Description
Blinds	Opens the screen in wide, even strips horizontally or vertically
Box In or Out	Redraws the screen from the center outward or from the outside to the center, using a box shape
Checkerboard	Changes the screen with a checkerboard pattern, either across or down
Cover	Redraws the screen as the new slide covers up the previous one
Fade Through Black	Fades away the old slide, shows black momentarily, and then fades in the new slide
Split	Redraws the screen by splitting it in different directions
Uncover	Opens the screen like a curtain, in a variety of directions
Wipe	Sweeps the screen in a choice of directions

The easiest way to add a transition is to use the Slide Transition Effects drop-down list, which is available on the Slide Sorter toolbar. Try adding some transition effects now.

To Use Slide Transitions

1 **Start PowerPoint, if necessary. Open** PP1-0701 **and save it as** Quality Children's Clothing.

2 **Click the Slide Sorter View button to display the presentation in Slide Sorter view.**
Notice that the Slide Sorter toolbar automatically displays whenever Slide Sorter view is used (see Figure 7.4). You can use the Slide Sorter toolbar to add or change transition effects.

Figure 7.4
You can use the Slide Sorter toolbar to add slide transitions.

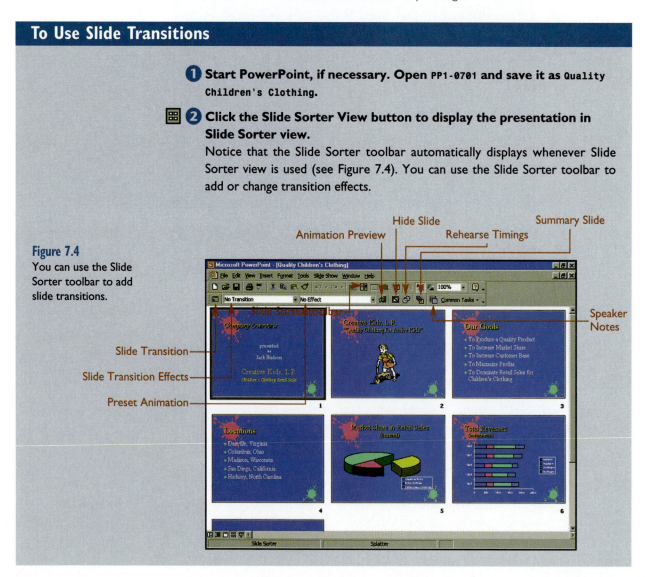

3 **With the first slide selected, click the Slide Transition Effects drop-down arrow.**

A list of transition effects displays, as shown in Figure 7.5. You can choose an effect, and then preview it in Slide Sorter view.

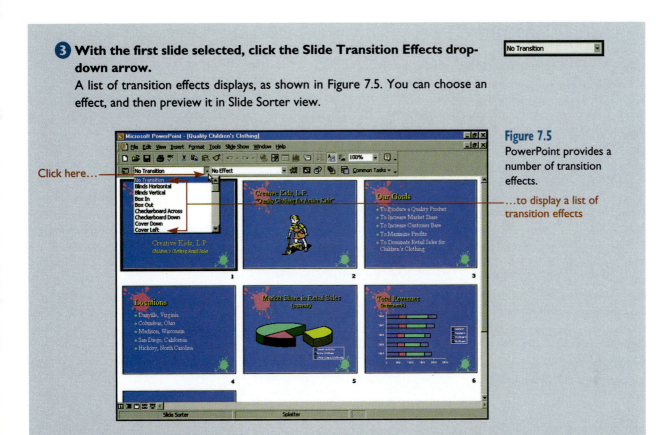

Figure 7.5
PowerPoint provides a number of transition effects.

...to display a list of transition effects

Click here...

4 **Choose Blinds Horizontal from the list.**

The transition effect is added for the selected slide and a slide transition icon is shown below the slide (see Figure 7.6). You can click this icon to preview the effect, which is handy because you don't have to run a slide show just to see how the transitions will look. Try using this feature now.

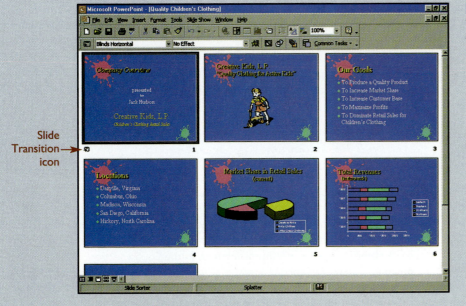

Figure 7.6
You can preview the transition effect quickly in Slide Sorter view.

Slide Transition icon

continues ▶

To Use Slide Transitions   (continued)

5 Click the Slide Transition icon for Slide 1.
Slide 1 displays a preview of the transition effect.

By now, you're probably convinced that it's helpful to add transitions to your slides judiciously. You'd like a more efficient method to do so than to add one transition at a time, however. Fortunately, you can select several slides and add the same transition to them simultaneously. Using this technique, try changing the transition effect for multiple slides at once.

6 Click Slide 2, press ⇧Shift, and click Slides 3 and 4.
A thick black line displays around each slide, indicating that they are selected.

7 Click the Slide Transition Effects drop-down list arrow, and then choose Checkerboard Across.
The transition effect is applied to the selected slides. Remember that you can tell whether a slide has a transition effect added because a slide icon displays beneath the slide.

Now see how your transitions look by running the presentation as a slide show.

8 Select Slide 1, and then choose View, Slide Show.

9 Click the left mouse button several times to advance completely through the slide show.
The transitions you specified are used as you move through the slides. When you finish the slide show, the presentation again displays in Slide Sorter view.

After viewing your transitions, you might decide that you want to remove one of them. (After all, too many transitions might become distracting to your audience!) You're in luck, because it's easy to remove a slide transition. Just select the slide, and then choose No Transition from the Slide Transition Effects drop-down arrow list.

10 Select Slide 3, click the Slide Transition Effects drop-down arrow list, and choose No Transition.
The transition is removed from the selected slide and the Slide Transition icon no longer displays. (If you wish, rerun the slide show to view this change before continuing with the tutorial.)

11 Save the presentation, but keep it open for the next exercise, in which you add animations to your bulleted text.

Adding Sounds to Transitions
If you have a sound card and speaker, you can spice up your presentation even more by adding sound during the transition. Choose Slide Show, Slide Transition to display the Slide Transition dialog box. In the Sound section, click the drop-down list arrow and choose a sound. Choose Apply to associate the sound with the selected slide or Apply to All to add it to all slides. When you run the slide show, the sound will play during the transition.

Lesson 2: Adding Text Animation

Another way to grab an audience's attention is to animate your text during a slide show so you can focus on important points, control the flow of information, or simply add interest to your presentation. For example, you can have your bullet points display one by one (a process that's generally referred to as *building* or *animating*) to prevent your audience from losing focus by reading ahead on a slide. Text animation is a feature that operates independently from the slide transitions feature that you learned about in Lesson 1. In other words, you can add a slide transition to a slide, text animation, or both.

Try adding animation to bulleted text on a slide now.

To Add Text Animation

1 **Make sure that the Quality Children's Clothing presentation is open in Slide Sorter view, and then select Slide 3, if necessary.**

Because Slide 3 has bullet points, you can set up the slide so that PowerPoint builds them separately.

2 **From the Slide Sorter toolbar, click the Preset Animation drop-down arrow.**

A list of available methods for building your bulleted list displays (see Figure 7.7). When you select one of these methods, PowerPoint automatically builds the text one point at a time.

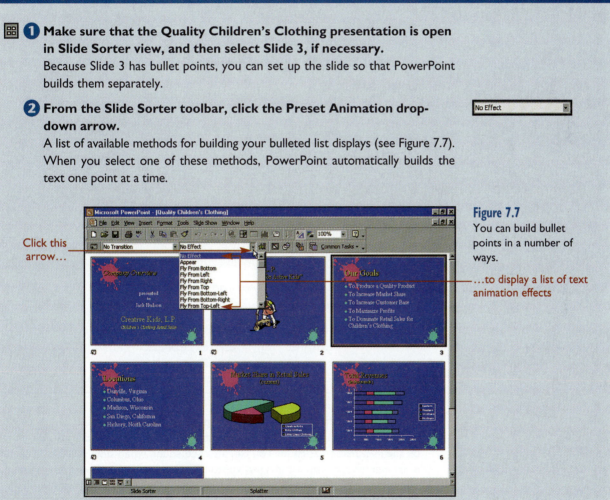

Click this arrow...

...to display a list of text animation effects

Figure 7.7
You can build bullet points in a number of ways.

3 **Select Fly From Bottom-Left.**

PowerPoint shows the way the animation looks on the slide, which helps you decide whether you want to use the animation or not. Additionally, a special Text Animation icon displays at the bottom of the slide, as shown in Figure 7.8, indicating that Slide 3 is a build slide. (If the animation occurred too quickly, you can replay it by clicking the Text Animation icon.)

continues ▶

To Add Text Animation (continued)

Figure 7.8
You can tell which slides have text animation by the icon.

Text Animation icon

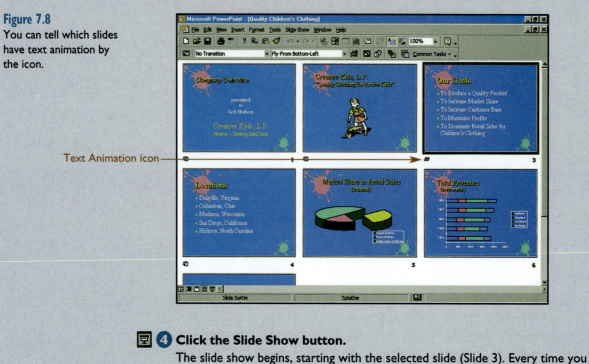

 4 Click the Slide Show button.
The slide show begins, starting with the selected slide (Slide 3). Every time you click the left mouse button (or press ↵Enter), PowerPoint displays a bullet point.

5 Click the left mouse button several times.
PowerPoint builds the slide, one bullet point at a time. When all of the slide text finishes displaying, the next mouse click moves to the next slide.

6 Press Esc to end the slide show and redisplay the presentation in Slide Sorter view.

7 Save the presentation and keep it open for the next lesson, in which you learn to customize your animation effects.

ⓘ **More Slide-Animation Features**
You can specify that the previous bullet point is dimmed (or even completely hidden) when you display each new point. This focuses your audience's attention on the information at hand. You can also add sound when slide objects (such as chart elements or clip art images) appear. To find out more about using animation on your slides, look at the `Animation` topic in the Help window.

Lesson 3: Timing the Slide Show Presentation

Because no one has an unlimited amount of time to give to a presentation, timing the slide show for the greatest impact is important. That's why PowerPoint includes a feature that you can use to find out how long you're spending on each slide, as well as to track the presentation's overall length.

You can set up your slide show to display a new slide automatically after a certain number of seconds, or change slides only when the left mouse button is clicked. If you plan to use the slide show as a self-running presentation (such as at a trade show), you may opt for the former method. If you are presenting the show to a live audience, you'll definitely want control by using manual advance. Keep in mind that you don't want to spend so long on a slide that your audience loses attention, however. The general rule when using manual advancement is to allow a maximum of two or three minutes per slide.

Even if you use manual advance, you can rehearse your presentation by using the slide timings. This is a good way of measuring the overall length of the presentation. Here's how: Click the Rehearse Timings button to start your presentation as a slide show. Talk through your presentation as if you're presenting it to a live audience. When you finish, you'll have a good idea of the overall length of the presentation, as well as the time spent on each individual slide.

In contrast, automatic advancement is great if you have an onscreen show that you want to run continually (at a trade show exhibit, for example). When using automatic advancement, you need to spend only as much time on a slide as the average person needs to read it. If the slide stays onscreen too long, people lose interest.

Keeping these benefits in mind, try rehearsing your timings now.

To Time the Slide Show Presentation

1 **Display the Quality Children's Clothing presentation in Slide Sorter view, and then select Slide 1.**

2 **On the Slide Sorter toolbar, click the Rehearse Timings button.**
The slide show begins—but with a difference. A Rehearsal dialog box displays and keeps track of how many seconds you show each slide. This dialog box also records the overall length of the presentation (see Figure 7.9).

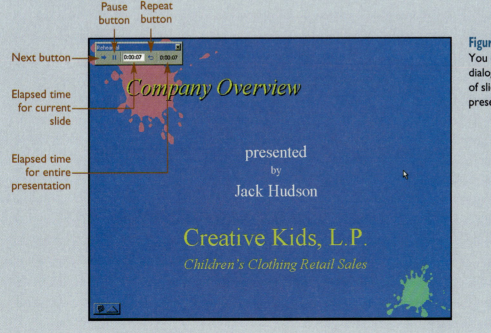

Figure 7.9
You can use the Rehearsal dialog box to keep track of slide and overall presentation length.

continues ▶

To Time the Slide Show Presentation (continued)

3 **After five seconds, click the left mouse button to advance to Slide 2.**

4 **In Slides 2–6, set timings of your choice (pause from 3–10 seconds per slide or bullet point before clicking the mouse button to proceed).**
When you finish going through the entire show, PowerPoint displays a message box, shown in Figure 7.10, so you can decide if you want to keep the timings as part of your presentation.

Figure 7.10
PowerPoint confirms that you want to save the new timings.

5 **Choose Yes.**
The slides display in Slide Sorter view, including the number of seconds after which each slide will advance (see Figure 7.11).

Figure 7.11
You can time your presentation, and then view the number of seconds each slide displays.

Slide timings

Now, view your electronic slide show with the new timings.

6 **Select Slide 1, and then click the Slide Show button to start the slide show.**
The show advances through the slides using the timings you specified.

7 **When the slide show finishes and the black screen displays, click to exit the slide show.**
The presentation displays in Slide Sorter view.

X By default, PowerPoint 2000 ends each slide show with a black slide so that the audience redirects their attention to you. It's possible that this option may have been turned off for your system, however. If you like the effect, here's how to turn it back on: Choose <u>T</u>ools, <u>O</u>ptions, and then click the View tab. Check the <u>E</u>nd with a black slide box before clicking OK to close the Options dialog box.

 8 Save the Quality Children's Clothing presentation, and then close it.
Keep PowerPoint open for the next lesson, in which you learn efficient methods of moving among slide show slides.

Setting Up Self-Running Presentations
If you want to use your slide show as a self-running presentation (such as at a trade show), set your slide timings just as you learned in this lesson. Then choose Sli<u>d</u>e Show, <u>S</u>et Up Show to display the Set Up Show dialog box. Choose <u>L</u>oop continually until 'Esc'. Click OK when you finish.

For even more control over a self-running presentation, you can choose Browsed at a <u>k</u>iosk (full screen) in the Set Up Show dialog box. This runs the slide show full-screen continuously and restarts the show after five minutes of inactivity. The audience can advance slides manually, but can't make changes to the presentation.

Finally, you can add *multimedia* effects, such as music, sound, and videos to your presentation. To find out how to enhance your presentation with these effects, look at the `Multimedia` topic on Help's <u>I</u>ndex page.

Lesson 4: Using the Annotation Pen

Have you ever wished that you could write or draw on a slide during a slide show? Perhaps you want to draw attention to specific information or recapture your audience's attention. Fortunately, PowerPoint provides an annotation pen, which is an electronic pen you control with the mouse to *annotate* the slide. Annotating is writing or drawing directly on the slide, and is an effective method of emphasizing information.

The comments you write are not permanent—when you display another slide, they're automatically erased. Alternatively, you can erase the notations but continue to display the slide.

For even more impact, you can change annotation pen colors. For example, you might use white for most of the points that you're trying to make, and then switch to orange for added emphasis. Try using the pen in a presentation now.

To Use the Annotation Pen

1 **Open** PP1-0702 **and save it as** Recruiting Technical Personnel.

2 **Display Slide 3, and then click the Slide Show button.**
The slide show begins. In order to use the pen, you must activate it. You do this by choosing P**e**n from the slide show shortcut menu.

3 **Right-click to display the shortcut menu, then choose P**o**inter Options, **P**en.**
The pointer changes to an electronic annotation pen. You can use this pen to draw by holding down the left mouse button and dragging.

4 **Drag to draw an arrow emphasizing the salary progression from Systems Support to Systems Analyst (refer to Figure 7.12).**

Figure 7.12
You can use the annotation pen to emphasize your points.

Use the annotation pen...

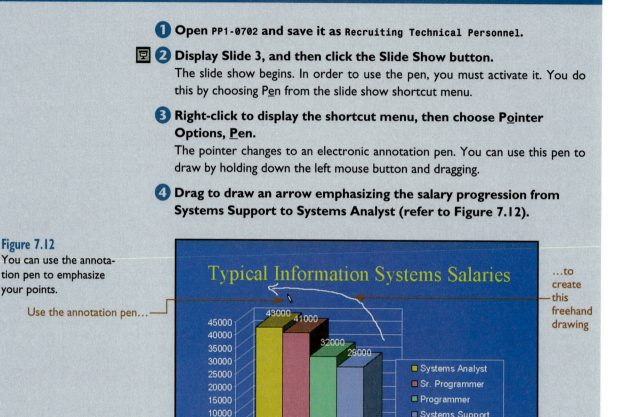

...to create this freehand drawing

The annotation is automatically erased whenever you move to another slide. If you want to continue to display the current slide (but erase the drawing), press E. Try this now.

5 **Press** E.
The drawing is erased. Notice that your pen is still active so that you can write other comments. Or you can activate the arrow, which automatically turns off the pen. The easiest way to turn off the pen is to press Esc.

6 **Press** Esc.
The arrow mouse pointer displays and the electronic pen is turned off.

Now, try an alternative method of turning on the pen—by pressing Ctrl+P. This method is not only quicker, but also more popular because the audience doesn't see the shortcut menu. Try activating the pen by using this technique.

7 **Press** Ctrl+P.
The electronic pen is activated. Now try changing the pen color.

8 **Right-click to display the shortcut menu, and then choose Pointer Options, Pen Color.**

A submenu displays with a list of available pen colors (see Figure 7.13).

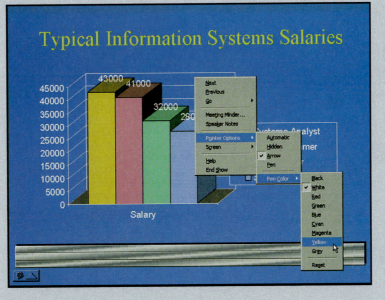

Figure 7.13
You can choose from a variety of pen colors.

9 **Choose Yellow, and then draw freehand on your slide to see the new pen color.**

The drawing displays, using the color you indicated.

Earlier in this lesson, you saw how to use the keyboard shortcut Ctrl+P to display the pen. Now try using a keyboard shortcut to switch back to the arrow.

10 **Press Ctrl+A.**

The pen icon changes to an arrow mouse pointer.

11 **Close your Recruiting Technical Personnel presentation without saving the changes.**

Keep PowerPoint open for the next lesson, in which you use the Meeting Minder.

Advancing Your Slide Show

When the annotation pen is active, clicking the left mouse button won't advance the slide show to the next screen; it just produces a dot on the screen. Press Esc (or Ctrl+A) to change the annotation pen back to an arrow, and then click.

Drawing Straight Lines with the Pen

To draw a perfectly straight line with the annotation pen, press ⬆Shift while you draw.

Lesson 5: Using the Meeting Minder

The Meeting Minder is a PowerPoint feature that helps you take notes during a presentation. You can use this tool to take minutes or record action items. Action items are any items that you want to assign to people during a meeting. You can display these items on a new slide at the end of your slide show or even print them.

The Meeting Minder is especially useful during an informal presentation, such as a staff meeting or brainstorming session. Try using this feature now.

To Use the Meeting Minder

1 Open **PP1-0703** and save it as **Recruiting Plan**.

2 Click the **Slide Show** button.
This starts the presentation, beginning with the current slide.

> ✗ If you forget how to move within an electronic slide show effectively, take a quick refresher course by referring to Project 2, Lesson 6, "Using the Slide Show Shortcut Keys."

3 Right-click the mouse to display the shortcut menu, and then choose **Meeting Minder**.
The Meeting Minder dialog box displays with two tabs: Meeting Minutes and Action Items (see Figure 7.14). You can click the tab you want, and then enter information.

Figure 7.14
You can use the Meeting Minder to document your meeting and create action items.

Action Items tab

Meeting Minutes tab

4 Click the **Action Items** tab to display the Action Items page (see Figure 7.15).

Figure 7.15
You can enter action items by using the Meeting Minder.

Assign the task to a person here

Type a general description here
Indicate the due date here
Click here to add the item to the list

5 In the **Description** text box, type **Attend job fairs at top colleges and universities to recruit employees**, and then press **Tab⇆**.
The text you typed is entered in the text box and the insertion point moves to the Assigned To text box.

6 **Type** L. Schmidt, **and then press** Tab⇄.

The insertion point moves to the D<u>ue</u> Date text box. By default, this text box displays the current system date.

7 **Enter** 6/12/99 **to replace the current system date.**

After you create the basic information for an action item, you add it to the list.

8 **Click** <u>A</u>dd **to place the item on the list.**

The action item displays on the list and the text boxes clear so that you can enter other tasks.

9 **Enter the following items in the Action Items page of the Meeting Minder dialog box:**

Description	Assigned To	Due Date
Coordinate advertising in national computer magazines	S. Black	2/7/99
Network with other businesses	J. Reams	3/24/99

10 **Choose OK to close the Meeting Minder dialog box.**

PowerPoint automatically creates a slide with the action items you entered and places it at the end of the presentation.

11 **Press** Esc **to end the slide show, and then press** Ctrl+End.

The slide show ends and the last slide—your action items—displays, as shown in Figure 7.16. You can display the slide, or print it to hand to your participants as they leave.

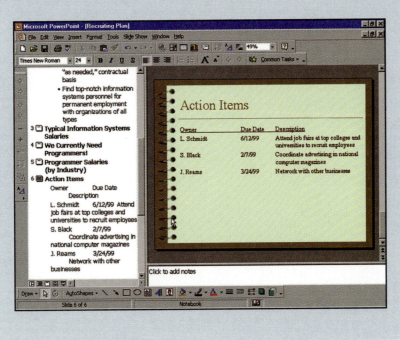

Figure 7.16
You can create an Action Items slide.

continues ▶

To Use the Meeting Minder   (continued)

⑫ With the Action Items slide displayed in Normal view, choose File, Print.
The Print dialog box displays.

⑬ Make sure that Current slide is chosen in the Print range section, and then choose OK.
The Action Items slide prints.

⑭ Save the presentation, and then close it.
Keep PowerPoint open if you plan to complete the Skill Drill, Challenge, and Discovery Zone exercises at the end of this project. Otherwise, make sure to exit PowerPoint and shut down Windows properly before turning off your computer.

Exporting Your Meeting Minutes to Word
You can export your meeting minutes (or action items) to Word. To do this, click the Export button in the Meeting Minder dialog box. In the Meeting Minder Export dialog box, check the box to Send meeting minutes and action items to Microsoft Word, and then click Export Now.

Summary

In this project, you learned some methods for spicing up your presentation when you run it as a slide show. You learned how to add transitions and text animation to your slides to control the flow of information and keep your audience's attention. You also learned how to rehearse and time a slide show, so you can check its overall length as a preliminary step when you're wanting your presentation to advance automatically. Finally, you practiced using the annotation pen and creating action items with the Meeting Minder feature.

To expand on your knowledge, spend a few minutes exploring Help on these topics. Additionally, complete some of the Skill Drill, Challenge, and Discovery Zone exercises.

Checking Concepts and Terms ✔

True/False

For each of the following, circle T or F to indicate whether the statement is true or false.

__T __F   **1.** You can use the Meeting Minder to create action items. [L5]

__T __F   **2.** After you assign slide timings, they display in Slide Sorter view. [L3]

__T __F   **3.** The only way to erase an annotation pen drawing is to advance to the next slide. [L4]

__T __F   **4.** You can't add both a slide transition and a text animation to the same slide. [L1–2]

__T __F   **5.** Annotation refers to the way bullet points are displayed on a slide. [L4]

Multiple Choice

Circle the letter of the correct answer for each of the following.

1. You can use the _____ to record action items. [L4–5]

   a. Minute Taker

   b. Meeting Minder

   c. Notes Pages view

   d. annotation pen

2. The annotation pen is used _____. [L4–5]

   a. to highlight information during an onscreen presentation

   b. to create a list of action items

   c. to take meeting minutes

   d. to draw objects in Slide view

3. When you use the Action Items feature, _____. [L5]

   a. PowerPoint automatically prints your presentation as an outline

   b. your speaker notes are updated

   c. an Action Items slide is automatically created

   d. action, or animation, is added to all bullet points

4. Blinds, Checkerboard Across, and Box In are all examples of _____. [L1, 4–5]

   a. annotations

   b. action items

   c. meeting minutes

   d. slide transitions

5. You might want to add text animation to your bullet points _____. [L2]

   a. to control the flow of information

   b. to keep your audience from reading ahead

   c. to increase interest

   d. all of the above

Screen ID

Identify each of the items shown in Figure 7.17.

Figure 7.17

A. Slide Transition Effects

B. Rehearse Timings

C. Animation Preview

D. Slide Transition

E. Slide timings

F. Slide Sorter toolbar

G. Hide Slide

H. Slide transition icon

I. Preset Animation

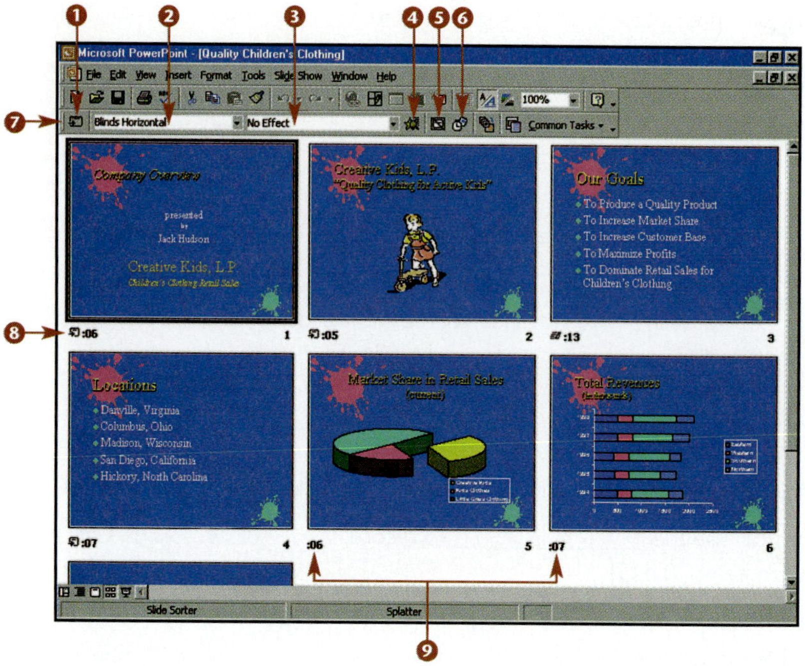

1. _____	4. _____	7. _____
2. _____	5. _____	8. _____
3. _____	6. _____	9. _____

Discussion Questions

1. Which PowerPoint feature would you use for each of the following situations? (*Note:* There might be more than one feature you could use for a couple of the situations.) [L1–5]

- You are conducting a brainstorming session and want to create a list of "to-do" items.

- You are running a staff meeting and want to generate some meeting minutes.

- You need to emphasize information while running a slide show.

- You want to prevent your audience from reading ahead on a slide.

- You want to capture your audience's attention.

2. Discuss the pros and cons for using each of the following PowerPoint features in your presentation. Also discuss the pitfalls of overusing the feature. [L1, 2, 4–5]

- Slide transitions

- Text animations

- Annotation pen

- Meeting Minder

3. Discuss the advantages of timing your presentation. Also discuss the differences between advancing a slide show manually and automatically. [L3]

Skill Drill

Skill Drill exercises reinforce project skills. Each skill reinforced is the same, or nearly the same, as a skill presented in the project. Detailed instructions are provided in a step-by-step format.

1. Using Help to Find Out About Slide Shows

You conduct a lot of meetings for a volunteer organization. To help you run the meetings more effectively, you use PowerPoint's slide show feature. To learn more about slide shows, you use Help. [L1, 3]

1. Start PowerPoint, if necessary, and then choose Help, Microsoft PowerPoint Help. If necessary, click the Show button to split the window into two panes.

2. On the Contents page, double-click the Running and Controlling a Slide Show icon. Click each of the following topics (write down what you learn about running a slide show before advancing to the next topic):

   - Take notes or meeting minutes during a slide show
   - Create a list of action items during a slide show
   - Write or draw (annotate) on slides during a slide show

   - Display a hidden slide during a slide show
   - Set up a slide show to run in a continuous loop
   - Slide show controls

3. Close the Help window.

4. Practice what you learned about running slide shows, using your notes as a guide.

5. Share what you learn with at least one other user. Keep PowerPoint open if you plan to complete additional exercises.

2. Adding Transitions and Animations

You're scheduled to conduct a new employee orientation session, but you're concerned that your audience will be bored with the information. To make the meeting more interesting, you decide to add slide transitions and text animations. [L1–2]

1. Open PP1-0704 and save it as Improved Orientation Session.

2. Display the presentation in Slide Sorter view and select Slide 1.

3. Click the Slide Transition Effects drop-down list arrow, and then choose Box In as the transition.

4. Select Slide 2, click the Slide Transition Effects drop-down list arrow, and choose Box Out.

5. Select Slides 3–4, click the Slide Transition Effects drop-down list, and choose Checkerboard Across.

6. Select Slide 5, click the Preset Animation drop-down list, and choose Crawl From Left.

7. Select Slide 6, click the Preset Animation drop-down list, and choose Spiral.

8. Select Slide 1, and then click the Slide Show button to run your presentation as a slide show.

9. Save the Improved Orientation Session presentation. Keep the presentation open if you plan to complete additional exercises.

3. Using Slide Show Timings

You're slated to conduct an orientation meeting for new employees at your company. To get an idea of the overall presentation length, you record it by using the slide show timings. [L3]

1. Make sure that the Improved Orientation Session presentation from the previous exercise is displayed in Slide Sorter view.

2. Select Slide 1, and then click the Rehearse Timings button to set slide timings. Make each slide display for 5–10 seconds (with the exception of Slide 5, which takes longer to display because the text animation is slow).

3. In the Microsoft PowerPoint message box, choose Yes to accept the slide timings, and then view them in Slide Sorter view.

4. Click the Slide Show button to automatically run the slide show with the slide timings you set.

5. In Slide Sorter view, click the Rehearse Timings button again and set new timings. Choose Yes to accept the slide timings.

6. Run the slide show again, and then save and close the presentation. Keep PowerPoint open if you plan to complete additional exercises.

4. Using the Annotation Pen

You're trying to convince your parents that you need more money for college expenses. To do so, you give a presentation to them on college expenses, using the annotation pen to emphasize your main points. [L4]

1. Open PP1-0705 and save it as College is Expensive.

2. Display the first presentation slide, and then click the Slide Show button.

3. When Slide 1 displays in the slide show, press Ctrl+P to display the annotation pen. Use the pen to underline the word successful on the slide.

4. Press Esc (or Ctrl+A) to switch the pen to an arrow. Display Slide 3 in your slide show.

5. Right-click on the slide to display the slide show shortcut menu. Choose Pointer Options, Pen Color, Red.

6. Draw a line from the 1st year column to the 3rd year column to illustrate the increasing costs of college. Circle the words Costs are rising!. Press Esc (or Ctrl+A) to switch the pen back to a pointer.

7. Press ↵Enter to display the last presentation slide. Use the pen to circle the word ME.

8. Press E to erase the annotation on the slide. Press Esc to end the slide show.

9. Save your College is Expensive presentation. Keep it open for the next exercise.

5. Adding Slide Transitions and Text Animations

To make the presentation you developed in the previous exercise more compelling, you add some slide transitions and animate your text. Then you add sound to a slide transition. [L1–2]

1. In the open College is Expensive presentation, click the Slide Sorter View button.

2. In Slide Sorter view, click Slide 1 to select it. Click the Slide Transition Effects drop-down list arrow, and then choose Fade Through Black.

3. Click Slide 2 to select it. On the Slide Transition Effects drop-down list, choose Dissolve.

4. With Slide 2 still selected, click the Preset Animation drop-down list arrow, and choose Zoom In From Screen Center.

5. Select Slide 3, and then choose Slide Show, Slide Transition from the menu bar. In the Effect section of the Slide Transition dialog box, click the drop-down list arrow. Choose Box In for the slide transition.

6. In the Slide Transition dialog box, click the So_u_nd drop-down list arrow, and choose `Cash Register` from the list. Click the _A_pply button to add the sound and transition effects to Slide 3.

7. Click Slide 4 to select it, click the Slide Transition Effects drop-down list arrow, and choose `Blinds Vertical`.

8. Click Slide 1, and then press F5 to run your presentation as a slide show. Press ↵Enter as many times as is necessary to completely advance through the slide show.

9. Save your `College is Expensive` presentation, then close it. Keep PowerPoint open if you plan to complete additional exercises.

Challenge

Challenge exercises expand on, or are somewhat related to, skills presented in the lessons. Each exercise provides a brief narrative introduction, followed by instructions in a numbered-step format that are not as detailed as those in the Skill Drill section.

1. Finding Out About Animation

You want to find out how to animate objects on your slides (such as drawn objects and clip art). To do so, you use Help. [L1–2]

1. In PowerPoint, choose _H_elp, Microsoft PowerPoint _H_elp. Click the Show button, if necessary, to split the Help window into two panes.

2. On the _C_ontents page, double-click the Designing Slide Shows icon. Double-click the Creating Animated Slides icon.

3. Research each of the following topics related to animating slide objects and text. Take notes on the procedures (or print the topics).

- ■ Animate text and objects
- ■ Animate the elements of a chart
- ■ Edit a text or object animation
- ■ Preview animation and transition effects in a slide

4. Share the information you learn with at least one other user. Practice using the features in a presentation you develop. Keep PowerPoint open if you plan to complete additional exercises.

2. Using Custom Animation

You are giving a short talk to the local Chamber of Commerce organization about your company. The meeting is during lunch (and you're concerned that people may get sleepy after eating a big meal). To keep their attention focused on your presentation, you add some animation. [L1–2]

1. Open `PP1-0707` and save it as `Talk to the Chamber of Commerce`.

2. Display Slide 2 in Normal view, and then choose Sli_d_e Show, Custo_m_ Animation.

3. Add check marks to both boxes in the Che_c_k to animate slide objects area. (This adds animation to the title and clip art object.) Click the _P_review button to see the effect, and then click OK.

4. Display Slide 6, `Total Revenues`, in Normal view. Choose Slide Show, Custom Animation.

5. Check the boxes for both the title and chart in the Check to animate slide objects area. Click the Preview button to see your effect.

6. Click the Chart Effects tab in the Custom Animation dialog box. Click the Introduce chart elements drop-down list arrow, and then choose by Series. Click the Preview button.

7. Change the way that the chart elements are introduced. Click the Introduce chart elements drop-down list arrow, and then choose by Category. Click Preview, and then choose OK.

8. Run your presentation as a slide show, starting from Slide 1.

9. Save your Talk to the Chamber of Commerce presentation, then close it. Keep PowerPoint open if you plan to complete additional exercises.

3. Adding Slide Transitions

For your college speech class, you're giving a talk on how to do presentations. To help hold the class's attention, you add slide transitions to your PowerPoint presentation. [L1]

1. Open `PP1-0708` and save it as `Presentation Guidelines`.

2. Display the presentation in Slide Sorter view. Use the Slide Sorter toolbar to add a transition of your choosing to each slide in the presentation. (*Hint*: Try combining opposite effects, such as using Box In for one slide, and Box Out for the next one. Another example of a possible combination is Cover Down/Uncover Up.)

3. Click the Slide Transition icon for each slide to preview the transition effect.

4. Add text animations to each slide that has a bulleted list. (Choose a different animation for each slide.)

5. Run your presentation as a slide show. Save the presentation. Keep the presentation and PowerPoint open if you plan to complete the next exercises.

4. Using Slide Show Timings

To help you time and practice your speech class presentation, you use PowerPoint's slide show timings. [L3]

1. Make sure that the Presentation Guidelines presentation from the previous exercise displays in Slide Sorter view.

2. Set slide timings by clicking the Rehearse Timings button, and then discuss the slide's contents—just as you would for a live audience.

3. View the timings that you set in Slide Sorter view. Run the presentation as a slide show.

4. Set up the slide show to play continuously (loop). (*Hint*: Use PowerPoint's Help to find out how to do this, or refer to information presented in Lesson 3 of this project.)

5. Run the slide show. When you finish viewing the show, press Esc to end it.

6. Save the `Presentation Guidelines` presentation. Keep the presentation open if you plan to complete the next exercise.

5. Using the Annotation Pen

To focus your audience's attention, you decide to use the annotation pen during your speech class presentation. To prepare for the presentation, you practice using the pen. [L4]

1. Select Slide 1 of the `Presentation Guidelines` presentation open from the previous exercise, and then run the presentation as a slide show.

2. Advance to Slide 4. Use the annotation pen to draw an arrow to each of the sub-points listed on the slide. Erase the drawing, and then change the pen color to blue.

3. Practice using the keyboard shortcuts and the shortcut menu to switch between the arrow and the pen.

4. On a blank area of the slide, practice drawing the following items:
   - arrow
   - square
   - circle
   - your name (in cursive)
   - your company or school name (in cursive)

5. Save your Presentation Guidelines presentation, and then close it. Keep PowerPoint open if you plan to complete additional exercises.

Discovery Zone

Discovery Zone exercises require advanced knowledge of topics presented in Essentials lessons, application of skills from multiple lessons, or self-directed learning of new skills.

1. Learning About Multimedia

You want to incorporate multimedia effects, such as music, sound, and video, in your presentation.

Using the Help system, find out about the following topics:
- How to add music background to a slide
- The difference between adding a clip from the Gallery and adding a clip from a file
- Adding a sound to a slide transition
- Adding a sound when a slide object or chart element is introduced
- Inserting a video in your presentation
- Resizing and moving a video

Write down what you learn. (If you're familiar with Word, you can use it to develop a table.) Then develop a PowerPoint presentation that incorporates multimedia effects. Use the knowledge you gain from the book to develop the best possible presentation. Finally, give your presentation to your class.

2. Creating Presentations

PowerPoint 2000 Essentials Basics covers the "key" features you can use to develop impressive presentations quickly. Use the knowledge that you gained from the book so far to develop and give at least three presentations. (If you forget how to perform a particular action in PowerPoint, use the Help system or the book to brush up on the concepts.)

Create each of the following types of presentations:

- A presentation you can use in a business setting
- A presentation you can use to promote a club, team, or organization
- A presentation you can use in a college class

Include the following elements in each presentation:

- A chart
- A bulleted list
- A clip art image
- An AutoShape
- Speaker notes

After you initially develop the content (and objects, such as clip art and charts) for the presentations, automate the presentations by using the following PowerPoint features:

- Slide transitions
- Text animation
- Multimedia clips (sound, music, or video)
- Chart animation
- Slide timings
- Action items

Give your presentations to your class. Use the feedback that your classmates offer to revise and improve the presentations. Then, present the slide shows a second time.

Save all your presentations. When you finish working, close the presentations and exit PowerPoint.

Project 8

Sharing Information with Other Programs

Objectives

In this project, you learn how to

➤ **Open a Word Document as a PowerPoint Presentation**

➤ **Use the Presentation Assistant to Fix Stylistic Problems**

➤ **Draw and Format a Table**

➤ **Copy and Paste Information Between Slides and Programs**

➤ **Copy Information from an Excel Worksheet to a Datasheet**

➤ **Insert a Picture from a File**

Key terms introduced in this project include

- docked
- floating toolbar
- integration
- move bars
- Presentation Assistant
- range

- sentence case
- stylistic problems
- table
- title case
- worksheet

Why Would I Do This?

One of the advantages of using Office 2000 instead of standalone packages is the built-in capability that the Office programs have to share information seamlessly with each other. This feature is called **integration**. Sharing information in this way saves time because you don't have to re-create it, and it helps ensure that accurate data is entered in your presentation.

For example, you might have an outline in Word that you'd like to use as the basis for a PowerPoint presentation. Instead of jumping through hoops to transfer the information from Word to PowerPoint, you can simply open the Word document in PowerPoint. Office 2000 also includes easy-to-use methods you can use to copy and paste information from one program to another. Finally, you can insert a picture file (such as a logo) into PowerPoint.

Visual Summary

In this project, you learn to use some of PowerPoint's integration features. You'll see how easy it is to open a Word outline within PowerPoint, quickly creating a presentation similar to the one shown in Figure 8.1.

Figure 8.1
It's easy to open a Word outline in PowerPoint.

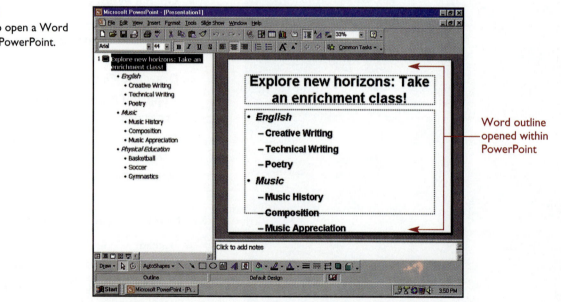

Word outline opened within PowerPoint

After you open the Word outline, you can use the **Presentation Assistant** to split the text into multiple slides (see Figure 8.2). You can also apply a design template to make the presentation more interesting.

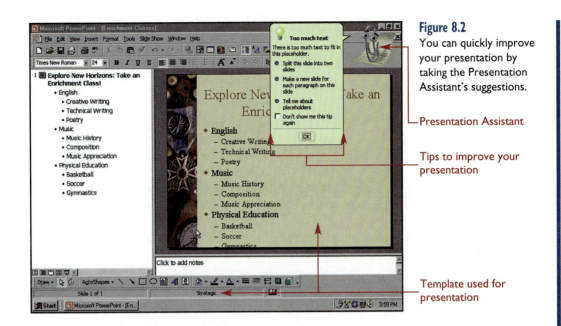

Figure 8.2
You can quickly improve your presentation by taking the Presentation Assistant's suggestions.

Presentation Assistant

Tips to improve your presentation

Template used for presentation

For this project, imagine that you're working for the Continuing Education department at Johnson University and are helping to set up summer enrichment classes. In order to create a presentation to give to area high schools, you use Office's integration features. When you finish working with the features in this project, you'll have developed a presentation similar to the one shown in Figure 8.3.

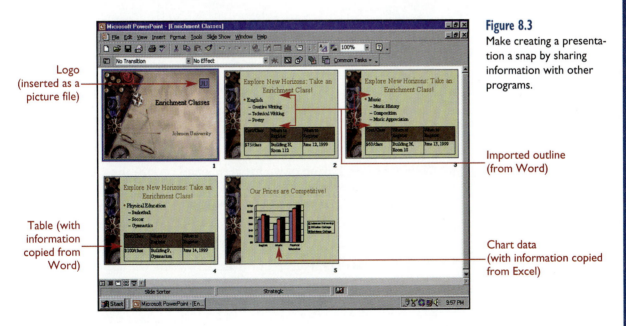

Figure 8.3
Make creating a presentation a snap by sharing information with other programs.

Logo (inserted as a picture file)

Table (with information copied from Word)

Imported outline (from Word)

Chart data (with information copied from Excel)

Because using integration features can save you time and effort, try sharing information with other programs now.

Lesson 1: Opening a Word Document as a PowerPoint Presentation

If you've worked with Office 2000 for a while, chances are you've prepared an outline in Word, and then wanted to use the same information as the basis for a PowerPoint presentation. Of course, you could re-create the information in PowerPoint, but it's much easier to open the Word document as a PowerPoint presentation. Fortunately, in PowerPoint 2000 you can do this! Try using this helpful technique now.

To Open a Word Document as a PowerPoint Presentation

1 **Start PowerPoint, if necessary, and then click the Open button on the Standard toolbar.**

The Open dialog box displays, as shown in Figure 8.4. Although you're already familiar with using this dialog box to open existing PowerPoint presentations, you've probably never opened a Word document in PowerPoint before. Fortunately, the steps for doing so are similar to those you use for opening a presentation: Just locate the file, and then click Open.

Figure 8.4
Use the Open dialog box in PowerPoint to locate and open Word documents.

Places bar

Click here to display file locations

Click here to display different file types

2 **Click the Look in drop down list arrow and choose the CD-ROM drive (D:), if necessary.**

Before you can open a file, you must first locate it. The files used in this book are located on the CD-ROM drive (unless your instructor has moved them elsewhere).

3 **Click the Files of type drop down list arrow and choose All Files from the list.**

All the files located on the selected drive and folder—whether created in PowerPoint or not—display (see Figure 8.5). Notice, too, that the icon next to PP1-0801 indicates that the file was created in Word.

Word file

Figure 8.5
You can display all files on a drive, even if they are not PowerPoint presentations.

Now that you've located the Word file that you want to use as the basis for the PowerPoint presentation, you can open it.

4 **Click PP1-0801, and then choose Open.**
The Word outline opens as a new PowerPoint presentation in Normal view (see Figure 8.6). The text from the outline extends beyond the lower (text) placeholder—not a very good design for a slide! For right now, however, don't worry about this. You learn how to use the Presentation Assistant to split the slide into multiple slides in the next lesson.

Notice that the presentation automatically uses a blank template. To liven up your presentation, try applying a different design template.

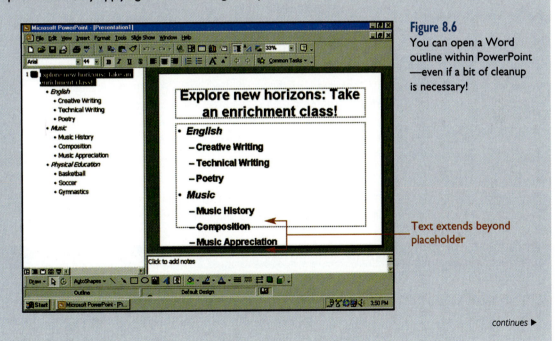

Figure 8.6
You can open a Word outline within PowerPoint —even if a bit of cleanup is necessary!

Text extends beyond placeholder

continues ▶

To Open a Word Document as a PowerPoint Presentation   (continued)

5 **Right-click on the slide (but not within a placeholder), and then choose Apply Design Template from the shortcut menu.**
The Apply Design Template dialog box displays. (You learned how to choose templates from this dialog box in Project 6, Lesson 1, "Using Templates.")

6 **Choose the Strategic template, and then click Apply.**
The template is applied to your presentation. Now save your newly created presentation. Remember, it's always a good idea to save (or resave) your presentations every few minutes.

7 **Save your new presentation as** `Enrichment Classes`**.**
Keep the presentation open and PowerPoint running for the next lesson, in which you learn how to better arrange the outline information by splitting it into multiple slides.

Lesson 2: Using the Presentation Assistant to Fix Stylistic Problems

In the previous lesson, you opened a Word outline as a PowerPoint presentation. You were probably impressed by PowerPoint's capability to open the Word file seamlessly, but at the same time may have been a bit distressed by its inability to logically arrange the information onto multiple slides.

Fortunately, you can use PowerPoint's Presentation Assistant to quickly fix problems such as these. The Presentation Assistant integrates several features from previous PowerPoint versions (such as the Style Checker and AutoClipArt). In a sense, the Presentation Assistant is an offshoot of the Office Assistant—designed to help you correct *stylistic problems* such as incorrect capitalization, too much text on a slide, and so on. To use the Presentation Assistant, you must first activate the Office Assistant. When activated, the Presentation Assistant flags potential problems by displaying a light bulb. You can click the light bulb to display a list of possible corrections for the problem and choose an option from the list.

In this lesson, you learn how to activate the Presentation Assistant and how to use it to split a single slide into multiple slides. Try working with this handy feature now.

To Use the Presentation Assistant to Fix Stylistic Problems

1 **Make sure that the Enrichment Classes presentation you created in the previous lesson is open in Normal view, and then choose Help, Show the Office Assistant.**

 In Project 1 of this book, you learned how to turn off the display of the Office Assistant. If the Assistant has been turned back on since you worked on that project, however, you can skip over Steps 1–2 and proceed directly to Step 3.

The Office Assistant appears onscreen. Remember that the Office Assistant must be displayed before the Presentation Assistant can show you suggestions for improving your presentation.

② Click outside the Office Assistant's message bubble (if necessary) to clear the bubble.

A light bulb displays near the title placeholder (see Figure 8.7). Whenever the light bulb appears, it's a sure sign that the Presentation Assistant has a tip or idea about how to improve your presentation.

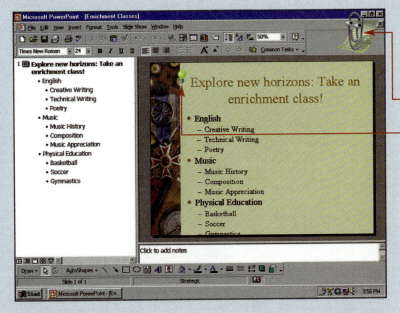

Figure 8.7
PowerPoint's Presentation Assistant helps you clean up presentations.

— Office Assistant

Click this light bulb to see a Presentation Assistant tip

③ Click the light bulb.

The Presentation Assistant indicates that the capitalization for the title placeholder should be in *title case*. Title case is the combination of upper- and lowercase letters used to capitalize the first letter of each word. You can choose to have the Presentation Assistant automatically change the text in the placeholder to title case or ignore its suggestion.

④ Click `Change the text to title case` (the first option button).

The text in the title placeholder is formatted as title case. At the same time, a light bulb appears next to the lower (text) placeholder, indicating that there is another stylistic or formatting problem that needs to be fixed.

⑤ Click the light bulb that appears next to the word `English`.

Again, the Presentation Assistant indicates that the text in the lower placeholder is not formatted according to the default setting of *sentence case*. Sentence case means that only the first letter of a sentence or phrase is capitalized. In this case, you should ignore the suggestion.

⑥ Click `Ignore this style rule for this presentation only` (the second option button).

A light bulb appears near the bottom of the lower placeholder (next to `Physical Education`).

continues ▶

To Use the Presentation Assistant to Fix Stylistic Problems   (continued)

7 **Click the light bulb.**

The Presentation Assistant indicates that there is too much text to fit in the placeholder (see Figure 8.8). You'll find that this is a typical problem when opening Word outlines in PowerPoint.

If you choose the `Split this slide into two slides` option, you'll end up with one slide that contains two of the main topics (`English` and `Music`). In contrast, if you choose `Make a new slide for each paragraph on this slide`, you'll create three slides, each with the same title, but having different topics for the bulleted points. Try splitting the single slide into multiple slides by using this technique.

Figure 8.8
Creating multiple slides is a snap when you use the Presentation Assistant.

Click here to split the slide into two slides

Click here to create a new slide for each main paragraph

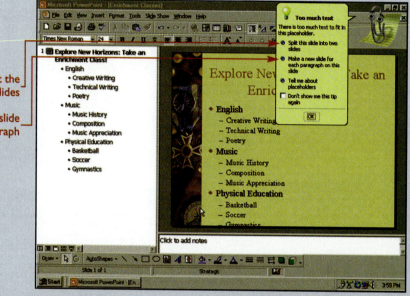

8 **Click** `Make a new slide for each paragraph on this slide.`

PowerPoint breaks the information included on the original slide into three individual slides. Each slide includes information for one of the main topics (such as `English`, `Music`, and `Physical Education`), but includes the same title.

9 **Press** PgUp **twice to scroll through the presentation and view your newly created slides.**

Now turn off the Office Assistant's display because you're finished fixing stylistic problems in this presentation.

10 **Right-click on the Office Assistant, and then choose Options.**

The Options page of the Office Assistant dialog box displays.

11 **Clear the Use the Office Assistant check box, and then click OK.**

The Office Assistant no longer displays.

12 **Save the Enrichment Classes presentation.**

Keep the presentation open and PowerPoint running for the next lesson, in which you draw and format a table.

Lesson 3: Drawing and Formatting a Table

One great way to organize your data is by drawing a **table**. A table is simply a grid of columns and rows that you can use to display your data in an organized manner. If you've worked with spreadsheet programs (such as Excel), you'll instantly recognize the similarities between the way a **worksheet** and a table are set up.

You can create a table within PowerPoint or by using Word. If you need to create only a simple table that doesn't need much formatting, use PowerPoint. On the other hand, if you want to have full access to more powerful formatting tools for your table, use Word. For now, focus on creating a simple table—right from within PowerPoint.

For this exercise, imagine that you need to create a table to display registration information for your classes. You want to locate a table at the bottom of each slide that includes the relevant information for the class. To do this, you create and format a table in PowerPoint. In the next lesson, you'll copy the table to all the slides where you need it. Try drawing and formatting a table now.

To Draw and Format a Table

1 Display Slide 1 in the Enrichment Classes presentation open from the previous lesson.
This is where you draw the table. After you create it, you'll copy its design and structure to the other slides.

2 On the Standard toolbar, click the Tables and Borders button.
The Tables and Borders toolbar displays (see Figure 8.9). This handy toolbar, which is universally available in the Office 2000 programs, enables you to draw a table electronically. To draw the table, make sure that the Draw Table button is activated, and then drag to create a table on your slide. If you make a mistake, just click the Eraser button and drag over the line(s) you want to remove. It's that easy!

> By default, the Tables and Borders toolbar displays as a **floating toolbar**, which means that it shows in its own window. Because of this, the toolbar on your screen may not display in the same location as the one in this book. If you'd like, just drag the toolbar's title bar to the location you want.
>
> Alternatively, the toolbar may be **docked**, or attached, to one side of the application window. You can convert it into a floating toolbar by moving it into the screen. To do so, drag the double bars (called **move bars**) on the toolbar.

continues ▶

To Draw and Format a Table   (continued)

Figure 8.9
The Tables and Borders toolbar puts tools for creating tables at your fingertips.

Draw Table tool

Table tool

Eraser tool

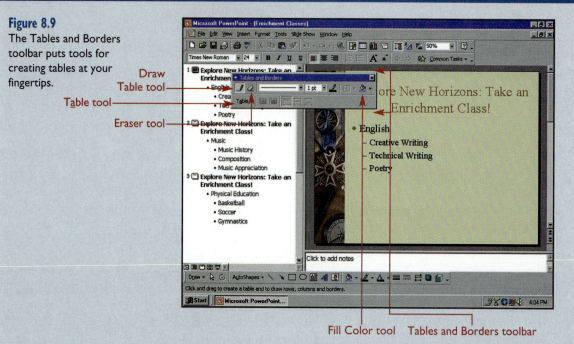

Fill Color tool   Tables and Borders toolbar

3 **If necessary, click the Draw Table tool, and then drag from immediately below the word** Poetry **to the lower right corner of the slide (see Figure 8.10). Release the mouse button.**
A rectangle is drawn in the lower half of the slide. Notice that the border includes selection handles so that you can resize the table. Additionally, the Draw Table pencil pointer remains active so that you can add more lines to your table.

Figure 8.10
Draw a table using the electronic pencil.

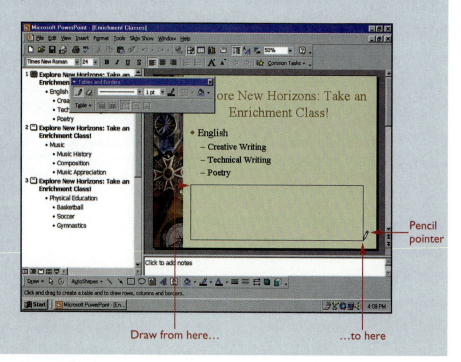

Pencil pointer

Draw from here...   ...to here

Now you're ready to add more lines to your table.

④ Drag to draw a horizontal line from the left center selection handle to the right center selection handle, and then release the mouse button.

A horizontal line divides the rectangle evenly, so that two rows are displayed. Now try adding two vertical lines so that you have three columns.

⑤ Drag to draw two vertical lines to create three columns that are approximately equal in width.

That's it! You created a table that includes three columns and two rows (see Figure 8.11). Next, you'll add shading to the top row to emphasize its information. First, select the row so that PowerPoint understands what part of the table you'd like to shade.

❌ If you can't seem to get the lines drawn exactly where you'd like, don't despair. Just click the Eraser tool, and then drag over the line you want to remove. Then "go back to the drawing board" by clicking the Draw Table tool, and try again.

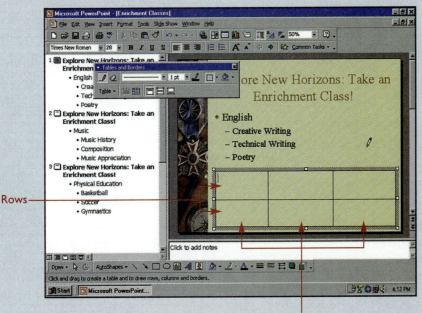

Figure 8.11
You can organize your data in columns and rows.

Tables are made up of a series of columns and rows that comprise a grid pattern. An intersection of a column and row is called a *cell*. To designate which part of the table you want to be affected by a command, you can click in a cell to select it. (If you want to select multiple cells, drag over them or select commands from the Table menu.)

⑥ Press Esc to turn off the Draw Table tool, and then click in any cell in the top row.

continues ▶

To Draw and Format a Table (continued)

 7 On the Tables and Borders toolbar, click the Table tool.
The Table menu displays (see Figure 8.12). This menu gives you a slew of choices related to working with your tables.

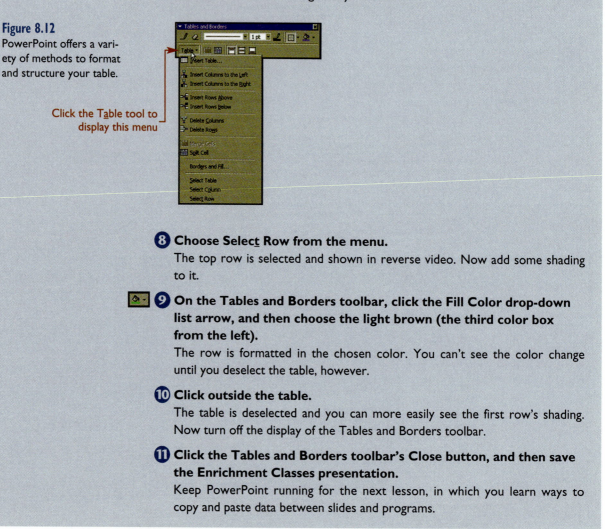

Figure 8.12
PowerPoint offers a variety of methods to format and structure your table.

Click the Table tool to display this menu

8 Choose Select Row from the menu.
The top row is selected and shown in reverse video. Now add some shading to it.

9 On the Tables and Borders toolbar, click the Fill Color drop-down list arrow, and then choose the light brown (the third color box from the left).
The row is formatted in the chosen color. You can't see the color change until you deselect the table, however.

10 Click outside the table.
The table is deselected and you can more easily see the first row's shading. Now turn off the display of the Tables and Borders toolbar.

11 Click the Tables and Borders toolbar's Close button, and then save the Enrichment Classes presentation.
Keep PowerPoint running for the next lesson, in which you learn ways to copy and paste data between slides and programs.

⚠ **Creating Tables**
Here's another option for creating a table: On the Standard toolbar, click the Insert Table button, and then drag over the number of columns and rows that you want to include in the table before releasing the mouse button.

Lesson 4: Copying and Pasting Information Between Slides and Programs

If you're like most people, you're interested in finding faster and more efficient ways to create a presentation. One way to streamline your work is to develop an object (such as a table) once, and then copy it to any other locations where you need it.

Fortunately, you can copy a variety of objects, including text, charts, clip art, or other objects from one PowerPoint slide to another. For example, you can quickly duplicate the table you created on Slide 1 of your presentation—including its structure and formatting—to other slides in the same presentation.

Even better, you can copy information from one Office 2000 program to another. For example, if the data you need already exists in Word or Excel, you don't have to recreate it. Instead, you can simply copy it electronically from one program to another.

Sharing information between PowerPoint and other programs is facilitated by the Windows Clipboard. The Clipboard is used in conjunction with the Copy and Paste commands. What, exactly, is the Clipboard? It is a temporary storage area in memory where data that is cut or copied is stored. From the Clipboard, you can paste (insert) the material in another program.

In this lesson, you experience firsthand how easy it is to copy and paste information. First, you'll copy the table from Slide 1 to the other presentation slides. Then, you'll copy text from Word into the PowerPoint tables. Try sharing information via the Clipboard now.

To Copy and Paste Information Between Slides and Programs

1 Click in the table on Slide 1 of the Enrichment Classes presentation, and then click the table's border.
You must first select an object before you can copy it. In this case, you have to click the table's border to select it.

> When you click within a table, the border displays with hatch marks, indicating that you placed the table in editing mode. Clicking on the table's border selects the table so that you can copy it. Make sure that the border appears as a series of tiny dots before proceeding with Step 2.
>
> Also, don't be dismayed if the Tables and Borders toolbar redisplays. By default, this toolbar displays whenever a table is selected, and it is hidden when you deselect the table.

2 Click the Copy button on the Standard toolbar.
This copies the selected object (the table) to the Clipboard. (If you prefer, you can copy by choosing Edit, Copy, or by pressing Ctrl+C from the keyboard.)

3 Press PgDn to display Slide 2, and then click the Paste button on the Standard toolbar.
The table is pasted on Slide 2. (If you want, you can paste items from the Clipboard by choosing Edit, Paste, or by pressing Ctrl+V.)

After an object is placed on the Clipboard, you can paste it multiple times. In fact, you can continue to paste the object until another item is copied (or cut) to the Clipboard.

4 Press PgDn to display Slide 3, and then press Ctrl+V.
The table is pasted on Slide 3. Now try copying and pasting text from Word into a PowerPoint table.

continues ▶

To Copy and Paste Information Between Slides and Programs (continued)

5 **Choose Start, Programs, Microsoft Word.**

Microsoft Word opens in memory and displays on the screen. PowerPoint remains open in memory. Whenever you have multiple programs open simultaneously, you can switch between them by clicking the appropriate button on the taskbar. For now, however, open the document in Word from which you need to copy information.

6 **In Word, open** PP1-0802.

This document includes information that you want to place in your PowerPoint tables, as shown in Figure 8.13. As usual, you must select and copy the text before pasting it.

Figure 8.13

You can copy text from a Word document to PowerPoint.

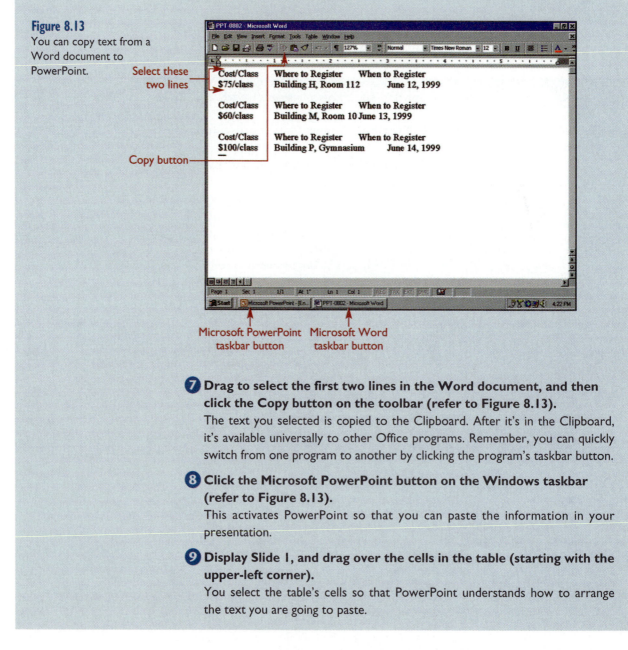

Select these two lines

Copy button

Microsoft PowerPoint taskbar button   Microsoft Word taskbar button

7 **Drag to select the first two lines in the Word document, and then click the Copy button on the toolbar (refer to Figure 8.13).**

The text you selected is copied to the Clipboard. After it's in the Clipboard, it's available universally to other Office programs. Remember, you can quickly switch from one program to another by clicking the program's taskbar button.

8 **Click the Microsoft PowerPoint button on the Windows taskbar (refer to Figure 8.13).**

This activates PowerPoint so that you can paste the information in your presentation.

9 **Display Slide 1, and drag over the cells in the table (starting with the upper-left corner).**

You select the table's cells so that PowerPoint understands how to arrange the text you are going to paste.

Make sure that all the cells in your table are selected. If you have trouble selecting cells via dragging, try this method: Click in the first cell in the table, press and hold down ⇧Shift, and then click the last table cell. If you're successful, all the cells in the table are selected.

🔟 **Click the Paste button on the toolbar.**

The text from the Word document is inserted in the PowerPoint table (see Figure 8.14).

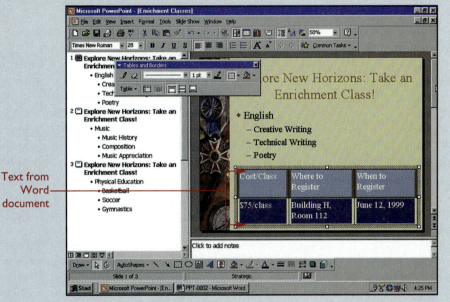

Text from Word document

Figure 8.14
It's easy to share information between Office programs.

ℹ️ **Changing Column Width**

If the columns in your table are not the width you like, you can move your mouse pointer over a vertical column divider until a two-headed arrow displays, and then drag left or right.

You can follow the same steps to copy text from the Word document to the other two tables in your presentation. Try this now.

⓫ **Using Steps 7–10 as a guide, copy lines 3–4 from the Word document to Slide 2's table. Then, copy lines 5–6 from the Word document to Slide 3's table.**

When you finish, you'll have copied the appropriate information from Word to your PowerPoint presentation. (If you want to, change the column width by using the previous "Changing Column Width" information as a guide.) Because you're finished using Word, you can close the document and exit the program.

⓬ **Right-click the taskbar button for Microsoft Word, and then choose Close from the shortcut menu.**

Word is cleared from memory.

⓭ **Save your Enrichment Classes presentation.**

Keep the presentation open and PowerPoint running for the next lesson, in which you learn how to copy information from Excel to a PowerPoint datasheet.

Lesson 5: Copying Information from an Excel Worksheet to a Datasheet

Another useful way to share information between programs is to copy information that already exists in Excel into PowerPoint. For example, you might have sales, production, or marketing data in an Excel worksheet, and want to base a PowerPoint chart on the information. By copying the data from Excel to PowerPoint, you minimize errors and save time.

For this lesson, you'll copy data comparing costs for your classes with costs from other colleges from an Excel worksheet to your presentation. Try using this application of the copy-and-paste feature now.

To Copy Information from an Excel Worksheet to a Datasheet

1 **In the Enrichment Classes presentation, press Ctrl+End to display the last slide (if necessary), and then click the New Slide button.**
The New Slide dialog box displays. You'll base your new slide on the Chart AutoLayout.

2 **Double-click the Chart AutoLayout, click in the title placeholder, and type Our Prices are Competitive!.**
Now you're ready to copy information from Excel. (If you need a refresher course on creating charts from within PowerPoint, refer to Project 5, "Working with Charts.")

3 **Choose Start, Programs, Microsoft Excel.**
Microsoft Excel starts and displays onscreen. Open the worksheet (the type of file used in Excel) on which you want to base your PowerPoint chart.

4 **In Excel, open PP1-0803.**
The Excel worksheet displays. This worksheet includes the information that you want to use for your PowerPoint chart. To select the exact information you want to copy, you can click in the first cell (the intersection of a column and a row), hold down the Shift key, and then click the last cell. Because cells are designated by a column letter (such as A) and a row number (such as 1), the first cell in the worksheet is cell A1.

5 **Click cell A1, press and hold Shift, and then click cell D4.**
A rectangular block of cells (called a *range*) is selected (see Figure 8.15). After you select the range, you can copy it to the Clipboard.

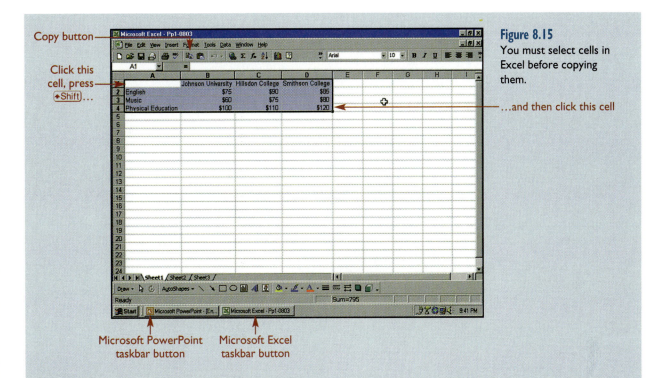

Figure 8.15
You must select cells in Excel before copying them.

6 **Click the Copy button on the toolbar.**
The cells you selected are copied to the Clipboard. Now paste them in a PowerPoint datasheet.

7 **Click Microsoft PowerPoint's taskbar button to switch to PowerPoint, and then double-click the chart placeholder.**
Microsoft Graph activates and the datasheet displays (see Figure 8.16). Now delete the existing sample data in the datasheet. The easiest way to do this is to click the Select All button, and then press Del. The Select All button is located in the upper-left corner of the datasheet (above the row headings and to the left of the column headings).

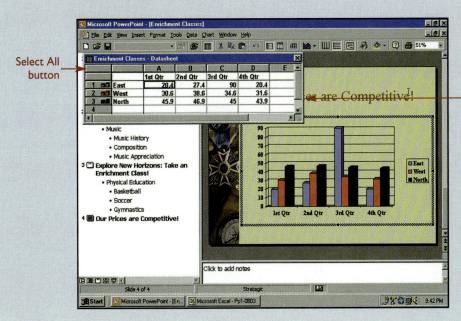

Figure 8.16
You can use the Select All button to quickly select an entire datasheet.

continues ▶

To Copy Information from an Excel Worksheet to a Datasheet   (continued)

8 **Click the Select All button and press** Del.
The existing data is erased from the datasheet.

9 **Click the Paste button on the toolbar.**
The data that you copied from Excel to the Clipboard is pasted into the datasheet. At the same time, a chart that includes the information is created (see Figure 8.17).

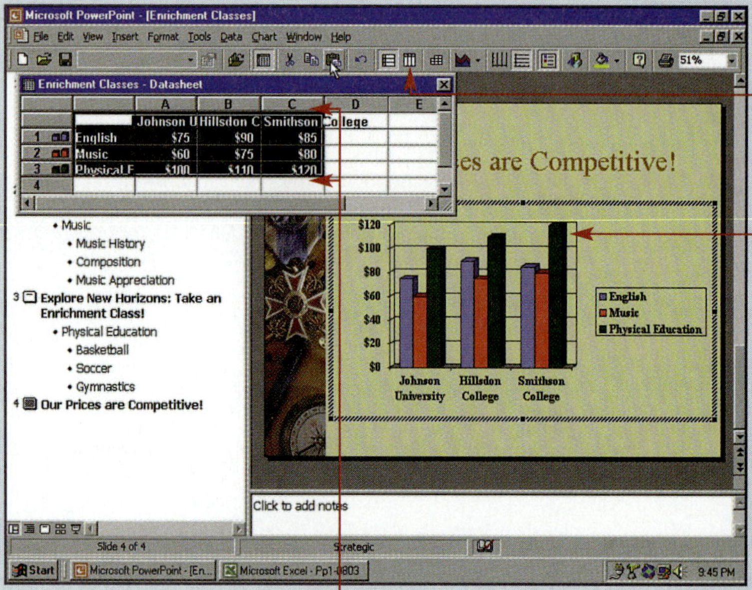

Figure 8.17
It's easy to create a PowerPoint chart based on existing data.

By Column button

New chart

Pasted information from the Clipboard

Now try displaying the information in a manner that highlights the difference between Johnson University's prices and your competitors.

10 **Click the By Column button on the toolbar.**
The chart displays by column (rather than by row).

11 **Click outside the chart to close Microsoft Graph, and then save the Enrichment Classes presentation.**

12 **Right-click on the Microsoft Excel taskbar button, and then choose Close.**
Excel is closed from memory. Keep PowerPoint running for the next lesson, in which you learn how to insert a picture file into your presentation.

Lesson 6: Inserting a Picture from a File

In Project 6, you learned how to use the Clip Gallery to insert pictures in your presentations. There's a wealth of other images available as well—those saved as picture files.

Where do these picture files come from? Scanned photographic images, pictures, and drawn images that are saved as .PCX files, bitmap (.BMP) files, .GIF files, etc., are all types of picture files that you can insert into your presentation.

For example, most businesses, schools, and other organizations have logos that they use to represent and identify themselves. Because of this, it's common to include the logo on presentations or other marketing materials. Instead of creating the logo from scratch, organizations usually make it available to their employees as a file on the company's network so that users can easily insert the logo into their presentations or other documents.

In this lesson, you put the finishing touches on your Enrichment Classes presentation by adding a title slide. You then insert a picture file (a logo for Johnson University) on this slide.

To Insert a Picture from a File

1 Display the Enrichment Classes presentation in Slide Sorter view, and then click to the left of the first slide.
A vertical bar displays, indicating the location for your title slide.

2 Click the New Slide button, and then double-click the Title Slide AutoLayout.
A title slide is inserted as the first slide in your presentation. Now switch to Normal view to add text and insert a picture file.

3 Double-click Slide 1 to switch to Normal view, and then type Enrichment Classes in the title placeholder and Johnson University in the subtitle placeholder.
The basic information you need for the title slide is entered. Now try inserting a picture file.

4 Choose Insert, Picture, From File.
The Insert Picture dialog box displays (see Figure 8.18). This dialog box looks very similar to the Open dialog box. Happily, you navigate it to find your picture file in the same way.

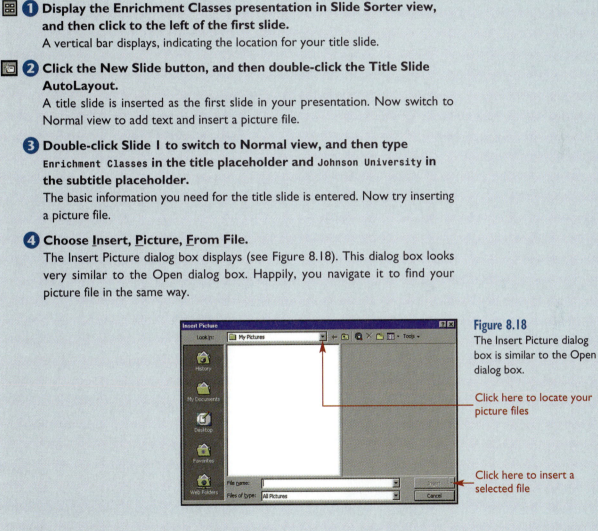

Figure 8.18
The Insert Picture dialog box is similar to the Open dialog box.

Click here to locate your picture files

Click here to insert a selected file

5 If necessary, click the Look in drop-down list arrow and choose the CD-ROM drive (D:) from the list.
A list of picture files displays.

6 Choose PP1-0804, and then click Insert.
Although the picture file is inserted on your slide as a selected object, it probably is not in the right location. Fortunately, it's easy to move the picture. Just make sure that it's selected, and then drag it to the desired location.

continues ▶

To Insert a Picture from a File (continued)

7 **Move your mouse pointer over the center of the picture object so that a four-headed arrow displays, and then drag the object to the upper-right corner of the slide. Release the mouse button.**
Your finished slide should look similar to the one shown in Figure 8.19.

Figure 8.19
It's easy to add a logo to your slide.

Selected picture object

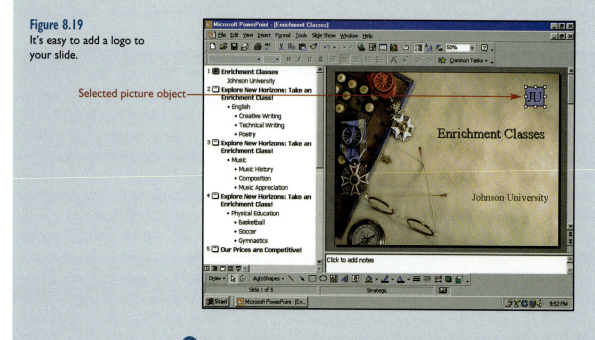

8 **Save the Enrichment Classes presentation, and then close it.**
Keep PowerPoint running if you plan to complete the Skill Drill, Challenge, and Discovery Zone exercises at the end of this project. Otherwise, make sure to exit PowerPoint and shut down Windows properly before turning off your computer.

 Adding a Picture to the Slide Master
You can quickly add a picture (such as a logo) to all slides in your presentation by placing it on the Slide Master. (If you'd like more information on using the Slide Master, refer to Project 6, Lesson 4, "Working with a Slide Master.")

Summary

Congratulations! After completing this book, you're "up and running" with PowerPoint 2000 and well on your way to creating presentations for home, school, or business.

In this project, you learned some effective methods of integrating PowerPoint with other programs. You learned how to open a Word document within PowerPoint, and how to use the Presentation Assistant to organize the information quickly and logically. Using Copy and Paste, you were able to quickly copy existing data from Word and Excel into PowerPoint. Finally, you built on your ability to use graphics by inserting a picture file into your presentation.

To expand on your knowledge, spend a few minutes exploring Help on these topics. Additionally, complete some of the Skill Drill, Challenge, and Discovery Zone exercises.

Checking Concepts and Terms ✓

True/False

For each of the following, circle T or F to indicate whether the statement is true or false.

__T __F **1.** You must have Word open in order to import a Word outline into PowerPoint. [L1]

__T __F **2.** Copying-and-pasting operations are facilitated by use of the Clipboard. [L4–5]

__T __F **3.** You cannot copy information in Excel and then paste it in PowerPoint. [L5]

__T __F **4.** Before you copy data, you must first select it. [L4–5]

__T __F **5.** You insert a picture into your presentation by using the Picture Gallery. [L6]

Multiple Choice

Circle the letter of the correct answer for each of the following.

1. In PowerPoint, you can _____. [L4–5]

  a. copy worksheet data from Excel to PowerPoint

  b. copy a table from one PowerPoint slide to another

  c. copy Word data into a PowerPoint presentation

  d. all of the above

2. The feature used to fix stylistic problems is called the _____. [L2, 4–5]

  a. Clipboard

  b. Stylistic Assistant

  c. Presentation Assistant

  d. Problem Solver

3. Use the _____ toolbar to facilitate drawing and formatting a table in PowerPoint. [L3]

  a. Drawing

  b. Tables and Borders

  c. Standard

  d. Picture

4. To open a Word outline within PowerPoint, _____. [L1]

  a. you must have Word open in memory

  b. you can open the Word outline from within PowerPoint

  c. you use the Import, File, Open command to perform the operation

  d. you must use Copy and Paste

5. PowerPoint flags potential stylistic problems by _____. [L2]

  a. underlining the words with a red squiggly line

  b. displaying a green check mark next to the problem

  c. displaying a light bulb next to the problem

  d. none of the above

Screen ID

Identify each of the items shown in Figure 8.20.

Figure 8.20

A. Columns

B. Rows

C. Draw Table tool

D. Table tool

E. Fill Color tool

F. Eraser tool

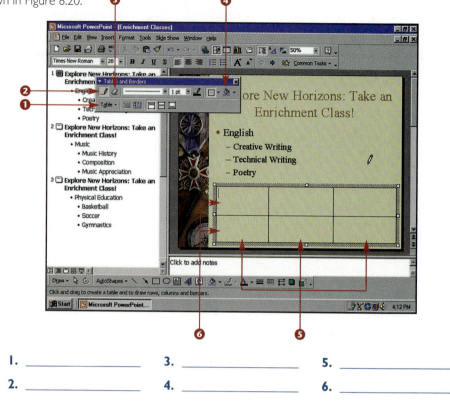

| 1. _____ | 3. _____ | 5. _____ |
| 2. _____ | 4. _____ | 6. _____ |

Discussion Questions

1. Which process or feature covered in Project 8 would you use for each of the following situations? [L1–6]

   - You have a chart in Excel, and you want to base a PowerPoint graph on it.

   - You have already developed an outline in Word, but you need to use the information for a PowerPoint presentation.

   - You want to insert your company's logo on a title slide.

   - You need to insert a picture of a machine that your company manufactures on a slide.

   - You have marketing statistics on a worksheet, and you want to create a PowerPoint chart based on the information.

   - You need to organize data in neat columns and rows.

2. Discuss the pros and cons of using each of the following integration features: [L1, 3–4, 6]

   - Copying and pasting

   - Inserting a picture file

   - Opening a Word document within PowerPoint

Skill Drill

Skill Drill exercises reinforce project skills. Each skill reinforced is the same, or nearly the same, as a skill presented in the project. Detailed instructions are provided in a step-by-step format.

1. Using Help to Find Out About the Office Clipboard

You're slated to give a presentation to coworkers on Office 2000's integration features. To prepare for the presentation, you spend some time researching the Office Clipboard, which allows you to collect and paste multiple items. You also research ways to use the Copy command more effectively. [L4–5]

1. Start PowerPoint if necessary, and then choose Help, Microsoft PowerPoint Help. If necessary, click the Show button to split the window into two panes.

2. On the Index page, enter Clipboard in the Type keywords text box. Click Search.

3. Research each of the topics listed on the Choose a topic list. Take notes on what you learn.

4. Enter copy in the Type keywords text box. Click Search.

5. Research the following topics on the Choose a topic list:

   ■ Copy Microsoft Excel data to PowerPoint

   ■ Copy a slide from one presentation to another

   ■ Copy data from another program into Microsoft Graph

6. Close the Help window. Share what you learn with at least one other user. Keep PowerPoint open if you plan to complete additional exercises.

2. Opening a Word Outline in PowerPoint

You are developing a presentation to give to your class about the different kinds of software on the market. You already created the information you need as a Word outline. Instead of re-creating the same information in PowerPoint, you simply open the Word document within PowerPoint. [L1]

1. Start PowerPoint, if necessary, and then click the Open button.

2. Use the Look in drop-down list arrow to locate the folder that contains your student data files.

3. Click on the Files of type drop-down list arrow and choose All Files.

4. Double-click PP1-0805.

5. Choose Format, Apply Design Template to display the Apply Design Template dialog box.

6. Choose the Network Blitz template, and then choose Apply.

7. Save the presentation as Software Types. Keep the presentation open and PowerPoint running if you plan to complete additional exercises.

3. Using the Presentation Assistant to Fix Stylistic Problems

In looking over the presentation you created in the previous exercise, you decide that there is too much text on the slide to be read easily. To fix this (and other stylistic problems), you decide to activate the Presentation Assistant. [L2]

1. Make sure that the Software Types presentation is open from the previous exercise.

2. Choose Help, Show the Office Assistant. Click outside the message bubble to turn off its display. (Don't complete this step if the Office Assistant is already displayed on your system).

3. Click the light bulb that appears next to Word Processing. Choose to ignore the style rule.

4. Click the light bulb that appears next to Presentation Graphics. Choose the Split this slide into two slides option button.

5. When you look over your presentation, you decide you'd rather split the original presentation slide into three (not two) slides. Click Undo to reverse your last action.

6. Click the light bulb that appears next to the Presentation Graphics text again. This time, choose the Make a new slide for each paragraph on this slide option. (If you accidentally turn off the display of the light bulb, you can reapply the design template and start the exercise again.)

7. Press (PgUp) twice to display Slide 1.

8. Right-click the Office Assistant and choose Options.

9. Clear the Use the Office Assistant check box, then choose OK.

10. Save the Software Types presentation, then close it. Keep PowerPoint open if you plan to complete additional exercises.

4. Inserting a Picture from a File

You developed a flyer to promote the Skiing Club's annual trip. To enhance the flyer, you insert a picture from a file. [L6]

1. In PowerPoint, open PP1-0806 and save it as Ski Trip.

2. Choose Insert, Picture, From File. If necessary, click the Look in drop-down list arrow and find the folder where your student data files are located.

3. Click the PP1-0807 file, and then choose Insert.

4. Right-click the slide, and then choose Apply Design Template.

5. Choose Ricepaper, and then click Apply. Center the text in the title placeholder so that you can more easily read it.

6. Save the Ski Trip presentation, and then close it. Keep PowerPoint open if you plan to complete additional exercises.

5. Drawing and Formatting a Table

You work for a training organization that conducts seminars for people who want to learn new software. To help organize class information, you draw and format a table. [L3]

1. In PowerPoint, open PP1-0808 and save it as Software Training Schedule.

2. Click the New Slide button, and then choose the Title Only AutoLayout. Click OK.

3. Enter Training Schedule in the title placeholder of your new slide.

4. Click the Tables and Borders button to display the Tables and Borders toolbar. Use the Draw Table tool to draw a rectangular table in the lower two-thirds of the slide.

5. Using the Draw Table tool, draw lines to create four columns and four rows for your table. (If necessary, use the Eraser tool to erase your lines and start over.)

6. Click in the first row, and then click the Table tool. Choose Select Row.

7. Click the Fill Color drop-down list arrow and choose the dark gray color box (the third box from the left). Click outside the table to see your changes.

8. Turn off the Tables and Borders toolbar by clicking the toolbar's Close button.

9. Save your Software Training Schedule presentation. Keep the presentation open if you plan to complete the next exercise.

6. Copying and Pasting Information

To complete your Training Schedule, you copy information and a graphic from a Word document into PowerPoint. [L4–5]

1. Make sure that the Software Training Schedule presentation is open from the previous exercise.

2. Start Word, and then open PP1-0809.

3. Select the lines of text (but not the graphic). Click the Copy button.

4. Switch to PowerPoint and select the table on Slide 2 of your Software Training Schedule presentation. Press Ctrl+V.

5. With the table still selected, click the Decrease Font Size button once. Resize the columns, as necessary, to properly display the text.

6. With the table still selected, click the Center button (to center the text).

7. Switch to Word. Click the logo (QST), and then press Ctrl+C.

8. Switch to PowerPoint and display Slide 1. Click the Paste button.

9. Move the logo to the lower-right corner of the slide.

10. Save the Software Training Schedule presentation, and then close it. Keep PowerPoint running if you plan to complete additional exercises, but close Word.

Challenge 💡

Challenge exercises expand on, or are somewhat related to, skills presented in the lessons. Each exercise provides a brief narrative introduction, followed by instructions in a numbered-step format that are not as detailed as those in the Skill Drill section.

[?] 1. Finding Out About Integration

You want to find out more ways to share information seamlessly between PowerPoint and other programs. To do so, you tap into PowerPoint's Help. [L1–6]

1. In PowerPoint's Help window, display the Contents page. Double-click Sharing Information with Other Users and Programs, and then double-click the Sharing Text, Data, and Graphics icon.

2. Research each of the subtopics listed, including the following:

- Ways to share information between PowerPoint and another Office program
- Drag information between programs
- How to import or convert files from another Office program
- Office programs that you can use to create a table
- Office programs that you can use to create an online or printed form
- Insert and edit a Word table
- Copy Microsoft Excel data to PowerPoint
- The format of information pasted from the Clipboard

3. Close the Help window. Share what you learned with another user. Keep PowerPoint running if you plan to complete additional exercises.

2. Creating a PowerPoint Presentation from a Word Document

You work for a travel agency that markets relatively inexpensive trips to college and university students. You're scheduled to set up a booth at open houses for several colleges, so you decide to create a PowerPoint presentation that you can use as a self-running slide show at your booth. And, because you already have the information in a Word document, you decide to initially create your presentation based on this information. [L1–2]

1. In PowerPoint, display the Open dialog box. Open PP1-0810 (a Word document) as a PowerPoint presentation.

2. Turn on the Office Assistant. Use the Presentation Assistant to fix any stylistic problems and to split the information from the Word outline into three slides. When you finish, turn off the Office Assistant.

3. Add a title slide at the beginning of the presentation. In the title placeholder, type `Great Adventures`, press `↵Enter`, and then type `Travel Agency`. In the subtitle placeholder, enter `Spring and Summer Trips`.

4. Apply a gradient fill effect to the background of all slides. Choose Format, Background, click the drop-down list arrow, and choose Fill Effects. On the Gradient page, choose the Ocean preset color. Also choose the From title Shading style, and choose the left variant. Apply the fill effect to all slides in your presentation.

5. Save the presentation as `Great Adventures Travel Agency`. Keep the presentation open and PowerPoint running if you plan to complete additional exercises.

3. Inserting Picture Files in a Presentation

To make your presentation more appealing, you decide to add several pictures to it. Fortunately, your travel agency has a wealth of picture files that you can quickly insert in your presentation. [L6]

I. Make sure that the title slide of the Great Adventures Travel Agency presentation is displayed in Normal view. Move the title placeholder to the top quarter of the slide. Move the subtitle placeholder to the bottom quarter of the slide. (*Hint:* Click in the placeholder, and then click and drag the placeholder's border.)

2. Insert the picture file, `PP1-0811`, on the title slide. Resize and move the picture so that it displays in the center of the slide.

3. Insert the picture file, `PP1-0812`, on Slide 2 (`Florida Sunshine Vacations`). Move the picture to the lower-right corner of the slide.

4. Insert the picture file, `PP1-0813`, on Slide 3 (`Alaskan Adventures`). Move the picture to the lower-right corner of the slide.

5. Insert the picture file, `PP1-0814`, on Slide 4 (`Virginia Horse Country Vacations`). Move the picture to the lower-right corner of the slide.

6. Save the Great Adventures Travel Agency presentation. Keep the presentation open and PowerPoint running if you plan to complete additional exercises.

4. Inserting and Formatting a Word Table

To quickly organize and summarize information about the trips—such as costs and length of each trip—you insert a Word table in your PowerPoint presentation. You then rely on Word's rich formatting features to format the table. [L3–4]

I. In the open Great Adventures Travel Agency presentation, press `Ctrl`+`End` to display the last slide. Click the New Slide button. Choose the Table AutoLayout (the last AutoLayout on the first row), and then click OK.

2. Add `Here's the Deal:` in the title placeholder of your new slide.

3. Double-click the lower (table) placeholder. In the Insert Table dialog box, choose to create a table with three columns and four rows. Choose OK.

4. Enter the following information in your table by using (Tab⭰) (and (⬆Shift)+(Tab⭰)) to move between cells:

Trip	Trip Length	Cost
Florida Sunshine Vacations	7 days	$795
Alaskan Adventures	10 days	$1895
Virginia Horse Country Vacations	7 days	$795

5. With your insertion point still in the table, choose Edit, Select All. Click on the Decrease Font Size button once. Also, click the Center button to align the text in the middle of each cell. If necessary, change the column width to better display your text.

6. Select the top row in your table and format it with a gray shading.

7. Add slide transitions to your slides. Set slide timings for your presentation so that each slide displays for approximately 15–20 seconds. Automate the show so that it runs continuously. (If you need a refresher course on how to perform these actions, see Project 7.)

8. View your slide show as a self-running presentation. Save the Great Adventures Travel Agency presentation, and then close it.

Keep PowerPoint running if you plan to complete additional exercises.

Discovery Zone

Discovery Zone exercises require advanced knowledge of topics presented in Essentials lessons, application of skills from multiple lessons, or self-directed learning of new skills.

1. Learning About Integration

For one of your computer classes, you're scheduled to give a presentation on Office 2000's integration features. Before plunging into creating the presentation, you spend a few minutes learning about integration features.

Using PowerPoint's Help system (and the Web, if you have access to it), find out about the following topics:

- Ways to insert and edit an equation in PowerPoint
- How to create a table and enter text
- How to add or delete rows from a table
- How to select items in a table
- How to add, change, or remove fill from a table cell
- How to merge and split cells in a table
- How to insert an Excel chart in a presentation
- How to change text and data in a chart
- How to change colors, patterns, and fills for a chart
- How to import chart data from other programs

Create a Word outline based on the information you find. Open the Word outline as a PowerPoint presentation. Use the Presentation Assistant to fix any stylistic problems you encounter and to split the information logically into multiple slides. Add a slide background or template to the presentation. If appropriate, create table(s) and chart(s) in the presentation to organize and emphasize information.

Give the presentation to your class. Save the presentation with a name of your choosing.

Keep PowerPoint running if you plan to complete the final exercise. [LI–6]

2. Creating a Presentation About Office 2000

You're in charge of the Information Technology Department at your business, and you want to upgrade your company to Office 2000. There's only one hitch: You have to convince management that the upgrade will be cost-effective because of all the new (and integrated) features included in Office 2000. Your boss has blocked out 20 minutes at next Monday's staff meeting for you to use to make your case. To use the time effectively, you decide to create a PowerPoint presentation that highlights the information.

Here's how to prepare for the presentation: Use the Help system in each of the Office programs (Word, Excel, Access, PowerPoint, and Outlook) to research the new features for each application. Also, find out what integration features are included in Office 2000. Additionally, review the PowerPoint techniques and features covered in Projects 1–8 of this book so that you can use them as you develop your presentation.

Next, create a Word outline that includes the information you find about Office 2000's new features. Open the Word outline as a PowerPoint presentation. Use the Presentation Assistant to fix stylistic problems and split the information logically into multiple slides. Add any other slides, charts, tables, and clips that will enhance your presentation. Rearrange, add, and delete other slides as necessary.

Format your text, bullets, and other slide elements by using techniques you learned in this book. Add a template and/or slide background to liven up your presentation. If you want to, make modifications to the slide master (such as adding the current date, your name, or your company's logo to a corner of the slide master).

Add speaker notes to your slides and print them out so that you'll have ready reference when you give your talk. Add slide transitions and text builds to control the flow of information. If you want to, use the slide timings as you practice giving your presentation to learn how to pace it.

Finally, review the use of the slide show shortcut keys, the annotation pen, and the Meeting Minder. Practice giving the presentation to a few friends, and then make revisions based on their feedback. When you're convinced that you've put together a top-notch presentation, give it to a larger audience (such as your class), and feel great that you're well on your way to becoming a "PowerPoint guru"! [LI–6]

Task Guide

A book in the *Essentials* series is designed to be kept as a handy reference beside your computer even after you have completed all the projects and exercises. Any time you have difficulty recalling the sequence of steps or a shortcut needed to achieve a result, look up the general category in the following alphabetized listing, and then quickly home in on your task at hand. For your convenience, some tasks have been duplicated under more than one category. If you have difficulty performing a task, turn to the page number listed in the third column to locate the step-by-step exercise or other detailed description. If a task does not include a page reference, it is a bonus task from the author that was not within the scope of the book. For the greatest efficiency in using this Task Guide, take a few minutes to familiarize yourself with the main categories and keywords before you begin your search.

To Do This	Use This Command	Page Number
Application and File Management		
AutoContent Wizard: use to create a presentation	Choose File, New to display the New Presentation dialog box; then click the General tab. Double-click the AutoContent Wizard icon.	[pg. 40]
AutoLayout: choose	Click the AutoLayout in the New Slide dialog box; then click OK.	[pg. 6]
Close a presentation	Choose File, Close.	[pg. 24]
Create a new, blank presentation	Choose File, New. In the New Presentation dialog box, click the Blank Presentation icon; then choose OK.	[pg. 6]
	Choose Blank Presentation in the PowerPoint Startup dialog box; then choose OK.	[pg. 6]
Exit PowerPoint	Choose File, Exit, or click the Application Close button.	[pg. 24]
Open an existing presentation	Choose File, Open; then double-click the presentation.	[pg. 72]
Print: action items	Display the Action Items slide, then choose File, Print.	[pg. 216]
Print: handouts	Choose File, Print. Click the Print what drop-down list arrow and choose Handouts.	[pg. 90]

continues ▶

To Do This	Use This Command	Page Number
Print: outline	Choose Outline View in the Print what section of the Print dialog box.	[pg. 56]
Print: speaker notes	Choose File, Print. Click the Print what drop-down list arrow and choose Notes Pages.	[pg. 89]
Save a presentation	Choose File, Save As.	[pg. 54]
	Click the Save button.	[pg. 54]
Start PowerPoint	Choose the Start button, Programs, Microsoft PowerPoint.	[pg. 3-4]
Startup dialog box: display	Choose Tools, Options; then click the View tab. Check the box for Startup dialog; then click OK.	[pg. 5]
Template: use to create a presentation	Choose File, New to display the New Presentation dialog box; then choose a template on the Design Templates page.	[pg. 38]
Windows 95: shut down	Click the Start button; then choose Shut Down.	[pg. 25]

Customization

Animation: customize	Display the slide in Normal view, then choose Slide Show, Custom Animation.	
Default settings: reset toolbars and menus	Choose Tools, Customize, Options. Click the Reset my usage data; then choose Yes.	[pg. 13-14]
Office Assistant: turn off	Right-click the Office Assistant and choose Options. Clear the Use the Office Assistant check box; then click OK.	[pg. 232] [pg. 23]
ScreenTips: turn on	Choose Tools, Customize, Options. Check the box for Show ScreenTips on toolbars; then click OK.	[pg. 10]
Startup dialog box: display	Choose Tools, Options; then click the View tab. Check the box for Startup dialog; then click OK.	[pg. 5]
Toolbars: display Tables and Borders toolbar	Click the Tables and Borders button on the Standard toolbar.	[pg. 233]
Toolbars: display or hide	Right-click on any visible toolbar; then click a toolbar from the list displayed.	
Toolbars: separate the Standard and Formatting toolbars	Choose Tools, Customize, Options; then uncheck the Standard and Formatting toolbars share one row box.	[pg. 13]

Charts—Data Charts

Change color or pattern	Select object(s) to change within the chart; then choose Format, Selected (name of object).	[pg. 144]

To Do This	Use This Command	Page Number
Change data	Enter information in the datasheet.	[pg. 138]
Create	Click the New Slide button and then an AutoLayout containing a chart placeholder.	[pg. 133]
	Click the Insert Chart button on the Standard toolbar.	
Datasheet: view or hide	Click the View Datasheet button.	[pg. 138]
Delete data	View the datasheet and select the cells, column(s), or row(s) you want to erase; then press Del.	[pg. 135]
Delete	Click the chart object to display the white selection handles; then press Del.	[pg. 145]
Edit	Double-click a chart object to activate Microsoft Graph.	[pg. 137]
Move	Move the mouse pointer to the middle of the selected chart until the pointer displays as a four-headed arrow; then drag to a new location.	[pg. 141]
Resize	Place the mouse pointer on a white selection handle to display a resizing arrow; then drag to resize.	[pg. 141]
Select	Choose the object from the Chart Objects drop-down list.	[pg. 144]
Sub-type: select	Choose Chart, Chart Type.	[pg. 143]
Type: change	Click the drop-down list arrow next to the Chart Type button; then select a chart.	[pg. 139]

Charts—Organization Charts

To Do This	Use This Command	Page Number
Add a job position	Click a job position box tool; then click the box to which it will be attached.	[pg. 150]
Add box color	Select the box and choose Boxes, Color.	[pg. 151]
Add box shadowing	Select the box and choose Boxes, Shadow.	[pg. 151]
Create	Choose the Organization Chart AutoLayout when creating a new slide.	[pg. 147]
Delete a box	Select the box and press Del.	[pg. 152]
Edit	Double-click the organization chart object.	[pg. 150]
Move a box	Drag the box to the box where you want it attached.	[pg. 152]

Graphics—Drawn Objects and Clipart

To Do This	Use This Command	Page Number
Clip Art: insert	Double-click a Clip Art placeholder	[pg. 188]
	Click the Insert Clip Art button on the Drawing toolbar	[pg. 190]
Drawing toolbar: display	Choose View, Toolbars, Drawing	[pg. 180]

continues ▶

To Do This	Use This Command	Page Number
Objects: change an object's line style	Click the Line Style button's drop-down arrow on the Drawing toolbar.	[pg. 186]
Objects: change color	Click the Fill Color button's drop-down arrow on the Drawing toolbar.	[pg. 186]
Objects: create	Select the tool from the Drawing toolbar; click and drag to draw.	[pg. 180]
Objects: delete	Select the object; then press (Del).	[pg. 185]
Objects: deselect all	Click outside selected objects.	[pg. 183]
Objects: deselect one	Hold down the (◆Shift) key, click the object, and release (◆Shift).	[pg. 183]
Objects: move	Move the mouse pointer to the middle of the selected object; drag to move.	[pg. 185]
Objects: resize	Move the mouse pointer across a selection handle until it turns into a two-headed arrow; drag to resize.	[pg. 184]
Objects: select multiple	Hold down the (◆Shift) key while clicking the objects.	[pg. 183]
	Using the Select Objects tool, draw a box around all objects.	[pg. 183]
Objects: select	Click the object.	[pg. 183]

Help

Expand or contract a Help topic	Double-click the book icon	[pg. 19]
Find Help by a keyword	Enter the topic in the Type keywords text box; then choose Search.	[pg. 20]
Find Help topics	Enter a question in the Assistant's balloon; then click Search.	[pg. 16]
Help dialog box: split into two panes	Click the Show button.	[pg. 18]
Help screens: move between	Click the Back or Forward buttons.	[pg. 18]
Office Assistant: display	Click the Microsoft PowerPoint Help button.	[pg. 15]
	Press (F1).	
Office Assistant: hide or show	Choose Help, Hide the Office Assistant (or Help, Show the Office Assistant).	[pg. 23]
Office Assistant: turn off	Right-click the Office Assistant and choose Options. Clear the Use the Office Assistant check box, and then click OK.	[pg. 232] [pg. 23]
Presentation Assistant: activate	Choose Help, Show the Office Assistant.	[pg. 230]
Presentation Assistant tip: display	Click the light bulb.	[pg. 231]

To Do This	Use This Command	Page Number
ScreenTip: display	Rest your mouse pointer over a button.	[pg. 9]
ScreenTip: turn on	Choose Tools, Customize, Options. Check the box for Show ScreenTips on toolbars; then click OK.	[pg. 10]
Slide Show: display keyboard shortcuts	Press F1 while running a slide show.	[pg. 52]

Integration

Clipboard: copy text or object to	Select the text or object; then click the Copy button (or press Ctrl+C).	[pg. 237]
Clipboard: paste text or object from	Click the Paste button (or press Ctrl+V).	[pg. 237]
Picture: insert from a file	Choose Insert, Picture, From File.	[pg. 243]
Word outline: open in PowerPoint	In PowerPoint, display the Open dialog box, click the Files of type drop-down list arrow and choose All Files from the list. Double-click the Word file.	[pg. 228]

Presentations—Animating

Animate bulleted points	Click the Preset Animation drop-down list arrow.	[pg. 207]
Animation: customize	Display the slide in Normal view, and then choose Slide Show, Custom Animation.	[pg. 221]
Slide transitions: add	Click the Slide Transition Effects drop-down list arrow; then choose an effect.	[pg. 205]
Slide transitions: remove	Choose No Transition from the Slide Transitions Effect drop-down list on the Slide Sorter toolbar.	[pg. 206]
Slide transitions: view	Click the Slide Transition icon under the slide (Slide Sorter view).	[pg. 206]

Presentations—Modifying Slides and Text

Alignment: change	Select the text, and then click the appropriate alignment button on the Formatting toolbar.	[pg. 112]
Bullets or Numbers: modify	Select the text; then choose Format, Bullets and Numbering to display the Bullets and Numbering dialog box.	[pg. 118]
Bullets: add or remove	Select the text, and then click the Bullets button on the Formatting toolbar.	[pg. 116]
Character attributes: change	Select the text, and then click the Bold, Italic, or Underline buttons on the Formatting toolbar.	[pg. 106]
Demote a point (indent more)	Click the Demote button on the Formatting toolbar or press Tab.	[pg. 81]

continues ▶

To Do This	Use This Command	Page Number
Font Size: change	Select the text, and then choose a size from the Font Size drop-down list.	[pg. 106]
Font: change	Select the text, and then choose a font from the Font drop-down list.	[pg. 107]
Formatting: apply	Select the text from which you want to copy formatting, click the Format Painter, and drag over the text to which you want to apply the formatting.	[pg. 109]
Move an entire line of text	Select the associated bullet in the Outline pane; then click the Move Up or Move Down buttons on the Outlining toolbar.	[pg. 83]
Move text	Select the text and choose Edit, Cut. Set the insertion point in the new location and choose Edit, Paste.	[pg. 83]
Numbering: add	Select the text, and then click the Numbering button on the Formatting toolbar.	[pg. 116]
Paragraph spacing: adjust	Select the paragraphs, and then choose Format, Line Spacing.	[pg. 113]
Promote a point (indent less)	Click the Promote button on the Formatting toolbar or press ♠Shift+Tab↹.	[pg. 81]
Text Color: change	Select the text, choose Format, Font, and choose a color from the Color drop-down palette.	[pg. 107]
Text: enter in a slide	Click in the placeholder; then type.	[pg. 7]

Presentations—Modifying Overall Design and Look

To Do This	Use This Command	Page Number
Color background: change	Choose Format, Background.	[pg. 172]
Color scheme: apply	Select Format, Slide Color Scheme.	[pg. 171]
	Right-click a slide to activate the shortcut menu, and select Slide Color Scheme.	[pg. 171]
Slide order: change	In Slide Sorter view, drag a selected slide to the new location.	[pg. 78]
Slide: add	Click the New Slide button on the Standard toolbar.	[pg. 75]
Slide: delete	Select the slide in Slide Sorter view; then press Del.	[pg. 75]
Spell check a presentation	Click the Spelling button.	[pg. 91]
	Choose Tools, Spelling.	
Template: apply	Choose Format, Apply Design Template.	[pg. 169]
Undo your last action	Click the Undo button.	[pg. 76]

To Do This	Use This Command	Page Number
Presentations: Navigating in Normal View—Move to		
First slide	Press Ctrl+Home.	[pg. 48]
Last slide	Press Ctrl+End.	[pg. 48]
Next slide	Press PgDn or click the Next Slide button.	[pg. 48]
Previous slide	Press PgUp or click the Previous Slide button.	[pg. 48]
Specific slide	Drag the scroll box to the corresponding location on the vertical scrollbar.	[pg. 49]
Slide Masters		
Date: insert	Display the slide master and select the area in which you want to place the date or time; then choose Insert, Date and Time	[pg. 177]
Footer: insert	Select the footer area placeholder on the slide master; then type the text.	[pg. 176]
Slide master: view	Choose View, Master, Slide Master.	[pg. 175]
Slide miniature: view	Choose View, Slide Miniature.	[pg. 175]
Slide numbers: insert	Display the slide master and select the area in which you want to place the slide number; then choose Insert, Slide Number.	[pg. 177]
Slide Shows		
Action Items: print	Display the Action Items slide; then choose File, Print.	[pg. 216]
Annotation pen: activate	Press Ctrl+P.	[pg. 212]
Annotation pen: erase a screen drawing	Press E.	[pg. 212]
Arrow mouse pointer: activate	Press Ctrl+A (or Esc).	[pg. 213]
Meeting Minder: use	Right-click in the slide show; then choose Meeting Minder.	[pg. 214]
Pen color: change	Right-click in the slide show; then choose Pointer Options, Pen Color.	[pg. 213]
Slide show: advance one slide at a time	Press ↵Enter or PgDn. Click the left mouse button.	[pg. 50]
Slide show: blacken or unblacken	Press B.	[pg. 53]
Slide Show: display keyboard shortcuts	Press F1 while running a slide show.	[pg. 52]

continues ▶

To Do This	Use This Command	Page Number
Slide show: display previous slide	Press (←Backspace) or (PgUp).	[pg. 50]
Slide Show: display shortcut menu	Right-click the mouse in the slide show.	[pg. 51]
Slide show: display specific slide number	Type the slide number, and then press (←Enter)	[pg. 51]
Slide show: end	Press (Esc).	[pg. 53]
Slide show: run continuously	Choose Slide Show, Set Up Show; then check Loop continually until 'Esc'.	[pg. 211]
Slide show: start	Click the Slide Show button, choose View, Slide Show.	[pg. 50]
	Press (F5).	[pg. 52]
Slide timings: rehearse	Click the Rehearse Timings button on the Slide Sorter toolbar.	[pg. 209]

Speaker Notes and Handouts

Add speaker notes	Type text in the notes box in Notes Page view (or in the Notes pane).	[pg. 87]
Format speaker notes	Select the text in Notes Page view; then use buttons on the Formatting toolbar.	[pg. 86]
Print handouts	Choose File, Print. Click the Print what drop-down list arrow and choose Handouts.	[pg. 90]
Print speaker notes	Choose File, Print. Click the Print what drop-down list arrow and choose Notes Pages.	[pg. 90]
Resize the Notes pane in Normal view	Drag the divider between the Notes pane and the Slide pane.	[pg. 88]
View speaker notes	Choose View, Notes Page.	[pg. 86]

Tables

Column width: change	Move the mouse pointer over a vertical column divider until a two-headed arrow displays; then drag left or right.	[pg. 235]
Draw table	Click the Draw Table button on the Tables and Borders toolbar; then click and drag on your slide.	[pg. 234]
Erase a table line	Click the Eraser button on the Tables and Borders toolbar; then drag over the line(s) you want to remove.	[pg. 235]
Fill: add to table cells	Select the table cells; then choose a color from the Fill Color button's palette.	[pg. 236]
Toolbar: display Tables and Borders toolbar	Click the Tables and Borders button on the Standard toolbar.	[pg. 236]

To Do This	Use This Command	Page Number
View		
Datasheet: view or hide	Click the View Datasheet button.	[pg. 138]
Full menu: display	Double-click the menu command.	[pg. 11]
Navigation pane: hide	Click the Hide button.	[pg. 21]
Preview a presentation in black and white	Click the Grayscale Preview button.	[pg. 56]
Rulers: display	Choose View, Ruler.	[pg. 180]
ScreenTip: display	Rest your mouse pointer over a button.	[pg. 9]
ScreenTips: turn on	Choose Tools, Customize, Options. Check the box for Show ScreenTips on toolbars; then click OK.	[pg. 10]
Slide master	Choose View, Master, Slide Master.	[pg. 175]
Slide miniature	Choose View, Slide Miniature.	[pg. 175]
Slide transitions	Click the Slide Transition icon under the slide (Slide Sorter view).	[pg. 205]
Switch between views	Click the associated View button.	[pg. 44]
	Choose the appropriate command on the View menu.	[pg. 47]
Toolbar button: display	Click the More Buttons button; then choose a button from the palette.	[pg. 10-11]

Glossary

All key terms appearing in this book (in bold italic) are listed alphabetically in this Glossary for easy reference. If you want to learn more about a feature or concept, turn to the page reference shown after its definition. You can also use the Index to find the term's other significant occurrences.

action items   Items that you assign to people during a slide show or meeting. [pg. 202]

animate   To use an effect in a slide show to enable you to focus on important points, control the flow of information, or simply add interest to your presentation (for example, to display bullet points one at a time). [pg. 202]

annotate   To write or draw directly on a slide during a slide show. [pg. 211]

annotation pen   A special mouse pointer that enables you to write or draw directly on a slide during a slide show. [pg. 202]

AutoContent Wizard   A wizard that helps you to create a presentation that includes a preset design and sample content. [pg. 36]

AutoLayout   A predefined slide layout option in PowerPoint. [pg. 6]

bullets   Objects, such as circles or squares, which are used to set off items in a list. [pg. 104]

cell   The intersection of a column and row in a datasheet. [pg. 133]

cell pointer   A darkened border around a datasheet cell, which indicates the location of the active cell. [pg. 135]

character attributes   Characteristics such as bold, italic, or underline that are applied to text for emphasis. [pg. 105]

chart   A pictorial representation of data. [pg. 130]

chart sub-types   Variations on the main chart types. [pg. 131]

clip art   Electronic pictures, available from various sources, that you can add to PowerPoint slides. [pg. 45]

Clip Gallery   A built-in collection of clip art, motion clips, and sound clips that you can add to slides. [pg. 167]

Clipboard   A temporary area of memory that holds material that is cut or copied to be pasted elsewhere. [pg. 82, 237]

color scheme   The underlying set of eight coordinated colors for a presentation. [pg. 170]

context sensitive   The way a menu displays the commands that are related to the area of the screen that you click. [pg. 51]

data charts   Charts that show numerical data in a pictorial manner. [pg. 130]

data series   A collection of values in a chart that pertain to a single subject. [pg. 144]

datasheet   A mini-worksheet that enables you to revise the information in a data chart. [pg. 130]

demote   To indent text on a slide so that it has less importance than the previous text item. [pg. 81]

design templates   (see **templates**)

docked toolbar   A toolbar that is attached to one side of the application window. [pg. 233]

drag-and-drop   A method of moving an object by selecting it, dragging it with the mouse to a new location, and then releasing the mouse button, dropping the object in place. [pg. 78]

drawn objects   Objects such as rectangles, ovals, lines, and arrows that you can draw on a slide to jazz it up or emphasize specific information. [pg. 178]

editing mode   A state in which you can enter or edit text in a placeholder. [pg. 7]

electronic slide show   A predetermined list of slides that are displayed sequentially. You can show the slides onscreen, or use a Liquid Crystal Display (LCD) panel and an overhead projector to cast the images from your computer onto a large screen. [pg. 2]

embedded object   An item created by one program and inserted into a document created by another program. [pg. 133]

floating toolbar   An onscreen toolbar that displays in its own window. [pg. 233]

font   (also called **typeface**) A collection of characters (letters, numbers, and special symbols) that have a consistent and identifiable appearance. [pg. 105]

footer area   The place at the bottom of each slide where you can add items such as your company name and a slide number. [pg. 42]

formatting   The way a presentation is set up to display (including text, alignment, bullets, margins, and so on). [pg. 104]

frame   A border that surrounds a slide element. [pg. 90]

full menu   A drop-down menu that includes all of PowerPoint's commands for a menu bar item. [pg. 11]

grayscale   Shades of white, gray, and black on printed output. [pg. 55]

handouts   Printed output that includes only the slides' contents, not the accompanying notes. [pg. 89]

horizontal text alignment   The way text displays horizontally in a placeholder. [pg. 111]

hyperlink   Underlined text, generally shown in a contrasting color, that you click to display related Help information. (The World Wide Web is, for all practical purposes, an endless mesh of hyperlinked pages that reside on countless computers.) [pg. 17]

icon bar   A special bar in Microsoft Organization Chart that displays box tools and its own menu bar so that you can use its commands. [pg. 147]

integration   The built-in capability that the Office programs have to share information seamlessly with each other. [pg. 226]

keyboard shortcuts   Combinations of keys you can press on the keyboard to perform actions. [pg. 47]

keyword   In PowerPoint, an item in a list of alphabetical Help topics that you can use to find all related topics. [pg. 20]
Also a topical word that you use to find related clips in the Clip Gallery. [pg. 167]

move bars   The double bars that appear at one end of a docked toolbar. They are used to move the toolbar to another location. [pg. 233]

multimedia   Special effects you can add to a presentation, such as music, sound, and videos. [pg. 211]

Navigation pane   The left pane of the Help window which helps you navigate through various topics by topic or keyword. [pg. 18]

Normal view   A tri-pane view that includes a Slide pane, an Outline pane, and a Notes pane. Each of these three panes offers a way to work with your presentation. [pg. 6]

notes box   An area of a slide where you can enter notes while in Notes Page view. [pg. 86]

Notes pane   An onscreen area that helps you to develop speaker notes. [pg. 7]

object   An item placed on a slide, such as a chart. [pg. 133]

Office Assistant   PowerPoint's Help system that supplies answers to your questions. [pg. 2]

organization charts   Charts that visually represent the structure of an organization. [pg. 130]

Outline pane   An onscreen area that organizes the content of the entire presentation and enables you to get a feel for the overall flow. [pg. 7]

output   The final product used in a presentation. In PowerPoint, you can choose from onscreen presentations, Web presentations, black-and-white overheads, color overheads, and 35MM slides. [pg. 42]

palette   A drop-down list of colors from which you can choose the colors that coordinate with your presentation's color scheme. [pg. 108]

parent box   An existing box in an organization chart to which you can attach new boxes. [pg. 149]

peripheral program   A program, such as Microsoft Graph, that starts every time you access a feature within the main program and place an object, such as a chart, on a slide. [pg. 133]

personalized menus and toolbars   Menus and toolbars that PowerPoint continually adapts to your work habits by displaying only the commands and buttons that you use most frequently. [pg. 13]

placeholder   An area on a slide that can accept different types of objects, such as graphics and text. [pg. 6]

point   A unit of measurement used to designate character height in a font. [pg. 106]

presentation   A series of slides that contains visual information you can use to persuade an audience. [pg. 2]

Presentation Assistant   An offshoot of the Office Assistant that is designed to help you correct stylistic problems in a presentation. [pg. 226]

presentation graphics program   A software package, such as PowerPoint, that helps you structure, design, and present information to an audience so that it is catchy and visually appealing. [pg. 2]

promote   To reduce the indent of text to indicate the relative importance of the text. [pg. 81]

pure black and white   All gray areas are converted to black or white on printed output. [pg. 55]

Random Access Memory (RAM)   The temporary storage space that a computer uses for programs that it is currently running. [pg. 4]

range   A rectangular block of cells in a datasheet. [pg. 240]

reverse video   The computer's method of highlighting text on the display so that dark text is shown as bright characters on a dark background. [pg. 73]

ScreenTip   A small box that displays the name of a button or object when you rest the mouse pointer on that object. [pg. 9]

sentence case   The first letter of a sentence or phrase is capitalized. [pg. 231]

short menu   A drop-down menu that displays an abbreviated list of commonly-used commands. [pg. 11]

shortcut menu   A list of context-sensitive commands that you display by right-clicking an object. [pg. 5]

slide image   A small-scale version of a slide shown in Notes Page view. [pg. 86]

slide master   A framework slide that controls the way presentation slides will look by governing characteristics such as font, background color, shadowing, and bullet style. [pg. 175]

Slide pane   An onscreen area that shows how an individual slide appears. You can add text, graphics, or other objects to a slide in this window. [pg. 7]

slide transitions   Visual effects that PowerPoint uses to change from one slide to the next slide in a slide show. [pg. 202]

speaker notes   Supporting data, quotations, or illustrations that you can use when giving a presentation. [pg. 85]

stylistic problems   Incorrect capitalization, too much text on a slide, and so on. You can use the Presentation Assistant to help avoid these problems. [pg. 230]

table   A grid of columns and rows that you can use to display slide data in an organized manner. [pg. 233]

templates   (also called design templates) "Blueprints" upon which you can base your presentation. Templates include the formatting, color, and graphics necessary to create a particular "look." [pg. 38, 168]

thumbnail   A miniature slide representation. [pg. 38]

title case   The combination of uppercase and lowercase letters that are used to capitalize the first letter of each word in a sentence or phrase. [pg. 231]

typeface   (see **font**)

views   The various perspectives PowerPoint provides to enable you to modify different aspects of your presentation. [pg. 36]

wizards   Interactive tools that guide you step-by-step through a process that might otherwise be complicated or awkward. [pg. 40]

worksheet   A spreadsheet document used in Microsoft Excel that can be imported into PowerPoint. [pg. 233]

Index